e-Governance in Africa

From Theory to Action

e-Governance in Africa

From Theory to Action

A Handbook on ICTs for Local Governance

Gianluca C. Misuraca

Africa World Press, Inc.
P.O. Box 1892
Trenton, NJ 08607
P.O. Box 48
Asmara, ERITREA

International Development Research Centre
Ottawa • Cairo • Dakar • Montevideo • Nairobi • New Delhi • Singapore

Africa World Press, Inc.

P.O. Box 1892
Trenton, NJ 08607

P.O. Box 48
Asmara, ERITREA

First Printing 2007

Jointly Published by
AFRICA WORLD PRESS
P.O. Box 1892, Trenton, New Jersey 08607
awprsp@verizon.net/www.africaworldpressbooks.com

and the
International Development Research Centre
PO Box 8500, Ottawa, ON Canada KIG 3149
info@idrc/www.idrc.ca
ISBN (e-book) 978-1-55250-369-0

Book and cover design: Saverance Publishing Services

Library of Congress Cataloging-in-Publication Data

Misuraca, Gianluca.
E-Governance in Africa, from theory to action : a handbook on ICTs for local governance / by Gianluca Misuraca ; with foreword by Joseph O. Okpaku.
p. cm.
Includes bibliographical references and index.
ISBN 1-59221-578-5 (hard cover) -- ISBN 1-59221-579-3 (pbk.)
1. Internet in public administration--Africa. 2. Information technology--Africa. I. Title.
JQ1875.A55A86 2007
352.3'802854678--dc22

2007012518

TABLE OF CONTENTS

FOREWORD

by Joseph O. Okpaku, Sr., Ph.D.

As is true of all new ideas and fields of human engagement, e-government (along with its collateral subject of e-governance) is knee-deep in the challenge of definitions as competing intellectuals, specialists and practitioners seek to clarify the many concepts and issues that define the concept, or to prevail in the choices of preferred definitions. On top of the list of concepts in transition, the dominant definitions of which are up for grabs, are: electronic Government or e-government, and its contradistinction with e-governance; e-Administration; the plethora of subsidiary (even if older) concepts such as e-Education, e-Health e-Voting and more, and overall, Information and Communication Technologies (ICTs) Development versus ICTs *for* Development.

In the process of seeking permanent space in the dual world of technology and governance, a process driven as much by equipment, applications and services vendors as by administrators, fresh opportunities are being created daily for the deployment of the tools of Information and Communication Technologies and the infrastructure that provides the platform on which they perform. Significantly, the systemic arena for e-government has advanced from global and regional, to in-country national, state, provincial, county and local levels of government. Not surprisingly, the field has also panned out to infuse itself with the by now predictable dichotomies of ICTs and e-government in industrialized countries versus in developing countries, for the rich versus the poor, the haves and the have-nots. An inevitable by-product of this process is e-government in Africa as a sub-sector, and here, many questions have been raised and attempts made to answer them. Already, there are more questions than the field can provide answers for, which is as it should be in a dynamic process that is driven by the search for answers to ever emerging questions, and the innovation and creativity that result.

In such an environment, *e-governance in Africa, From Theory to Action: A Handbook on ICTs for Local Governance* by Gianluca Carlo Misuraca, is a timely and significant effort to provide a comprehensive framework for understanding the theme of e-governance in Africa, its many challenges and opportunities, and the state and dynamics of the fast evolving situation on the ground. Together with the handful of similar works before it, this book offers a very valuable synopsis of the scholarship to date on the subject, especially as it seeks to provide the author's own definitions of key concepts in e-government and e-governance, and his interpretations of those of other scholars.

e-governance in Africa, From Theory to Action is presented in three parts: In Part I, "Conceptual Framework: Towards a Multi-dimensional e-governance", the author diligently and successfully seeks to provide a summary of the key positions in the debate on the theoretical framework for examining the real or potential (or, for that matter, the absence of) impact of the deployment of Information and Communication Technologies and their applications for the administration of governance, otherwise, e-governance. He attempts to track the conceptual migration from e-government to e-governance, seeking to demonstrate a distinction between the two. In the process, Misuraca presents his own evolution of the conceptualisation of e-governance, and offers what he calls a "working definition" of e-governance as:

The use of ICTs, and especially of the Internet, to adopt a new conception and attitude of governing and managing where participation and efficiency are required of all partners linked in a network.

He goes on to call e-governance "a new way of coordinating, planning, formulating and implementing decisions and operations related to governance problems, using ICTs as a medium of communication and partnership-development," or simply, " Governance with and of ICTs".

Misuraca argues forcefully about the benefits of e-governance, specifically for local government (what the trade calls Local e-government or e-Local Governance), and especially in Africa. He postulates that this process can enable local governments to "re-invent" themselves, and maintains that a good deal of the promise of democratic governance can be more readily accomplished through the embodiment of networked electronic facilities in local government administration.

These claims are by no means self-evident or universally accepted. There are those who argue equally coherently that the cost of migrating local governance (and perhaps all government administration) to an e-governance platform in a context of competing demands of abject financial resources cannot be justified. I for one also maintain that the unmitigated deployment of e-governance can inadvertently serve to undermine direct contact between the people and those who govern them, a crucial, fundamental and non-negotiable pre-requisite of good, representative, responsive and responsible governance. If nothing else, the efficacy of the claims of the *de facto* incontrovertible benefits of e-governance is clearly yet to be proven, given the still questionable success of e-governance even in materially much richer regions of the world. In common parlance, the jury is still out on this subject. But the presentation of much of the argument on the subject by Gianluca Misuraca is very informative and most useful in providing support or fodder for either side of the argument.

Which is what makes Part Two of the book, "Case Studies on ICTs for Local Governance", a summary of four case studies in Africa, and the core of this book, most relevant. The selection of the locale of the case studies, with one in French-speaking West Africa (Senegal), one in English-speaking West Africa (Ghana), one in East Africa (Uganda), and one in southern Africa (Cape Town, South Africa), attempts to provide a representative continental sampling. Each case study differs significantly from the other, providing a broad spectrum of experience even if, for the same reason, this limits the authority or justification to draw cross-cutting conclusions from such disparate experiments.

The Senegal Case, is a study of the impact of ICTs on the decentralization of government based exclusively on a review of the *Senegal ACACIA Strategy (SAS)*, which is a project of the International Development Research Centre (IDRC) of Canada, and which was begun in 1996. The author reviews various phases of this project, and concludes that despite initial gains, after a decade of effort, there is no significant impact of the introduction of electronic resources on the decentralization of governance in Senegal. The reasons for this are perhaps as important as the outcome, perhaps significantly more so. Misuraca identifies a good number of questions that need to be answered in seeking to deploy ICTs for the decentralization of government and empowering local administrations.

The Ghana Study, which examines ICTs and Traditional Governance, reviews a number of projects that seek to use Information and Communication Technologies to enhance the effectiveness of governance by traditional chiefs and their collaboration and coordination with the central (elected) government. These include the locally-developed ICTs for Accelerated Development (ICT4AD) strategy, the Chieftaincy, Governance and Development project developed by the Institute of African Studies at Ghana's premier tertiary institution, the University of Legon, and sponsored by the Ford Foundation, and in particular the Governance, Culture and Development project, funded by the Open Society Initiative of West Africa (OSIWA).

This case study is a particularly complex one to seek to draw conclusions from because the core tension in the experiments involved in the projects is not so much e-governance as it is the dynamics between traditional governance and authority as represented by traditional chiefs (who remain very powerful in Ghana) and the contemporary state governance as led by elected officials. The struggle for power between traditional rulers and elected officials was a major challenge at Ghana's Independence in 1956 as it was in that of Nigeria (1960) and other West African states in which traditional chiefs once represented the prime authority of governance. Seeking to ascribe kudos for a greater working relationship between the two to the use of ICTs risks being far-fetched. Nonetheless, Misuraca offers some sound observations, including, for example, that traditional leaders need to acquire a working knowledge of modern instruments of public administration while securing the benefits of long-standing trust by the people that is inherent in chieftaincy.

The Ugandan case study is of the District Administrative Network Programme (DistrictNet). DistrictNet came out of the Roundtable Workshop on "ICTs for Rural Development" held by the Government of Uganda in March 2001 as a pilot project in four districts of the country's administrative system. Sponsored partly by the International Institute for Communication Development (IICD) and the Department for International Development (DFID) of the government of the United Kingdom, DistrictNet's purpose was to promote the establishment of facilities and capacities for adopting data management and the use of electronic communication to enhance the delivery of administrative services. Misuraca highlights the achievements of this programme and its promise as it migrates from pilots to nationwide implementation.

He, however, identifies several challenges that will need to be carefully managed in order for this transition to be successful.

In the last case study, the author reviews the extensive efforts made by the City of Cape Town in South Africa, to create a "Smart City" through a series of projects, some internally driven, other externally, but all aimed at streamlining the administration of government services while promoting business. He provides good descriptions of the various projects and the results that have emerged from the effort. He concludes that the class (and, in South Africa, therefore, racial) distinctions that are part of the social fabric remain essentially unaltered despite the ICTs programmes, mainly because of the imbalance in the relative ability of people and enterprises to pay for the cost of access and service.

In Part III, "Conclusions and Way Forward", Gianluca Misuraca provides his own conclusions from the case studies and his views on the overall challenges of the use of ICTs for local governance. Amongst them are that: no one strategy fits all; local content is important; engaging large numbers of the focus population is difficult but important; the high cost of ICTs equipment, applications and services remains a deterrent to the adoption or successful implementation of Local e-government programmes; and local conditions must be considered rather than seeking to import external models wholesale.

The final chapter in this section, "One Way Forward: LOG-IN Africa", presents the Local Governance and ICTs Research Network which "Project Idea" was formulated by the author himself. LOG-IN Africa is funded to the tune of 1.5 million Canadian dollars by IDRC and was successfully established under the leadership of Gianluca Misuraca as Project Leader and Research Network Coordinator in 2006.

Finally, the Annex, "Review of Key Experiences of ICTs Impacting on Governance in Africa", serve as very useful research tools as much for the student and scholar, as for the practitioner and the administrator.

This book is by no means a comprehensive or exhaustive study of e-governance in Africa, but a case study of selected experiments on e-governance in local government in Africa. This notwithstanding, the author is to be congratulated for what he has addressed, without being held responsible for what he has not. To get the most out of this book, the reader might wish to focus a bit more on what it covers and offers, and the value of the conclusions that the author has extrapolated from these case studies (even as focus points for debate) rather than on what it has not but might have offered or covered. This is particularly important because the permutation of what could be addressed is so vast that no one book, not even in electronic form, can be fully comprehensive and yet comprehensible. This is why the author proscribed the scope of the work in the subtitle of the book, as a handbook. What it does do that is important, is that it provides a valuable compendium of the debate on the subject.

A major obstacle to gaining useful and meaningful value from the output of research on matters concerning Africa, derives in serious part from the nature of their sponsorship. Unfortunately, more often than is acceptable or desirable, many such research tend to be advocacy and agenda-driven, and the footprints of such a pedigree tend to be strewn all over the reports and their recommendations. These what one might call "sponsor imprints" vary from subtle suggestions to heavy-handed pre-determined "institution self-serving" conclusions which often fly in the face of evidence, and often of common sense. This often not only subjects the results of the studies to what one might call "benign notice", but more often than not leads to the corresponding benign neglect of their recommendations, and to their failure if implemented.

In this regard, IDRC, especially through its ACACIA initiative, has had an illustrious and consistent track record of promoting ICTs in Africa for a long time. This study, sponsored by it, inevitably would seek to provide justification (and justifiable reinforcement) for the efforts and investment. Significantly, to the credit of both the author and to IDRC, Misuraca has delineated numerous challenges, obstacles and even failures in the once presumed self-evident and incontrovertible benefits of ICTs for accelerating governance and overall development, especially in Africa. He may not have covered the reasons for this shortfall in efficacy. But one might suggest that they possibly lie, at least in part, elsewhere in global strategic, intellectual, cultural and policy assumptions that are eminently questionable, even though loud in their advocacy, and compelling in the power behind them. But providing a comprehensive explanation for such shortfalls may not belong to the purview and context of this book.

e-governance in Africa, From Theory to Action: A Handbook on ICTs for Local Governance is a important contribution to the literature on the subject of e-governance in general, and e-governance in Africa in particular, as well as of ICTs and Development in Africa.

This volume reflects Gianluca Misuraca's vast knowledge of the field, including his practical experience while working for UN-DESA on secondment to the Tangier-based African Training and Research Centre in Administration for Development (CAFRAD), domicile of the *e-Africa Initiative* of the New Partnership for Africa's Development (NEPAD) of the African Union. Misuraca himself originally formulated the *e-Africa Initiative* on behalf of CAFRAD and UN-DESA in 2002.

I highly recommend it, as a significant work at an important phase in a scholarship process that is still in its puberty, with much debate and maturation, and the corresponding adjustment in the conceptual framework, yet to come.

Joseph O. Okpaku, Sr., PhD
President and CEO
Telecom Africa International Corporation
New Rochelle, N. Y. USA

Dr. Joseph O. Okpaku, Sr., President and CEO of Telecom Africa International Corporation, is a globally renowned expert in teleCommunication, Information and Communication Technologies, Strategic Development and Governance. He has lectured and is extensively published worldwide on the subject of ICTs, Governance and Development, including *eGovernment for Results: A Programme Document for the Implementation of the Tangier Plan of Action for the e-Africa Initiative on Good Governance; Creating a Desirable 21st Century Africa: The Role of Leadership and Governance; Knowledge and the Translucency of Government: The Opportunities and Challenges of eGovernment for Strategic Development; SMART e-GOVERNMENT---Adopting Information and Communication Technologies to Enhance Strategic Development Without Undermining Fundamental Human Priorities*, and *Information and Communication Technologies for African Development: An Assessment of Progress and Challenges Ahead (ed.)*.

PREFACE

"...let us resolve to bridge the Digital Divide between countries, between rural and urban areas, between educated and illiterate populations, and between men and women. And let us act urgently so that all the world's people can benefit from the potential of the ICT revolution...."

—U.N. Secretary General Kofi Annan
2002 "World Telecommunication Day"

Information and Communication Technologies (ICTs) are bringing about major changes in the way in which local and regional authorities operate, interact and communicate internally or with other administrations, enterprises and citizens. As the closest level of government to the citizen and the main providers of public services, local and regional authorities are in the front line in the development of e-government and e-governance initiative.

e-government can be defined in many ways, but this work identifies it as the composite trend of governments at all level, mainly through their operational arm, the administration and, subsidiarily through the access of citizens to public affairs, aimed at promoting 1) a better and more efficient administration, 2) more effective inter-administration and administration-enterprise relationships and 3) user-empowering servicing and more transparent access of citizens to political decision-making.

e-governance is instead generally referred to as the capacity of ICTs to harness changes, looking not only at the increasing use of ICTs as a technological tool for delivering services online and improving the efficiency of administrations, but as a new paradigm for opening up government services to citizens, thereby increasing transparency and participation, and making government more responsive and centred upon its citizens' needs.

But this is a limited definition of the potential of e-governance, in fact, the conceptualisation of e-governance that I propose in this work is that e-governance concerns a rapidly evolving multi-dimensional, multi-actor, multi-level and inter-sectoral area of application, influenced not only by the ICT-revolution, but mainly by globalisation, international economic competition and state transformation. It also takes place in a very specific environment and contextual atmosphere about which we must understand and learn, in order to best guide the process. This overall change can be identified as manifold, although producing a composed impact on our lifestyle, level of wealth and relationships, inter-regionally and inter-nationally speaking.

In this respect, exchanges of experiences can provide a valuable tool in helping local and regional authorities to rise to the challenge and meet the expectations and needs of citizens in the digital era. This does not involve imposing a model, especially imported from the North to the South, but instead, pooling the wealth of knowledge that we have together and tapping this resource through the creation of a platform for the dissemination of practices and the localisation of solutions to promote regional development and good local governance.

However, as technology changes rapidly, so does the study of ICT-related issues. This is especially true with regard to a subject such as e-governance, that is still in its infancy, with a limited literature, no demonstrated results from applied research and which is evolutionary by definition.

Therefore, the findings and conclusions of this work should be considered both as a starting point and as a basis for further research and analysis.

This is also because from the time I started investigating in the area of e-governance to the publication of this work, there has been an emerging interest in the subject and, at the same time, some first applications of the hypothesis of the positive impact of ICTs on governance are also showing their limitations.

My own observations of the issues related to ICTs and governance have been subject to evolution. In fact, this research is the result of my "learning journey" on e-governance in Africa, started actually when, from e-Europe I went to e-Africa. It began in 2002 when I was working with the United Nations, and it was enriched by the experience gained at the Executive Master in e-governance at the Ecole Polytechnique

Fédérale de Lausanne (EPFL), of which I am now the Managing Director, after being a "pioneer" participant in its first edition in 2005.

During this period I have been looking at the interrelation between ICTs and governance, and it is now clear to me that, as one of the most recognised and appreciated scholars in this field, and a pioneer in the area, Prof Claudio Ciborra, already mentioned in his inaugural lecture at the London School of Economics in October 2002, "New approaches are desperately needed".

It is with this recommendation in mind that I am also looking at the relationship of ICTs and Governance, not only from a technological point of view, but mainly as the framework in which institutional redesign can take place.

I wish you pleasant reading.

Gianluca C. Misuraca

ACKNOWLEDGEMENTS

During my previous and current working experience I learned a lot from Africa and Africa changed my life ... As happened to many before me, and will still happen after, Africa conquered me and many friends consider myself "African by adoption"....

I wish therefore to thank all the people I met in my "learning journey", and especially during my many travels across Africa.

In particular, I wish to thank Prof Tijjani Muhammad Bande, former Director General of the African Training and Research Centre in Administration for Development (CAFRAD), where I spent three unforgettable years, and all CAFRAD's "family" and all other "African" colleagues, as well as Mr. Guido Bertucci, Director of the Division for Public Administration and Development Management of the United Nations Department of Economic and Social Affairs (UNDESA), and Ms Haiyan Qian, Chief of UNPAN, my supervisors during the two years I spent as Associate Expert serving the UN.

I also wish to thank Prof Matthias Finger and especially my friend Dr Pierre Rossel of the Ecole Polytechnique Fédérale de Lausanne (EPFL) for their mentoring during my Executive Master first and, afterward, as colleagues in the implementation of the Master itself, and for the common development of a new conceptualisation of e-governance as well as the establishment of a platform for global knowledge dissemination.

I am grateful to Prof. Mike Martin and his wife Bernadette for reviewing my text, and for most valuable comments and, of course, a special thanks go to Jo Okpaku, that accepted to write the foreword of the book. It enriches enormously my work, and I am delighted to be associated with one of the most relevant scholar on ICTs for Development in Africa.

Of course, I also need to thank "my government", Souad, and all my family for the patience and the support they provided me during my professional and research activities.

Last but not least, I wish to thank the International development Research Centre (IDRC) and the United Nations Economic Commission for Africa (UNECA) which gave me the opportunity to conduct this research and supported me throughout its execution, and allowed me to travel again, ...from e-Africa to... LOG-IN Africa, the Research Network on Local Governance and ICTs for Africa, approved for funding by IDRC and executed by CAFRAD, established under my leadership, in 2006.

INTRODUCTION

The advent of the Information Society is creating unprecedented conditions for bridging the digital divide through supporting government operations to strengthen the establishment of efficient, effective and transparent governance systems. Electronic tools can significantly improve the services and information flows from administrations to their constituencies. Communication among administrations and citizens and businesses can be enhanced and, at the same time, Information and Communication Technologies (ICTs) offer unique opportunities for the re-use and exploitation of public sector information within the emerging digital economy. Bringing out this potential will create vast economic opportunities for developing countries[1]. However, there are different aspects and configurations of the Digital Divide: Infrastructural, Information, Knowledge, Intellectual, Human Resource Capacity, Cultural, Content[2]. Therefore, the Digital Opportunity also presents a "divide" among developed and developing countries. This needs different actions in different contexts and a holistic approach to solve, in an integrated manner, the various gaps existing in developing countries and, in particular, Africa.

The centrality and importance of strengthening the political and administrative frameworks in African countries is commonly recognised. In the context of development, improved governance has several implications. In particular, however, it facilitates the design and pursuit of a comprehensive national strategy of development. It ensures capacity, reliability and integrity of the core institutions of the modern state. It implies improving the ability of government to carry out governmental policies and functions, including the management of implementation mechanisms. It means accountability for actions and transparency in decision-making and also signifies the opportunity for people to participate openly in the democratic process. Improved governance requires an effective, efficient and responsive public administration system[3].

In the light of the above, and within the framework of enhancing governance in Africa, there's a clear recognition of challenges and opportunities particularly relating to the development of a widespread «Knowledge-based Society» to be created using e-governance as a tool. As underlined by the United Nations Development Programme - Human Development Report 2001 *"Making New Technologies Work for Human Development"*, "*technology networks are transforming the traditional map of development, expanding people's horizons and creating the potential to realise in a decade progress that required generations in the past*"[4]. There is no doubt that the need for all-round improvement of performance is a very urgent one for African governments and that ICTs are valuable in decision making, planning and management support in all sectors of the economy[5]. The Information Society is in fact already being overcome by the "Network Age", that is changing how technologies are created and diffused. But gaps among rich and poor countries and risks of mismanagement of the enormous opportunities and power given by ICTs have to be carefully taken into consideration.

The international debate and several United Nations documents, such as the Millennium Declaration and the Monterrey Consensus, have highlighted the centrality and importance of good governance for sustainable development. Sound economic policies, solid democratic institutions responsive to the needs of the people and improved infrastructure are understood as being the basis for sustained economic growth, poverty reduction and employment creation.

ICTs provide a powerful tool in support of development strategies and the establishment of efficient and effective governance systems. Electronic tools can significantly improve service delivery, transparency and accountability and two-way communications between administrations and their constituencies.

Contexts and institutional frameworks within African countries are changing rapidly and policymakers and private and public telecommunications service providers have introduced reforms. Reforming countries are reaping the benefits through improved infrastructure, increased applications and better accessibility and affordability of ICTs equipment and services. However, one of the major challenges confronting Africa is to develop the capacity, strategies, and mechanisms necessary to take full advantage of the opportunities offered by ICTs especially at the local level.

The Fifth African Governance Forum (2002) and the Declaration of the World Summit of Cities and Local Authorities on the Information Society (Lyon, 5 December 2003), both identified development at the local level as the key to good governance including through the use of ICTs. Notably, the Digital Solidarity Fund, the new financial mechanism officially established and funded as a follow-up to the first phase of the World Summit on Information Society (WSIS), has the specific aim of supporting projects and activities in the area of ICTs for local governance in developing countries. However, despite the recognition of its importance little empirical evidence exists, especially in Africa, on the effects of ICTs on local governance.

Decentralisation and locally controlled administration are increasingly identified as basic components of democratic governance and provide an enabling environment in which decision making and service delivery can be brought closer to the people, especially the poor and the marginalised. Community participation in decision making, planning, implementation and monitoring and backed by appropriate institutions and resources; along with effective decentralisation can, through ensuring greater accountability, responsiveness and participation, result in local services that are more efficient, equitable, sustainable and cost-effective.[6]

The integration of ICTs in these processes can greatly enhance the delivery of public services to all citizens and thus, the overall objective of improving the performance of governance systems at all levels, as well as increase the democratic governance framework of the society at large.

But the potential for e-governance in developing countries remains largely unexploited,[7] perhaps because of the difficulty in achieving the revised organisational structures and skills; the degree of decentralisation of decision making;[8] new forms of leadership; transformation toward public-private partnerships; and the effective involvement of stakeholders that is required.[9] Moreover, local governance is in general given little attention within national e-governance policies and strategies.

However, the broad assumptions that decentralisation policies can influence good local governance and that the use of ICTs can greatly increase this influence have yet to be proven. To date there is little empirical evidence of the "multi-dimensional" effects of ICTs on local governance, which can in turn inform national e-governance policies. While, there are some examples of linkages between ICTs and local governments, the causal connection between ICTs and innovation in local governance for socio-economic development is little understood. Also, recognition of the potential of ICTs for local governance comes from a few successful pilot applications around the world. Attempts are currently underway to critically evaluate some of these projects so that the real extent of their impact can be understood and the factors inhibiting that impact can be identified. However, there is no common assessment framework from which lessons can be drawn in examining the link between ICTs and good local governance which is defined as "the exercise of economic, political, and administrative authority to better manage the affairs of a locale".[10]

With this research I intended to initiate the move away from anecdotal analysis of strengthening local governance with ICTs, towards a more rigorous, evidential and outcomes-based analysis of developing trends and implementation of ICTs in local governance and so develop the basis for a Research Agenda on ICTs for Local Governance in Africa.

In fact, drawing on an "institutionalist" framework, on the one hand I have started to investigate how ICTs affect policy outcomes within a given institutional setting and, on the other hand, what are the key drivers or factors of success in implementing strategies and programmes that include integrating ICTs at local governance level.

The theoretical framework underpinning the practical work assumes not only a direct intervening effect of ICTs on policy outcomes, but furthermore a possible indirect effect of ICTs on the institutional settings themselves.

The analysis focusses on four selected projects being implemented in Africa, as case studies, to start creating an environment of lessons to be learned from each other and to inform about the factors of success in relation to enhancing governance and reinforcing democracy using ICTs.

The preparation of the case studies is based upon "field-missions" undertaken within the framework of the Acacia & Connectivity Africa Dissemination Activities of the International Development Research Centre (IDRC), and on behalf of the United Nations Economic Commission for Africa (UNECA), in preparation of the Second Phase of the World Summit on Information Society – WSIS-II (Tunis 2005), as well as to support the development of a broader Research Network Activity to be initiated and funded by IDRC and executed through the African

Training and Research Centre in Administration for Development (CAFRAD) as a follow-up to the WSIS-II (Tunis, November 2005).

The case studies, identified following the decisions of the "Partnership for ICTs in Africa" (PICTA) meeting (Tunis, 2003), where an assessment of tools for local government, compiling stories on different PICTA member partners' experiences in this area, has been indicated as a priority action, are the following:

1. The role of ICTs in Decentralisation Policy in Senegal;
2. ICTs and Traditional Governance in Ghana;
3. The District Administrative Network Programme in Uganda;
4. The Cape Town's "Smart City" Strategy in South Africa.

By investigating the relationships between ICTs and local governance, my research was intended to provide empirical evidence of the dynamics, outcomes and implications for policy and practice of the integration of ICTs in local governance systems in Africa. Also, key drivers for effective integration of ICTs into local governance systems have been identified and discussed, based on concrete examples and discussing them within the local context of effective implementation.

Conclusions, more than a definitive set of recommendations for implementation of ICTs at the local level should be seen as some lessons learned from experience, and the starting point of further research in the emerging area of e-Local governance, and e-governance in general.

Notes

1. Misuraca Gianluca, "e-Africa initiative for good governance: building e-governance capacity in Africa", Paper presented to the International Conference on e-government, SITEXPO, Casablanca, Morocco, 18-21 February 2004.
2. Okpaku Joseph, Ownership of Problems, Intellectual Property and the Digital Divide: The Enabling Challenge of Solutions - An address to the WIPO Second International Conference on Electronic Commerce and Intellectual Property, Geneva, September, 2001.
3. UNDESA, Economic Governance: Guidelines for Effective Financial Management, New York, 2000.
4. UNDP, Human Development Report, 2001, www.undp.org

5. e-Africa 2002: Building e-governance capacity in African countries, Tangier, 2002, Project Proposal, prepared by Gianluca Misuraca on behalf of the African Training and Research Centre in Administration for Development, CAFRAD.
6. Report of the Workshop on Poverty Alleviation and Decentralization for Ten West African countries, organized jointly by UNDESA and the Government of Senegal, Dakar, July, 2003.
7. D.V. Ndou, "e-government for Developing Countries: Opportunities and Challenges", *The Electronic Journal on Information Systems in Developing Countries*, 18,1,1-24, 2004.
8. Dr. A. Aliyu, "Nigerian Experience of Decentralization as a Means to Improve Governance and How It Contributes to Combating Poverty", 2003.
9. Fifth African Governance Forum (AGFV), "Local Governance for Poverty Reduction in Africa", Maputo, Mozambique, 23-25 May 2002.
10. LOG-IN Africa Project Proposal, Gianluca Misuraca on behalf of CAFRAD for IDRC, November 2005.

PART I

CONCEPTUAL FRAMEWORK: TOWARDS A MULTI-DIMENSIONAL E-GOVERNANCE

1

THE POTENTIAL OF ICTS FOR GOOD GOVERNANCE: BASIC CONCEPTS AND DEFINITIONS

Today's world is more and more referred to as being "networked" due to the advancement of ICTs but also because of the growing phenomenon of the involvement of non-state or non-governmental actors into policy-making, either in a consultative way or through the development of new participatory approaches, often enabled or enhanced by the use of ICTs.

This is dispersing State power into autonomous local governance systems, while the industrial revolution in the past centralized it. The opportunity of using ICTs for communicating on a global scale has added new dimensions to possibilities for pursuing national, regional and local development; that is where economic and social impacts can be more valuable to the administration users and the citizens.

Recognising the importance of information for democratic and civic life, in principle, it is required to increase knowledge and information capacities to operate in a context where institutions and infrastructure are needed to facilitate the flow of information, its availability and access. Some indicates in a straightforward positive way that "Information and knowledge are closely intertwined: to produce information, a knowledgeable agent processes new findings and data, acceptable to society, and the resulting commodity is the increase of knowledge through improvement of access". In this way, "The increment in knowledge reduces uncertainty with regard to the organisation of economic and social activities, providing the capacity to effectively use available information and reach informed decisions"[1].

However, as a matter of fact, information is not knowledge neither competence. Information access and sharing, as well as expert data handling, necessitate a lot of knowledge. Information is not the first stage towards knowledge, neither the pre-condition of it. Often it is quite the opposite. Similarly, the increase of participation in the usage of ICTs is no automatic and linear step towards a deep, effective, sustainable or democratic evidence. On the contrary, one has to stress that to carry out a collective learning of some significance through ICTs, more horizontal processes, empowerment and trial and error linked with experience sharing must somehow take place "upstream" or at least considered quite early in an ICT-based project to constitute a democratic enhancement chance.

In this context, the relations between ICTs and governance are multiple. Governance supported by the development of ICTs can have more powerful information transmission, stimulate debate and participation and, at the same time, the establishment of information systems and knowledge management tools can facilitate governmental processes. However, it should be underlined that, when discussing integration of ICTs in administration, the focus is in the promotion of governance using ICTs as a tool, rather than the ICTs being an end in themselves[2].

To this extent, it is necessary to identify and to try to define the basic concepts we are dealing with, from Government to Governance, at central and local level, and including the potential role of the ICTs as a tool for good governance as well as giving a perspective on how ICTs can enhance citizens' participation.

In fact, there are many definitions and views of the same concept, and interpretations are so varied and sometimes conflicting that makes this task difficult and could generate controversial conclusions. In this context, with particular regard to the use of ICTs in public administration, some assert that "trying to establish a single definition for such complex and diverse issues and challenges may be unworkable at best and unhelpful at worst"[3].

Therefore, what I try to do here is to discuss basic concepts and present some commonly recognised definitions aiming at providing a contribution to the establishment of a common understanding on what we are talking about, in order to build a shared framework within which an operational dialogue among different actors and stakeholders, with different backgrounds, viewpoints, interests and objectives, can work together. This is done utilising international literature and especially recent background papers produced within the context of the Global Forum on Re-inventing Government and the UN World Public Sector Reports[4].

First of all, everyone thinks they know what a government is, but its "simple" definition given by the United Nations, introduces other concepts that are not always effectively considered by all governments.

Definition of Government:
a public organization – is part of a broader governance system. It is a means to a goal.
These days, government is seen predominantly as a public organization set up by a society for the purpose of pursuing that society's development objectives. This comprises articulating the society's development-related demands, proposals and needs, aggregating them and implementing responsive solutions. Enjoyment of public consent constitutes the source of government's legitimacy. Transparency is a condition sine qua non for government's accountability vis-à-vis its oversight body.
(*U.N. World Public Sector Report, 2003 – www.unpan.org*)

In its broadest sense, government refers to a body that has the authority to make and the power to enforce laws within a civil, corporate, religious, academic and other organization. At a nation level, government commonly refers to the administration of a state, in general to the executive function or branch of the body of the exercising authority. The level of government responsible for running a district, province or city is also referred as local government in contrast with bodies at nation-state level (I will be back on this later).

1.1. GOVERNANCE, GOOD GOVERNANCE AND DEMOCRATIC GOVERNANCE

When most people hear the word governance they think of government. After all, both have the same root word (*κυβερνᾶν*) from the Greek language, which means "to steer". But governance is about more than just government. It is a complex yet universal force that exists in all societies. People use governance in their daily lives to manage human relationships, just as corporations and countries do to manage their interactions and activities[5].

In this regard, and considering its meaning in the Greek language, an useful metaphor to describe governance is referred to steering a ship. "Steering a ship, in fact, is not only a matter of keeping the ship afloat and in forward, backward, or sideways motion. It is knowing the direction to be taken and ensuring that the ship is constantly on course in that direction. Above all, for everyone in the ship and those waiting for its arrival, a captain can claim good seamanship only when the ship gets to where it is expected"[6]. As an act of steering a people's development, governance is about processes not about ends.

The **World Bank** has identified three distinct aspects of governance: 1. the form of political regime; 2. the process by which authority is exercised in the management of a country's economic and social resources for development; 3. the capacity of governments to design, formulate and implement policies and discharge functions (World Bank, 1997).

For **UNDP**, governance is viewed as the exercise of economic, political and administrative authority to manage a country's affairs at all levels. It is about the process by which government, the private sector, citizens and groups articulate their interests, mediate their differences, and exercise their legal rights and obligations (UNDP, 1997).

For **UNESCO**, governance refers to the exercise of political, economic and administrative authority in the management of a country's affairs, including citizens' articulation of their interests and exercise of their legal rights and obligations.[7]

The concept of governance defined by **OECD** denotes the use of political authority and exercise of control in a society in relation to the management of its resources for social and economic development (OECD, 1995). This broad definition encompasses the role of public authorities in establishing the environment in which economic operators function and in determining the distribution of benefits as well as the nature of the relationship between the ruler and the ruled.

According to the **Institute of Governance**,[8] governance comprises the institutions, processes and conventions in a society which determine how power is exercised, how important decisions affecting society are made and how various interests are accorded a place in such decisions (Institute of Governance, 2002).

The **Commission on Global Governance** defines it as the sum of the many ways individuals and institutions, public and private, manage their common affairs. It is a continuing process through which conflicting or diverse interests may be accommodated and co-operative action may be taken. It includes formal institutions and regimes empowered to enforce compliance, as well as informal arrangements that people and institutions either have agreed or perceive to be in their interest (Commission on Global Governance, 1995).[9]

As we have seen, definitions of governance by leading institutions and studies converge on the term as meaning by which power is exercised.

Having now made clear the concept of governance as a "participatory process", we can better understand why it has become a truism to say that **good governance** is essential for successful development. But what is good in good governance and what are the implications for development ?

The concept of governance in the context of the promotion of sustainable economic development comprises efficient government, effective civil society and a successful private sector. Good governance has many characteristics. Good governance systems are participatory in that the members of governance institutions have a voice in the decision making process based on democratic traditions. The procedures and methods of decision making reflect transparency to ensure effective participation. The governance system aims at bringing about **sustainable development**, which is defined as "improving economic efficiency, protection and restoration of the environment and enhancing wellbeing of people" (International Institute of Sustainable Development, 1995).

While governance is a neutral concept, good governance addresses the allocation and management of resources to respond to collective problems. A universally agreed position on what constitutes good governance is hard to come by. However, conceptually, it is characterised by the principles of participation, transparency, accountability, rule of law, effectiveness, equity and strategic vision (UNDP, 1997).

By definition, good governance is the positive aspect of governance. But what about bad governance?

Bad governance is defined by Weiss as "the personalisation of power, lack of human rights, endemic corruption and unelected and unaccountable governments"[10]

When we speak of the quality of a country's governance, then, we mean the degree to which its institutions and processes are transparent and accountable to the people and allow them to participate in decisions that affect their lives. It is also the degree to which the private sector and organisations of the civil society are free and able to participate[11].

Good governance is a concept that has come into regular use in political science, public administration and, more particularly, development management. It appears alongside terms such as democracy, civil society, participation, human rights and sustainable development. In the last decade, it has been closely associated with public sector reform. As indicated by the Secretary General of the United Nations Kofi A. Annan **"Good governance is perhaps the single most important factor in eradicating poverty and promoting development"[12].**

According to the United Nations, good governance promotes equity and equality of treatment to all based on the concept of non-discrimination. The basic consideration in good governance is being able to develop the resources and methods of governance. In the context of social development parameters, it promotes gender balance, enables synthesis of diverse perspectives and mobilises resources for social purposes. Good governance strengthens indigenous mechanisms and ensures efficient and effective use of resources. All civilised societies are supposed to be based on the rule of law which is an essential component of good governance and that should engenders and commands respect and trust.[13]

According to OECD, good governance has eight major characteristics. It is participatory, consensus oriented, accountable, transparent, responsive, effective and efficient, equitable and inclusive and follows the rule of law. It assures that corruption is minimised, the views of minorities are taken into account and that the voices of the most vulnerable in society are heard in decision making. It is also responsive to the present and future needs of society.[14]

Participation by both men and women is a cornerstone of good governance. Participation could be either direct or through legitimate intermediate institutions or representatives. It is important to point out that representative democracy does not necessarily mean that the concerns of the most vulnerable in society would be taken into consideration in decision making. Participation needs to be informed and organised. This means freedom of association and expression on the one hand and an organised civil society on the other.

Consensus oriented: considering there are several actors and as many viewpoints in a given society, good governance requires mediation of the different interests in society to reach a broad consensus on what is in the best interest of the whole community and how this can be achieved. It requires a broad and long-term perspective on what is needed for sustainable human development and how to achieve the goals of such development. This can only results from an understanding of the historical, cultural and social contexts of a given society or community.

Accountability is a key requirement of good governance. Not only governmental institutions but also the private sector and civil society organisations must be accountable to the public and to their institutional stakeholders. Who is accountable to whom varies depending on whether decisions or actions taken are internal or external to an organisation or institution. In general an organisation or an institution is accountable to those who will be affected by its decisions or actions. Accountability cannot be enforced without transparency and the rule of law.

Transparency means that decisions taken and their enforcement are done in a manner that follows rules and regulations. It also means that information is freely available and directly accessible to those who will be affected by such decisions and the enforcement of those decisions. It also means that enough information is provided and that it is provided in easily understandable forms and media.

Responsiveness: Good governance requires that institutions and processes try to serve all stakeholders within a reasonable timeframe.

Effectiveness and efficiency: Good governance means that processes and institutions produce results that meet the needs of society whilst making the best use of resources at their disposal. The concept of efficiency in the context of good governance also covers the sustainable use of natural resources and the protection of the environment.

Equity and inclusiveness: A society's wellbeing depends on ensuring that all its members feel that they have a stake in it and do not feel excluded from the mainstream of society. This requires that all groups, but particularly the most vulnerable, have opportunities to improve or maintain their wellbeing.

Rule of Law: Good governance requires fair legal frameworks that are enforced impartially. It also requires full protection of human rights, particularly those of minorities. Impartial enforcement of laws needs an independent judiciary and an impartial and incorruptible police force.

In brief, according to the general principle of International Organisations, good governance is when the authority of the government is based on the will of the people and is responsive to them. It is when open, democratic institutions allow full participation in political affairs and when human rights protection guarantees the right to speak, assemble and dissent. And it is when government and governmental institutions are pro-poor and promote the human development of all citizens. In short, it distinguishes between the institutions and processes of governance and their content and quality.

A definition that summarises the concept of governance and good governance which can be universally recognised is the following:

Definition of Governance and Good Governance:
A multifaceted compound situation of institutions, systems, structures, processes, procedures, practices, relationships, and leadership behaviour in the exercise of social, political, economic, and managerial/administrative authority in the running of public or private affairs.
Good Governance is the exercise of this authority with the participation, interest, and livelihood of the governed as the driving force.
(*Governance and Public Administration Branch, Division for Public Administration and Development Management, Department of Economic and Social Affairs, General Secretariat, United Nations – GPAB/DPADM/UNDESA*)

Building on these ideas, the UNDP Human Development Report 2002[15] elaborated the concept of **democratic governance**, that is, governance that would promote human development. Like the concept of good governance, democratic governance seeks efficient institutions and a predictable economic and political environment necessary for growth and effective functioning of public services.

It is defined as follows:

Definition of Democratic Governance:
Good governance from a human development perspective.
At its core it means:
- People's human rights and fundamental freedoms are respected, allowing them to live with dignity;
- People have a say in decisions that affect their lives;
- People can hold decision-makers accountable;
- Inclusive and fair rules, institutions and practices govern social interactions;
- Women are equal partners with men in private and public spheres of life and decision making;
- People are free from discrimination based on race, ethnicity, class, gender or any other attribute;
- The needs of future generations are reflected in current policies;
- Economic and social policies are responsive to people's needs and aspirations;
- Economic and social policies aim at eradicating poverty and expanding the choices that all people have in their lives.

(UNDP, Human Development Report, 2002)

The concept of democratic governance shares with humane governance the concerns with political freedom and human rights and the removal of discrimination as central objectives. A reform agenda would aim not only at building institutions and rules that are not just efficient but also fair, and that are developed through a democratic process in which all people have a real political voice. Democratic governance thus incorporates the notion of good governance for development, democratic processes and institutions and a concern with the securing of political and civil rights and freedoms as human rights.

Democratic governance is therefore considered as the most "human-development-friendly system of governance"[16]. However, we should also consider that democracy is a value that has different meaning in different cultures, and especially, that it is not only participation as it is often – in a simplistic way – referred to. And this is particularly true when it comes to ICTs.

In many cases, in fact, it is argued that introducing ICTs in Government can increase democracy, because it enlarges participation to public affairs. But this is not always the case, and, more important, it is not enough to enable changes.

1.2. LOCAL GOVERNANCE AND DECENTRALISATION

If we recognise the concept and definition of government and governance as indicated above, then we can discuss their implications at local level, trying to define the major forms of public sector decentralisation arrangements. But first of all what do we intend for local government?

In modern nations, local governments usually have fewer powers than national governments do. They usually have some power to raise taxes, though these may be limited by central legislation. In some countries local government is partly or wholly funded by subventions from central government taxation. The question of Municipal Autonomy - which powers the local government has, or should have, and why - is a key question of public administration and governance.

The institutions of local government vary greatly between countries, and even where similar arrangements exist, the terminology often varies. Common names for local government entities include state, province, region, department, county, district, city, township, town, borough, parish and village. However all these names are often used informally in countries where they do not describe a legal local government entity.

Local Government can therefore be defined as follows:

Definition of Local Government:
Local governments are administrative offices of an area smaller than a state. The term is used to contrast with offices at nation-state level, which are referred to as central government, national governments or (where appropriate) federal governments.
(Wordiq.com http://www.wordiq.com/definition/Local_government)

Now, if we consider the concept of governance at a local level, we will then have the definition of Local Governance.

Definition of Local Governance:
Local governance refers to the exercise of authority at local community level.
(*GPAB/DPADM/UNDESA*)

But not all governance practices at a local level would constitute local governance. It is possible to have central governance or even foreign governance at local level. "What determines whether governance is local or not is the extent to which the local population is involved in the steering (i.e. in determining the direction) according to their local needs, problems and priorities"[17].

In this sense, governance ceases to be a matter of government only. It is a situation of multiple inter-linkages and relationships in which different and various actors in the public and private sectors as well as civil society – at local, national and international levels – play different roles sometimes mutually conflicting and sometimes mutually reinforcing and complementary, focussing on satisfying the interests of the local community.

In this framework, local governance is not good by definition, but it can be assumed that good local governance involves a good management of administration at local level, including inter-administrative and inter-sectoral linkages.

Thus, the definition of Good Local Governance can be as follows:

Definition of Good Local Governance:
the exercise of economic, political, and administrative authority to better manage the affairs of a locale. (*LOG-IN Africa, CAFRAD/IDRC*)

Linked to the concept of local governance is of course the idea of decentralisation.

Conceptually, decentralisation relates to the role of, and the relationship between, central and sub-national institutions, whether they are public, private or civic.

The concept and definition of decentralisation has evolved over time and has acquired several shades of meaning. The "Classic" Decentralisation, as Mawhood and Davey described it, has rarely taken place.

Instead, regimes in developing countries modified the term to fit different types of administrative setups.[18]

Classic Decentralization is based on the following five principles:

1. Local authorities should be institutionally separated from central government and assume responsibility for a significant range of local services (primary education, clinics and preventive health services, community development and secondary roads being the most common).
2. These authorities should have their own funds and budgets and should raise a substantial part of their revenue through local direct taxation.
3. Local authorities should employ their own staff, although in the initial stage the regular civil service staff could be employed temporarily.
4. Councils, predominantly composed of popularly elected representatives, would govern the authorities internally.
5. Government administrators would withdraw from an executive to an advisory and supervisory role in relation to local government.

(Mawhood and Davey, 1980)

According to the Fifth African Governance Forum V, decentralisation is defined as follows:

Definition of Decentralization:
a gradual process expected to enhance the opportunities for participation by placing more power and resources at a closer, more familiar, more easily influenced level of government. In an environment with poor traditions of citizens' participation, therefore, decentralization is perceived to be an important first step in creating opportunities for citizen-state interaction.
(African Governance Forum V - Concept paper 2002)

Organisationally, decentralisation, or decentralised governance, refers to the restructuring of authority so that there is a system of co-responsibility between institutions of governance at central, regional and local levels according to the "principle of subsidiarity", thus increasing the overall quality and effectiveness of the governance system, while increasing the authority and capacities of sub-national levels.[20]

Broadly speaking, according to the United Nations, decentralisation can take the form of either devolution, deconcentration, delegation, or outsourcing, defined as follows:

Devolution:
is the closest to 'classic' decentralization. It implies that responsibilities and resources are transferred to local governments with a high degree of autonomy to decide how to use the resources.
Deconcentration:
refers to institutional changes that shift the authority to make certain types of decisions from the center to dispersed locations. In this arrangement, staff and resources are transferred from headquarters to lower units of administration, under officers who could take operational decisions without reference to the headquarters.
Delegation:
refers to transfer of authority to public corporations or semi-autonomous bodies or public enterprises. The central government sets the objective of the delegated agencies and transfers resources to them on the basis of approved plans and budgets. However, these agencies have a fair degree of autonomy in performing their functions and may even have autonomous revenue sources.
Outsourcing/transfer-partnership:
a relatively new phenomenon, refers to transfer of responsibility for public functions to private enterprises or voluntary organizations.

Of the four forms of decentralisation described above, deconcentration represents the least amount of transfer of power to local people. Delegation also does not by itself transfer power to the locals, although the delegated agencies have the scope for involving local people in their decision making process. It is the two other forms, namely devolution and outsourcing/transfer-partnership when it is referred to civil society organisations that provide the largest scope for developing genuinely local level governance based on popular participation, through mobilizing the capacity and initiatives of civil society organizations working for social and economic development. Overall, according to studies and analysis, in Africa, decentralisation has, to a different degree, by and large taken the form of deconcentration and delegation.[21]

1.3. ICTS, E-GOVERNMENT, E-GOVERNANCE AND E-PARTICIPATION

The overall objective of improving the governance systems and the performance of the public administration at all levels, enhancing the delivery of the public services to all citizens, can greatly benefit from the integration of ICTs in the process of decision making, planning, co-ordination and management carried out by governments. But what are ICTs and why should we integrate ICTs in the government process?

On a point of definition we talk of ICTs, adding "communications" to the more familiar "Information Technology". This reflects the increasing role of both information and communications technologies in all aspects of society. Generally speaking, ICTs are defined by Stevenson in his 1997 report to the UK government and promoted by the new National Curriculum documents for the UK in 2000 as: "The study of the technology used to handle information and aid communication"[22]. But what we are interested in, more than the study of technologies, is the application to improve and "channel" information through any means of communication, based on different infrastructure. So it is important to understand what is information and what is communication. The World Bank defines ICTs as a generic term, which includes Information Technology (hardware and software) and the telecommunication infrastructure, equipment and services.

According to J. Habib Sy, "Information refers to knowledge, strategic and non-strategic research results as well as patented or licensed information increasingly commoditised in public and private channels at a cost commensurate with its technological, commercial, military, educational or social value". Despite being a bit complicated, this means that information is an essential ingredient in any historical communication system and a central condition for capital accumulation and wealth generation. "Communication refers instead to processes and effects within a given social context in which senders and receivers of messages enter into transactions of some sort". For Sy, "ICTs refer mainly to people and the way they relate to each other either individually or in a group rather than the technology. Technology, in this context, is neither a necessary and sufficient condition for social progress nor a means for leapfrogging"[23].

Therefore, recent literature uses interchangeably the word ICTs and Info-communication to signify the following:

Definition of ICTs / Info-communication:
The combination of all those areas traditionally known as telecommunication, information technologies, radio and television broadcasting, online publishing and postal services, including the ultimate multimedia.
(E. Olekambainei and M. A.Sintim-Misa, in "Info-communication for Development in Africa", in ICTs for African Development, edited with Introduction by Joseph O. Okpaku, Sr., UN ICT Task Force Series 2, New Rochelle, N. Y. Third Press. 2003.)

Thus, what is important about ICTs is their capacity for improving the communication between people: that is defined as the quintessential aspect of human society. In fact, human beings have always used communication to inform, learn, define concepts and viewpoints, deliberate and reach agreements, in private and public life. The electronic features of modern ICTs can be put into this timeless communication process and benefit from doing so[24].

The definition of the Quintessence of ICTs made by Dr. Joseph Okpaku in one of his instructive papers is instrumental in this regard.

The Quintessence of ICTs:
The tool for conducting the development process, the tool for engaging men and women, young and old, rich and poor, in crafting a common future on the wealth of culture and experience, positive and negative, the tool which enables us to express ourselves articulately in our own context, and for others to hear us some distance away, and for us to hear them too, is the fundamental element of ICTs. The enhancement of this process to give it speed and distant reach, to store it for future use, even far from its origin, the application of the innovation of science and technology to enable us to conduct this critical dialogue faster, more widely and more frequently: this is the quintessence of ICTs.
(Okpaku Joseph Sr., The Role of ICTs in the African Development Agenda, 2002[25])

In this respect, ICTs either as a tool or structural productivity lever, support both ordinary communication and innovation networking environments; they also, along the way, modify lifestyles, organisational boundaries and institutional adaptation capabilities. They help solve problems but also feed divides of various natures. They are supposed to define a new social paradigm, the Information Society, a world of promises, still to a large extent to be verified.

The e-world developed in this context, the Internet was the tool that, in the area of already existing computing instruments and applications, changed it all. Private initiatives came first, pioneering sectors being the banks, tourism, aviation, the military, then as somewhat a post Internet bubble remedy, but certainly in the continuation of messianic announcements by Al Gore and Martin Bangemann in the early nineties, state-supported efforts to develop converging strategies emerged, in OECD countries first, before expanding as a standard programme or at least an expectation in all countries, regions and municipalities of the world[26].

In this connection, it is worth underlining the role of ICTs as a tool for development, and not as a goal in itself. Using ICTs can help achieve development goals. This is particularly true in relation to government operations and governance in general. The integration of ICTs in governmental operations introduces the concept of Electronic Government, Digital Government or – in short – e-government.

This development has started in some isolated cases somewhat before the Internet (digital cities, like Amsterdam, for instance), but of course, the nineties were the period during which all this really took off. Measuring the deployment of e-government became a considerable business, benchmarking countries and regions in terms of initially, how much they could show as far as computer and Internet accesses were concerned, then various forms of "readiness" or administrative sophistication they could report upon became a "must to". More recently, measurement started to become a more scientific endeavour, coping with complex and partially contradicting features to benchmark efficiency, effectiveness, openness, etc. This debate is now open to emphasising real impact or track effectiveness with figures and verifiable models and all indications show that we are only at the beginning of this process.

Technological evolution may also soon prove to be a strong modifier of the initial e-government development framework, wireless solutions, satellite coverage and access and even more, mobile phone expanding potential.

After a few hesitations about terms, digital government, e-administration and others led to a more consensual formulation to this underpinning effort, and the e-government era emerged. In fact, there are many definitions of e-government, and the term itself is not universally used. The differences are not just semantic and may reflect priorities in government strategies.

According to Prof. Claudio Ciborra, in literature, e-government is mainly referred to as having three levels:

- the relationship (transaction) between the administration and the citizen (customer) and the related re-engineering of the activities internal to the administration (Bellamy and Taylor, 1998);
- the way in which the boundaries between the state and the market are redrawn, by the creation of an electronic, minimal state, more transparent, agile and accountable (Heeks, 1999, Stiglitz and Orszag 2000);
- the purpose of aid policies aimed at introducing e-government into developing countries, to improve accountability and transparency as key characteristics of good governance (UNDP, 2001)[27].

According to the OECD, the definitions of e-government fall into three groups:

- e-government is defined as Internet (online) service delivery and other Internet-based activity, such as e-consultation;
- e-government is equated to the use of ICTs in government. While the focus is generally on the delivery of services and processing, the broadest definition encompasses all aspects of government activity;
- e-government is defined as a capacity to transform public administration through the use of ICTs or indeed is used to describe a new form of government built around ICTs. This aspect is usually linked to Internet use.

The definition of e-government of the **OECD** is therefore simply "The use of ICTs, and in particular the Internet, as a tool to achieve better government"[28].

Adding a level of complexity, the **European Union Commission** defines e-government as "the use of ICTs in public administrations combined with organisational change and new skills in order to improve public services and democratic processes and strengthen support for public policies"[29].

For the **World Bank**, e-government refers to the use by government agencies of information technologies (such as Wide Area Networks, the Internet, and mobile computing) that have the ability to transform relationships with citizens, businesses, and other arms of government. These technologies can serve a variety of different ends: better delivery of government services to citizens, improved interactions with business and industry, citizen empowerment through access to information, or more efficient government management. The resulting benefits can be less corruption, increased transparency, greater convenience, revenue growth and/or cost reductions.[30]

In a simpler and easy manner, Prof. Dele Olowu, in a book published by **UNECA**, defines e-government as "all the information and communication technology platforms and applications in use in the public sector or the use of the internet for delivering government information and services to citizens"[31].

If we consider the ICTs as a "facilitator" in improving governance, through "re-inventing" the role of governments, providing tools to support public service reforms, enhance public administration management and public sector performance vis-à-vis the private sector and the citizens, we arrive at the concept of **Transformational e-government.** This, at its best, can be viewed as the process of creating **public value** with the use of modern ICTs, where public value is defined by Kelly and others (2001) as "the value created by Government through services, laws, regulations and other actions", or, by the United Nations in a simpler (or maybe too simplistic) way, as "the things that people want"[32].

A definition of e-government in this sense, that is comprehensive and summarises the concept of transformational state, is provided by the private sector, and in particular **Gartner Research**, which has been one of the pioneers in this area. It also reflects the operational approach that is typical of the business-oriented experience of private companies, and is as follows: "the continuous optimization of Government service delivery, constituency participation, and governance by transforming internal and external relationships through technology, the Internet and new media. In particular, e-government technologies can improve significantly the capacity of co-ordination among different branches and bodies of government, and communication among governments, citizens and business"[33].

The model of development for this pervasive effort is the famous stage concept of Gartner (2000), which has since been reformulated with minor variations. It supposed stages of phases and complexity through which government and, in most cases it should be more accurate to say the administration, deploys means of providing information and gradually more interaction-based service access to the users, online.

According to the **United Nations** "World Public Sector Report 2003: e-government at the Crossroads", "e-government is a government that applies ICTs to transform its internal and external relationships. Through the application of ICTs to its operations, a government does not alter its functions or its obligation to remain useful, legitimate, transparent and accountable. If anything, this application raises society's expectations about the performance of government, in all respects, to a much higher level"[34].

An evolution of this concept (2005; 2006; UNDESA) brings about the definition of E/M-Government (e-government / Mobile Government) as follows.

"The application of ICTs within and by the public sector, that provides government, the citizen and business with a set of tools that can potentially transform the way in which interactions take place, services are delivered, and public administration reform and good governance goals are met[35].

In this regard, it is assumed that "the strategic use of ICTs in government can result in a more inclusive, effective, efficient, transparent and accountable public administration, which will be key to improved economic development and competitiveness. Moreover, in enhancing the quality and delivery of public services through ICTs - especially in education, health, social security and social welfare - government may be better positioned to reduce poverty, redress inequality, and promote sustainable development"[36].

This definition and conceptual framework is, in my opinion, appropriate to identify the developmental role of ICTs and the transformative potential of the impact of ICTs. However, it also highlights the limitations of e-government as a real transformative process in itself, considering its focus on only one of the functions of the State, namely the service delivery.

Therefore, considering the numerous definitions of e-government, the working definition of e-government that I propose here is "a middle-of-the-road concept", that is as follows:

Definition of e-government:
e-government is the composite trend of governments at all levels, mainly through their operational arm, the administration, and subsidiarily through the access of citizens to public affairs, aimed at promoting:
1) a better and more efficient administration;
2) more effective inter-administration and administration-enterprise relationships; and
3) user-empowering servicing and more transparent access of citizens to political decision-making.
(Misuraca G, Rossel P., Finger M., EPFL, CDM, e-Gov, 2006)[37].

Considering instead the combination of ICTs with governance in the sense we formulated it above, e-government is more and more moving towards e-governance, where the concept of e-governance further encompasses e-government. e-governance is a growing phenomenon around the world and is emerging as a significant discipline, initially within the field of public administration reform, but that is now being realised as not only being a "government business", but a societal challenge as well.

e-governance is defined by the **Inter-American Development Bank** as being "beyond the scope of e-government.......", and in particular by Blake Harris that, to summarise, says that "e-governance is not just about government websites and email, etc..." and that " ....it will change how citizens relate to governments as much as it changes how citizens relate to each other"[38].

UNESCO defines e-governance as "the public sector's use of information and communication technologies with the aim of improving information and service delivery, encouraging citizen participation in the decision-making process and making government more accountable, transparent and effective"[39].

The **Pacific Institute of Management** in India equates e-governance with smart governance and uses the acronym SMART to define it as the "application of ICTs to the process of government functioning to bring out Simple, Moral, Accountable, Responsive and Transparent governance". The government of India has used this as the basis for its vision statement for e-governance and for the development of strategic initiatives and further objectives as outlined in what was termed an Indicative Roadmap to enact that vision.[40]

Different approaches are that of Gordon, who defines e-governance rather more narrowly as "the use of ICTs to improve the quality and efficiency of all phases of the life cycle of legislation". Vikas Nath, active on the Internet, defines e-governance as "Governance processes in which ICTs play an active and significant role". Gurstein and others emphasise the role of citizen as the basis for e-governance as in "the use of ICTs as a means to enhance the role of citizens in relation to their capacity and opportunity for effective participation in the broad structures of governance"[41].

A working definition of e-governance for Africa has also been developed -with my support- by the **African Training and Research Centre in Administration for Development (CAFRAD)** within the framework of the e-Africa Initiative for Good Governance: Building e-governance capacity in African countries. It defines e-governance as "the use of ICTs, and especially the Internet, to adopt a new conception and attitude of governing and managing where participation and efficiency are required of all the partners linked in a network: e-governance is therefore a new way of co-ordinating, planning, formulating and implementing decisions and operations related to governance problems. Governments can utilise e-governance to re-invent themselves, get closer to the citizenry and forge closer alliances and partnerships with diverse communities of interest, practice, expertise, conviction and inter-dependence within the context of national and international development agendas"[ap]. This definition is probably, in my opinion, the more appropriate to the African context, and it highlights how, as a concept and an emerging practice, e-governance seeks to realise processes and structures for harnessing the potentialities of ICTs at various levels of government and beyond, of the public sector, for the purpose of enhancing good governance and, in particular, citizens' participation.

But it is clear that the concept of e-governance is not commonly recognised and shared worldwide. Quite the contrary. For many, e-governance is just one more buzzword for e-government. For others, who aim at specific identifications, e-governance is merely an indication of the impact of e-government outside the administration boundaries, in particular when private economy actors are active stakeholders.

Looking at prevalent literature and definitions, as pointed out by Finger (2003, 2004 and further elaborated by Finger, Rossel and Misuraca, 2005, 2006), we can identify three main conceptualisations of e-governance: 1) e-governance as customer satisfaction; 2) e-governance as processes and interactions and 3) e-governance as tools[43].

The first and probably most widespread conceptualisation refers to customer satisfaction. Indeed, the term e-governance is not only used here as being synonymous of e-government, it is moreover synonymous with satisfying the citizen/customer by means of delivering the services through the Internet. Generally, this is the view of promoters of new public management who see in the ICTs a significant contribution to, and the next step in, improving service delivery and especially customer satisfaction. For this conceptualisation, the main unit of analysis is the government or rather the administration, whose interface with the citizens the ICTs are said to be going to improve. As a matter of fact, citizens are seen here as more or less passive recipients of digitalised information and services, i.e., as customers. In other words, at the heart of this conceptualisation it is not the process to which the ICTs are being applied, but merely the delivery of information and sometimes services. Needless to say that this view does not take into account the possible other policy levels that the state may need to cope with and, also, it does not mention the emergence of non-state actors who become increasingly involved in policy-making, service delivery and to a lesser extend regulation - the three main functions of the state[44].

In the second conceptualisation e-governance is seen as a decisional process. The **International Centre of e-governance** says for example, “Governance is not government, nor is it the act of governing. It is more usefully seen as a process: the process by which institutions, organisations, companies and societies guide themselves. It is also about how these bodies interact with each other, with their clients and with the public. At its most basic level, it is about how society organises itself for collective decision making, and also provides transparent mechanisms for seeing those decisions through. E-governance is a shorthand term for the use and impact of technology, in particular ICTs, in governance systems." Similarly, the **e-governance Institute of Rutgers University** states: "e-governance involves new channels for accessing government, new styles of leadership, new methods of transacting business, and new systems for organizing and delivering information and services. Its potential for enhancing the governing process is immeasurable." Here, the focus is clearly on processes and interactions, which the ICTs are said to foster or at least to facilitate. Potentially, the conceptualisation could also be extended to transactions. However, the view of the state remains quite traditional: indeed, it means interactions between the citizens and the private sector on the one hand and the state on the other. However, the state remains always at the centre of the process.

The third conceptualisation sees e-governance as a set of tools in the hands of government, or rather in the hands of the administration. In other words, the starting point here is not the state or its transformation, but the possibilities that ICTs offer. According to the **Commonwealth Centre for e-governance (CGeG)**, it is the movement of governments online to deliver their services and programmes, to provide government information, and to interact with the citizen, all electronically. This is resulting in the formation of new relationships between the citizen and the state.

In particular, CGeG says: "e-governance is a tool. And like any other tool, no matter how powerful, it has limited value and relevance in itself. Its value arises from its application to specific goals and objectives. E-governance is really about choice. It is about providing citizens with the ability to choose the manner in which they wish to interact with their governments." ..."E-governance is the commitment to utilise appropriate technologies to enhance governmental relationships, both internal and external, in order to advance democratic expression, human dignity and autonomy, support economic development and encourage the fair and efficient delivery of services"[45].

Following this and other research, in particular from the **Riley Reports**, the Commonwealth Centre for e-governance notes that "e-governance differs from e-government in the sense that e-government constitutes the ways public sector institutions use technology to apply public administration principles and conduct the business of government: it is government using new tools to enhance the delivery of existing services. E-governance includes the vision, strategies, planning, leadership and resources needed to carry this out: it is the way that political and social power are organised and used"[46].

This is parallel to the discussion by Okot Uma (2001 and 2005), which focusses on the direct contribution that the "e" plays in advancing principles of governance and particularly good governance. Indeed, he says, "e-governance seeks to realise processes and structures for harnessing the potentialities of information and communication technologies at various levels of government and at the public sector and beyond, for the purpose of enhancing good governance". Better governance, thanks to the ICTs, would improve, according to Okot-Uma, democracy and ultimately peoples' lives[47].

Not surprisingly, e-governance is not structured along concepts of state transformation, but rather along technological possibilities. Says Perri, one of the representatives of this conceptualisation of e-governance: "one way to classify e-governance systems is roughly according to the main tool for which they are used. There are tools for 1) generating understanding simple data; 2) collecting data or observations through search agents; 3) organising and analysing data on events, conditions, problems and processes; 4) supporting communication and transaction e-mail, electronic conferencing, video-conferencing systems; 5) modelling decisions and advising on possible consequences spreadsheets; 6) and environments that provide integration and storage for the other categories".

In other words, this conceptualisation is characterised by a strange combination of quite unreflected use of ICTs on the one hand and visionary (or even normative) statements on democracy and "good governance" on the other. It clearly puts the ICTs before the state, and actually operates with, in the opinion of Finger and others (2003, 2005), a quite simplistic and old-fashioned, and in any case naïve vision of the State. In particular, it is not dynamic, as it does not see the implications of the ICTs on operations, nor on state transformation.

In summary, looking at the main, currently prevalent conceptualisations of e-governance, it can be seen that there are still quite different understandings of what e-governance is, ranging from naïve and promotional views (e-governance as tools for democracy) to simplistic and unambitious ideas of using the ICTs for enhancing service delivery only (e-governance as customer satisfaction), passing through the one which sees e-governance as a dynamic process, i.e., mainly as an enhancement of interactions between actors (citizens/consumers, administration, private sector, civil society)[48].

Given the above, I postulate that there is a need to consider a more radical paradigmatic shift. As a complementary activity but inherently different from e-government, e-governance is the field of activity where co-ordination, arbitration, networking and regulation (just to mention essential steering functions), with ICTs, but also of ICTs, involved with all sorts of non-state actors, the state representatives being at best one of the stakeholders[49].

There are basically two converging processes that support the activities in the e-governance arena. One which stems from insufficient coverage, by the state, of problems that need to be solved but in which most solutions, experiments and expertise, from design to usage, are mainly carried out by non state actors, as innovative moves or as survival needs.

The other process, emerging from technology or service users, as inhabitants or as specific customers of a given economic market, individuals, communities or local enterprises, expresses some form of bottom-up creativity in which the state may play a role but only after the interactions and processes tackled reach a certain level of consistency. It is particularly true in the ICT area, where new services, habits, components or even technological ecosystems (let us think of Ipod, digital photography, smartphone applications or GPS-based services) emerge with barely any state presence of any kind.

E-governance is an intermediation arena in which negotiations, experiments and networking make important use of ICTs and in turn may also be dealing with some regulation of ICTs. After a while, in particular in the second case, the state tries to control it, sometimes with success (standardisation in WIFI for instance), sometimes not (governance of the Internet). In other cases, the issues are still open (pornography, intellectual property rights of ICT multimedia products, etc.).

In an attempt to advocate a "muddling through approach" rather than an idealistic one, in my opinion, and in this supported by research carried out in the last few years, I summarize the analysis by saying that differently from e-government, e-governance stresses the importance of the several components and multi-dimensional capacity of ICTs, the learning residing much more in the causality chain than the other way around.

For each technological implementation, for each e-service delivered, beyond their obvious instrumental level, there is in fact an organizational and institutional dimension, more governance-oriented, to be taken care of, in which ICT-deployment must be defined within the framework of a policy-compliant and inter-stakeholder knowledge management-effective perspective. This allows the slide from e-government to e-governance.

Society in fact is not harmonious and just saying that e-governance, like governance is about the transactional aspect of inter-actor life would not account for the complexity of what really takes place, it is also confrontational. Stakeholders have to muddle their way through even when they are not fundamentally friends, inter-industry-wise and inter-level-wise. This is why e-governance can be seen as the expression of a "dynamic tension" between institutional frameworks and ICTs.

Therefore, in a point of conceptualisation, we must take into consideration the multi-dimensional aspects of ICTs when discussing e-governance. In this regard, in a simple but, in my opinion very effective way, e-governance can therefore be defined as: **the Governance "with and of" ICTs**[50].

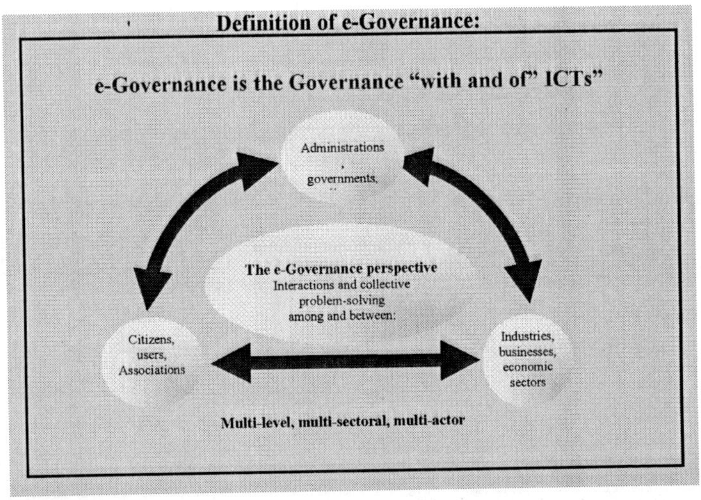

There are in fact, two side of the coin: "with" means basically "bureautic", web-based and connective type of technologies and applications or rather said mediation-supportive technologies and applications; meanwhile governance of ICTs means dealing in terms of innovation and regulation with all the technologies of the Information society (from tele-surveillance to GPS, through transport telematics and virtual community management applications, just to mention a few). (I will be back on this).

Complementary to the concept of e-governance, are the concepts of **e-Participation** and **e-Democracy**, which deal with how the citizen interacts with government and influences the legislative or public sector process. These concepts and emerging movements seek to engage the citizen with government and legislatures through the use of ICTs. According to some activists, this new dynamic that is developing between the citizen and government can actually result in giving some measure of power to the citizen. The distribution of information (if critical) can in fact produce some distribution of power since government information is no longer restricted to the political and bureaucratic elite.[51]

But before I present some definitions of e-Participation and e-Democracy that this approach involves and which is becoming popular on the web and among practitioners, despite it is evident that it is more a wishful thinking that a proven reality, it has to be considered that for countries, especially in the developing regions, there is the need to ensure (before even thinking of "going e", the correct introduction and utilisation of ICTs and e-government applications. Of particular importance is therefore the concept of **"e-readiness"**, as defined by Richard Heeks:

> Definition of e-Readiness:
> refers to available technological infrastructures, legal frameworks, institutional and human resources and political will. *(Heeks Richard – IDPM, University of Manchester www.man.ac.uk/idpm)*[52]

In this regard, it has to be considered that included in the vision of the UN General Assembly Millennium Declaration, is the reaffirmation by the member states that they "....resolve to work collectively for more inclusive political processes, allowing genuine participation by all citizens in all countries... and the right of the public to have access to information....."[53] Within this framework, e-Participation has been defined as follows:

Definition of e-Participation:
Participatory, inclusive, deliberative process of decision-making. This can be achieved via:

a) Using ICTs to increase the supply of information useful in the process of consultation and for decision-making;
b) Using ICTs to enhance consultation; and
c) Using ICTs to support decision-making by facilitating people's participation within the framework of G2C and C2G interactions.

(United Nations, "World Public Sector Report 2003: e-government at the Crossroads", New York, 2003, www.unpan.org)[54]

Looking at the concept of e-participation, according to the methodology and results of the UN Global e-government Survey, which presents a ranking of countries in the world referring to two primary indicators (e-government Readiness Index and e-Participation Index), the following e-Participation framework has been devised:

e-Participation Framework:

1. **e-Information:** Government Websites offer to citizens policies and programme documents; budgets; laws and regulations; briefs on key issues of public interest. Tools for dissemination of information exist for timely access and use of public information, including web fora, email lists, news-groups and chat rooms.
2. **e-Consultation:** Government Websites explain e-Consultation mechanisms and tools. They also offer a choice of public policy topics on line for discussion, with a real-time and archived access to audios and videos of public meetings. The Government encourages citizens to participate in discussions; and
3. **e-Decision-Making:** Government indicates it will take citizen input into decision-making and provides actual feed-back on the outcome of specific issues.

(United Nations, "World Public Sector Report 2003: e-government at the Crossroads", New York, 2003, www.unpan.org)[55]

Much of the analysis and the literature on the issues of e-governance, e-participation and e-democracy, highlights that, so far, governments are mainly concerned with organising ways for a better delivery of their services to the citizens, while there is little evidence that the citizen is having any significant input into how e-government will evolve.

It is not the objective of this work to analyse and discuss in-depth the issue of e-democracy, especially because there are as many interpretations of what constitutes e-democracy as there are interpretations of democracy. Moreover, since this concept is in its early stages, there remains much confusion about what it encompasses and how to clearly define it[56].

However, to take advantage of the studies undertaken by individuals on this subject, a definition of e-democracy by Steven Clift is referred to[57]:

> Definition of e-Democracy:
> represents the use of information and communication technologies and strategies by democratic actors within political and governance processes of local communities, nations and on the international stage. Democratic actors/sectors include governments, elected officials, the media, political organizations, and citizen/voters" *(Steven Clift, www.publicus.net)*

In conclusion, what can be said here is that this new participatory approach to running governance affairs, involving both the public sector, the private sector and the civil society, despite represents for the time being only an optimistic hypothesis should be implemented taking into consideration that the development of ICTs, and especially that of the Internet, is in principle able to improve the quality of life and blurring national boundaries. Through "e-space", the traditional concept of citizenship can be transformed into "active citizenship" and the next step is likely to be the establishment of systems based on online consultation and participation, according to some experiences already available in both industrialised and developing countries[58]. However, if this will automatically enhance democracy is yet to be proven.

Notes

1. Okpaku Joseph, "e-Culture, Human Culture and In-Between: Meeting the Challenges of the 21st Century Digital World", Address to the ITU Conference on "Creating New Leaders for e-Culture", Coventry, UK, August, 2001
2. Misuraca Gianluca, Overview of the e-Africa initiative for good governance: building e-governance capacity in Africa, Encyclopedia of Developing Regional Communities with Information and Communication Technology, IDEA May 2005.
3. e-government Policy Network of the Privy Council Office (PCO) "Transforming Government and Governance for the 21st Century", www.publiservice.pco-bcp.ga/egov-cybergouv 2003
4. The Global Forum on Re-inventing Government (and related publications and reports) is organized (every two years now) by the Division for Public Administration and Development Management of the United Nations Department of Economic and Social Affairs (DPADM/UNDESA). Gianluca Misuraca was a member of the organizing committee of the 4th Global Forum on Reinventing Government, Marrakech, Morocco, 2002, and contributed in the 5th Global Forum on Reinventing Government, Mexico City, 2003. See also www.unpan.org
5. Cheema Shabbir and Maguire Linda, "Democracy, and Development: A Conceptual Framework"; Background Paper of the 4th Global Forum on Re-inventing Government - Citizens, Businesses and Governments: Dialogue and partnerships for Development and Democracy, Marrakech, Morocco, 10-13 December 2002, UN, New York 2002. www.unpan.org - www.globalforum.ma
6. Kauzya John-Mary, "Local Governance Capacity Building for Full Range Participation: Concepts, Frameworks, and Experiences in African Countries"; Background Paper of the 4th Global Forum on Re-inventing Government - Citizens, Businesses and Governments: Dialogue and partnerships for Development and Democracy, Marrakech, Morocco, 10-13 December 2002, UN, New York 2002. www.unpan.org - www.globalforum.ma
7. www.portal-unesco.org, 2003
8. The Institute on Governance is a NGO based in Ottawa, Canada, www.iog.ca
9. Fukuda-Parr Sakiko and Ponzio Richard, "Governance: Past Present and Future"; Background Paper of the 4th Global Forum on Re-inventing Government - Citizens, Businesses and Governments: Dialogue and partnerships for Development and Democracy, Marrakech, Morocco,

10-13 December 2002, UN, New York 2002. www.unpan.org - www.globalforum.ma

10. Weiss Thomas, "Governance, Good Governnace and Global Governance: Conceptual and Actual Challenges", Third World Quarterly, Vol. 21, n.5, 2000
11. Cheema Shabbir and Maguire Linda, "Democracy, Governance and Development: A Conceptual Framework"; Background Paper of the 4th Global Forum on Re-inventing Government - Citizens, Businesses and Governments: Dialogue and partnerships for Development and Democracy, Marrakech, Morocco, 10-13 December 2002, UN, New York 2002. www.unpan.org - www.globalforum.ma
12. Kofi Annan, Millennium Declaration, United Nations 2000.
13. UNDESA, Economic Governance: Guidelines for Effective Financial Management, New York, 2000.
14. This definition of good governance is taken from an OECD e-book entitled Citizens as Partners - Information, Consultation and Public Participation in Policy-Making, 2001
15. UNDP, Human Development Report 2002, "Deepening democracy in a fragmented world", UN, NY, 2002.
16. Falk Richard, Prof, "On Humane Governance", University Park, The Pensyllvania State University, 1995.
17. Kauzya John-Mary, "Local Governance, Health and nutrition for all: problem magnitude and challenges with examples from Uganda and Rwanda", Paper presentation to the Global Forum on Local Governance and Social Services for All, Stockholm, Sweden, 2-5 May 2000.
18. Report of the workshop on Poverty Alleviation and Decentralization for ten West African countries, organized jointly by UNDESA and the Government of Senegal, Dakar, July, 2003.
19. The subsidiarity principle, as it is conceived in the Treaty of the European Union, is intended to ensure that decisions are taken as closely as possible to the citizen and that constant checks are made as to whether action at Community level is justified in the light of the possibilities available at national, regional or local level. Specifically, it is the principle whereby the Union does not take action (except in the areas which fall within its exclusive competence) unless it is more effective than action taken at national, regional or local level. It is closely bound up with the principles of proportionality and necessity, which require that any action by the Union should not go beyond what is necessary to achieve the objectives of the Treaty, www.europa.eu.int
20. Work Robertson, "The Role of Participation and Partnership in Decentralized Governance: Lessons from Nine Local Case Studies on Service

Delivery to the Poor"; Background Paper of the 4th Global Forum on Re-inventing Government - Citizens, Businesses and Governments: Dialogue and partnerships for Development and Democracy, Marrakech, Morocco, 10-13 December 2002, UN, New York 2002. www.unpan.org - www.globalforum.ma

21. Report of the workshop on Poverty Alleviation and Decentralization for ten West African countries, organized jointly by UNDESA and the Government of Senegal, Dakar, July, 2003. See also Katsiaouni, 2003.
22. Stevenson, 1997, in Computing Dictionary, http://www.hyperdictionary.com
23. Sy, J. Habib, "Critical and Prospective Views on ICTs and Governance in Africa", in "Africa Networking: Development Information ICTs and Governance, United Nations Economic Commission for Africa, UNECA, Addis Ababa, 2004
24. Osorio C., "Public Ends by Digital Means: Some Thoughts for Creating Public Value", National Science Foundation, Digital Government Workshop, White Paper 2002.
25. Okpaku Joseph O. Sr., "The Role of ICTs in the African Development Agenda", keynote address to the CAFRAD, UNDESA, NEPAD e-Africa 2002: Regional Workshop on Building e-governance capacity in Africa, Johannesburg, South Africa, 28-31 October 2002.
26. Gianluca Misuraca, Matthias Finger, Pierre Rossel, "Governance with and of ICTs: the need for new institutional design in a changing world", egov magazine, Volume II – Issue 5, May 2006,
27. Ciborra Prof. Claudio, U., "Unveiling e-government and Development: Governing at a distance in the new war", Inaugural lecture at LSE on 24 October 2002
28. OECD, e-government Studies, "The e-government Imperative", 2003, www.oecd.org
29. EU, Communication from the Commission to the Council, the European Parliament, the Economic and Social Committee and the Committee of the Regions – The Role of eGovernment for Europe's Future, 26 September 2003
30. World Bank, 2002 – www.worldbank.org
31. Olowu Dele, "Bridging the Digital Divide in Africa: Making the Governance Discourse Relevant", in Africa Networking: Development Information, ICTs and Governance, UNECA, Addis Ababa, 2004
32. For a complete definition of Public Value see United Nations, "World Public Sector Report 2003: e-government at the Crossroads", New York, 2003, www.unpan.org (Box 2, pag. 3).

33. Gartner Group, www.gartner.group.com
34. United Nations, "World Public Sector Report 2003: e-government at the Crossroads", New York, 2003, www.unpan.org
35. UNDESA/DPADM, www.unpan.org, 2005.
36. Idem.
37. This is a working definition that comes out of the evolutionary research framework developed by the author in collaboration with his colleagues within the framework of the Executive Master in e-governance at EPFL. For an overview of this conceptual framework see: Gianluca Misuraca Matthias Finger, Pierre Rossel, "Governance with and of ICTs: the need for new institutional design in a changing world", egov magazine, Volume II – Issue 5, May 2006, and also http://egov.epfl.ch
38. www.iadb.org/ict4dev/governance.htm
39. www.portal-unesco.org, 2003
40. www.pimanagement.org
41. For these definitions and discussions see: Gordon T.F., eGovernance and its value for Public Administration", White paper, e-government Competence Centre, Fraunhofer Institute for Open Communications Systems (FOCUS), Berlin, Germany, May 2006; Gurstein Michael, "From e-government to e-governance: an approach from effective use", Canadian Civil Society and the WSIS Conference on Paving the Road to Tunis, May 2005; and www.digitalgovernance.org
42. CAFRAD, e-Africa 2002: Building e-governance capacity in African countries, 2002, Project Proposal, edited with technical assistance of Mr Gianluca Misuraca.
43. See for example, Finger Matthias, Pecoud Gaëlle, "From e-government to e-governance? Towards a model of e-governance", 3rd European Conference on e-government, Trinity College Dublin, Ireland, 3-4 July 2003. See also EPFL-e-Gov, working papers; and Rossel, Finger, From e-government to e-governance: implications for technology management, 2005
44. For a discussion about the State Transformation see, among others, Finger Matthias.
45. Gilbert Riley Cathia, "The Changing Role of Citizen in the e-governance & e-Democracy Equation", CceG, 2003, www.electronicgov.net
46. On this see also Sheridan and Riley (2006) and Riley 2003.
47. Okot-Uma Rogers W'O., "Electronic Governance: Re-inventing Good Governance", Commonwealth Secretariat, London, 2000.
48. Finger, Pecoud, op. cit.

49. The claim for new institutional designs is the results of both the professional activities I have carried out and the research I am involved within the framework of the Executive Master in e-governance at EPFL.
50. This is a working definition that comes out of the evolutionary research framework developed by the author in collaboration with his colleagues within the framework of the Executive Master in e-governance at EPFL. For an overview of this conceptual framework see: Matthias Finger, Gianluca Misuraca and Pierre Rossel, "Governance with and of ICTs: the need for new institutional design in a changing world", egov magazine, Volume II – Issue 5, May 2006, and also http://egov.epfl.ch
51. Gilbert Riley Cathia, "The Changing Role of Citizen in the e-governance & e-Democracy Equation", CceG, 2003, www.electronicgov.net
52. Richard Heeks - Institute for Development Policy and Management of the University of Manchester www.man.ac.uk/idpm .
53. United Nations Millennium Declaration, A/RES/55/2, 18 September 2000, www.un.org/millennium
54. United Nations, "World Public Sector Report 2003: e-government at the Crossroads", New York, 2003, www.unpan.org.
55. United Nations, "UN Global Survey on e-government", New York, 2003, www.unpan.org.
56. For a comprehensive analysis on this issue see Gilbert Riley Cathia, "The Changing Role of Citizen in the e-governance & e-Democracy Equation", CceG, 2003, www.electronicgov.net, Other definitions of e-Democracy are available on www.portal-unesco.org or from the International Teledemocracy Centre, Scotland, the UK-based Dialogue by Design, or by Ake Gronlund, from Umea, University of Sweden.
57. For a deeper analysis of e-Democracy, see also the e-Democracy Centre www.edc.org
58. IDEA, Conference on "Democracy and the Information Revolution, Stockholm, June 2001, www.idea.int

2

DECENTRALISATION AND LOCAL GOVERNANCE: BENEFITS AND LIMITS

2.1. BENEFITS OF DECENTRALISATION

Decentralisation and local governance are increasingly recognised as basic components of democratic governance, since they provide an enabling environment in which decision making and service delivery can be brought closer to the people, especially to the poor.

Decentralisation is instrumental in the overall issue of re-inventing government and is essential to achieving the internationally set Millennium Development Goals (MDGs). Under the combined pressure of accelerating globalisation and persistent demands for deeper and expanded democratisation, central governments are seeing their traditional roles continuously challenged. Re-inventing government would then require revisiting the nature and role of the state itself and the sharing of political power and administrative responsibilities.[1]

But which are the benefits of decentralisation? and how does decentralisation contribute to the process of poverty reduction?

If we recall the key elements of good and democratic governance, and we consider them both for economic growth and as a means of achieving the MDGs, especially that relating to poverty reduction, decentralisation increases popular participation in decision making because it brings government closer to people, making it more accessible and knowledgeable about local conditions and more responsive to peoples' demands.

Central governments located far away and preoccupied mostly with national and regional issues, fall short of adequately and efficiently providing services essentially local in nature. The case for decentralisation can, in fact, be made on a number of grounds such as the following:

i. Local authorities tend to act more in line with local preferences and conditions, and their response to local needs is more expeditious. Decentralisation provides opportunities to marginalised sectors of the community, like women in some countries, minorities etc., to participate at the local level, enabling a more sensitive approach to policy formulation and implementation.
ii. Because decentralisation tends to enhance transparency and accountability, the amount of money wrongfully diverted away from development often declines. The Human Development Report (2003)[2], underlines that in 55 countries, decentralisation of government spending was closely associated with lower corruption among bureaucrats and reduced rent seeking by private parties - leaving more money to spend on basic services for poor people.
iii. Decentralisation increases effectiveness in service delivery, like reducing absenteeism among government employees, for example, in local schools and health clinics because elected officials receive complaints from their constituents and can improve discipline.
iv. Decentralisation provides bureaucrats with early warnings of potential disasters, enabling quick remedial action.
v. Decentralisation makes development projects more sustainable and cost effective because local people are more likely to be involved in their design, execution, and monitoring.
vi. Decentralisation encourages communities to find solutions to their everyday problems, yielding innovative ideas, which are more attuned to local conditions.
vii. Decentralisation provides opportunities for more people, including the under-represented groups (like women in some countries, the poor, minorities etc.) to participate in decisions that affect their lives.

To summarise, because of a greater degree of accountability, responsiveness and participation, effective decentralisation can make a big difference by making the provision of local (social and economic) services more efficient, equitable, sustainable and cost-effective. Through community participation in decision making, planning, implementation and monitoring and backed by appropriate institutions and resources, it can go a long way in improving the quality of life, particularly of the poorer and marginalised sectors of the population, thereby alleviating poverty.[3]

2.2. CONSTRAINTS OF DECENTRALISATION

But does decentralisation always work? And which are the constraints of decentralisation? For the process of decentralisation to be complete and for it to be successful, there are certain preconditions which may not exist in a country at a given time.

According to the UNDP Human Development Report (2003), these prerequisites include:

1. Effective state capacity;
2. Empowered, committed and competent local authorities; and
3. Engaged, informed and organised citizens and civil society.

Decentralisation requires co-ordination between levels of government and more regulation -not less- to ensure basic transparency, accountability and representation. The state also has to raise adequate fiscal resources to support decentralisation. For the above to be achieved, effective state capacity is necessary. Furthermore, to ensure that the decentralisation effort is not hijacked by the local elites, and there is broad based participation, both a strong state and a mobilised civil society are required.

Decentralisation is influenced by a country's size, population, its political and institutional inheritance and diversity. These attributes have an important effect on the design and modalities of decentralisation, which are crucial for its success. Appropriateness of functions to be decentralised, adequacy of fiscal resources to be transferred to the sub-national government, efficacy of administrative and legal setups and sufficiency of technical/skilled personnel at all levels of government are important ingredients for successful decentralisation.[4]

However, politicians have more often than not used the slogan of decentralisation as rhetoric to strengthen their own power base rather than improve governance. In practice, the lack of willingness of the centre to relinquish or share power has been a major impediment to effective decentralisation. In fact, the inability to make the transition to a people-centred governance, with its commensurate implications for participation and empowerment is perhaps a bigger bottleneck in the process of decentralisation than legislative changes, which in their own right are also crucial.[5]

Finally, lack of public awareness and an absence of a culture of participation and a weak "voice" of particularly the poor and marginalised sections of the population has inhibited the development of: firstly, a two way accountability system whereby local governments are not only supervised by an effective state government from above but also a strong civil society from below; secondly, a local government system which is responsive to the needs of all sections of populations, particularly the poor and the marginalised. As a matter of fact, the decision making process is dominated by local elites and government functionaries with little, if any, participation by the masses.

2.3. PARTICIPATION, ENGAGED GOVERNANCE AND THE ROLE OF THE CIVIL SOCIETY

However, "a process for participation does not ipso facto lead to empowerment, and to be consulted does not mean that one's voice had weight in decisions taken": one way of achieving this is through "engaged governance" whereby an attempt is made, through new forms of collaboration between citizens' groups and the public sector, to link social capital into the development management process of a country.[6]

Engaged Governance:
is both a process and a form that attempts to link social capital into the development management processes of a country. This form of management goes beyond the realm of public administration and other formal institution and links itself to civil society organizations to help mainstream citizen or community inputs into the process of policy formulation. Though engaged governance is an emerging concept, there are examples where it has been successfully implemented. For example, in South Africa citizens' groups actively participate in budgeting and fiscal policy processes. In Australia, the state government of Queensland has established an Engaged Government Unit within the Premier's Department to ensure community's inputs into policy deliberations. The concept is finding support in other developing countries also.
(Katsiaouni, Workshop on Poverty Alleviation and Decentralisation for ten West African countries, organised jointly by UNDESA and the Government of Senegal, Dakar, July, 2003)

In this context, the role of the Civil Society for Poverty Reduction can be instrumental. Recent years have witnessed a considerable surge of interest throughout the world in the broad range of social institutions that operate outside the confines of the market and the state. Known variously as the 'non-governmental organisations' (NGOs), 'Civil Society' or 'third' sector, this set of institutions includes within it a wide array of entities – hospitals, universities, professional organisations, human rights organisations, job training centres and many more.

A growing number of political leaders, community activists and international donors have come to see such civil society organisations as strategically important participants in the search for a middle way between sole reliance either on the market or on the state. In fact, even governments are now increasingly viewing NGOs as an integral part of the institutional structure particularly for addressing the poverty problem. This is reflected in the poverty reduction strategy put in action by governments in most developing countries in Asia and now increasingly so in Africa.

But what is the link between civil society and poverty alleviation? And what role can NGOs play to help tackle the problem of poverty?

Potentially, NGOs, both local and international, can respond to the growing problem of poverty in a number of ways. Their responses can be categorised into the following: advocacy, social mobilisation, delivery of social services, providing livelihood programmes, training and relief and rehabilitation.[7]

NGOs, through advocacy, can potentially play a very significant role in influencing economic and political policies that have an impact upon the poorer sections of population. The agents of an active civil society, for example, can: give useful input on the thrust and design of economic policies; bring specific issues of social concern such as the environment, labour rights, gender equality and public health into the public spotlight. In some cases even help to change prevailing social norms; contribute to greater transparency and accountability and thereby curtail patronage, powerful special interests and corruption; ensuring that government policies are carried out in the manner intended and thereby significantly contribute to good governance.

Civil society can mobilise the masses, empower them and give them a "voice", supplement government in the provision of services, particularly social services, design and implement income generating programmes and micro-credit, improve community skills through technical/vocational and entrepreneurial training, and perform relief and rehabilitation functions. Another, albeit often overlooked, contribution of civil society groups to poverty alleviation is as a potential source of financial support to carry out various development programmes. A lot of the work undertaken by the NGOs is on a self-help basis and financed by philanthropic contributions, a source which otherwise would have perhaps remained untapped.

In conclusion, civil society organisations can potentially play an important role in poverty alleviation in developing countries.

2.4. DECENTRALISATION AND LOCAL GOVERNANCE IN AFRICA

One of the major findings of the Fifth African Governance Forum, is that the fundamental challenge for good governance in Africa is to strengthen the political will in support of decentralisation. The first step in this direction would be for leaders of the African countries to show their real commitment to decentralise. In many African countries, clear constitutional principles as well as legislative and regulatory frameworks, which are key for decentralisation, are not yet in place. Other major constraints to effective political participation by the citizenry include: scarcity of resources, poorly trained cadres at the local government level, intra-partisan rivalries and non-responsive political parties, weak governance structures to control corruption and to promote accountability and transparency, and inadequate attention of local authorities to the importance of decentralisation.[8]

But if we analyse the situation in Africa, most of the important prerequisites for successful decentralisation are almost non-existent or in the very early stages of development, especially considering that some countries are emerging or have just emerged from conflict or crisis. Which are then the imperatives and reasons for decentralisation in Africa?

For a long time, worsening poverty levels in Africa were explained in terms of poor economic performance. Emerging evidence, however, shows that economic growth alone is not sufficient to bring about, in a sustainable way, the needed reduction in poverty. In fact for some African countries, GDP growth has come hand in hand with worsening social indicators, validating an established fact that while economic growth is important for poverty alleviation, particularly in the medium and long term, it is definitely not sufficient by itself. In the African context, the lack of responsiveness of poverty to the economic stimulus is attributed in part to problems with governance, especially at the local level.[9]

In pro-poor interventions, one of the primary hurdles is how to effectively target the poor. Proper targeting has generally proved to be elusive. The other challenge is how best to ensure that there is local ownership of the interventions. These considerations bring to the fore the issues of local governance. One of the lessons from past failures of poverty-focussed interventions is the importance of avoiding a 'top down' approach to project design and implementation as this invariably results in ineffectiveness of the interventions.[10]

Also, concerns regarding central administrative capacity, fiscal constraints and the limited accountability at all levels of government have led African leaders to place increased emphasis on the importance of decentralisation and developing local governance capacities. The other supporting argument for decentralisation is the need for improved government effectiveness in the delivery of goods and services and revenue collection.

External pressure by funding agencies like the World Bank, UN etc. have also been important motivations for decentralisation in many countries.[11]

Furthermore, a good number of African countries see decentralisation as a solution not only to the enhancement of the state's capacity to accelerate local development but also as a way to enhance the voice and power of the poor in the continuing fight against poverty. On the political side, decentralisation has been opted for as a solution to political challenges that seem to threaten national cohesion. Countries with a history of tensions (linguistic, ethnic/tribal, religious) have often found the federal approach to national governance as most suitable. Central politicians also tend to support decentralisation to appeal to voters and win elections as a means of undercutting the power base of rivals.[12]

However, despite the political and developmental motivations, decentralisation is perhaps much more of a challenge in Africa than elsewhere in the world. It is, therefore, important that there is consensus on the decentralisation policy, which is not centrally or donor driven, and which has a holistic framework, focussing on all levels of government and civil society simultaneously. It should be based on improving the enabling environment and building capacities and not on projects. The need for immediate success and quick results can lead to quick fixes, which are unsustainable. As such, it is important that decentralisation is viewed with a long-term perspective. African leadership will have to demonstrate patience and uninterrupted and determined commitment for the successful implementation of decentralisation in the continent.

2.5. ELEMENTS FOR EFFECTIVE LOCAL GOVERNANCE – DECENTRALISATION POLICIES

Given the above, capacity development - that will enable participation of key stakeholders - is crucial to achieving sustainable development. Experience has shown that there is a gap between existing capacities and demand for services and accountability at the local level. This situation calls for the creation of awareness, clear articulation of roles, and harnessing of the potentials of the different actors involved.

Decentralisation policies sometimes call for establishing new structures, participatory mechanisms and accountability systems. However, the option of strengthening existing traditional structures should not be totally discounted.

According to studies and analysis conducted in several countries, for effective local governance decentralisation policies, strategies, legal frameworks, programmes and activities should be conceived from two planes[13]:

- The vertical plane: involving the transfer of authority functions, responsibilities and resources from central government to local government;
- The horizontal plane: involving the empowerment of grass-root communities to enable them to determine, plan, manage and implement their own socio-politico-economic development.

While vertical decentralisation requires shifts in central government policy, laws as well as institutional and structural arrangements to provide for the sharing of powers, authority functions and resources and enable local governments to perform fully, horizontal decentralisation may take place without necessarily making adjustments in the laws. However it requires determined mobilisation and organisation of local communities to participate fully in the planning and implementation of socio-economic activities that are aimed at strengthening their capacity to determine and enjoy their livelihood.

An important linkage between vertical and horizontal decentralisation is that in countries used to highly centralised governments and/or dictatorships, horizontal decentralisation empowers local populations and prepares them to be able to positively receive and utilise the powers, authority and resources transferred to them via the vertical decentralisation.

It is always of great use to engineer efforts of decentralisation on the two planes involving all stakeholders: horizontal decentralisation will empower local communities and, vertical decentralisation will create conducive structural arrangements and transfer of powers, functions, responsibilities and resources that will supplement the empowerment created by vertical decentralisation.

Conceiving the two planes of decentralisation is also useful in the situation where the debate and agreement on formal vertical decentralisation, involving the transfer of powers, authority, functions, and resources from central government to local governments, for various reasons takes a long time. In such cases it is possible and advisable to start on programmes, projects and activities that empower local communities via, for example, NGOs or Community Based Organisations (CBOs).[14]

In conclusion, based on the experiences and lessons learned in this field by eminent experts and practioners, the key policy messages and recommendations for local governance-decentralisation, or **Decentralised Governance**, can be summarised as follows:

1. Decentralised governance for poverty reduction is a long-term learning and development process that requires a sustained commitment from, co-ordination of, and strengthened capacities of all stakeholders at various levels;
2. At the national/central level, there must be an enabling environment to ensure that devolution of authority/power to the local level would succeed for community empowerment;

3. For decentralisation to contribute to poverty reduction, it is necessary to give due attention to administrative and fiscal decentralisation and not just to political decentralisation;
4. For decentralisation to be effective, adequate emphasis should be placed on ensuring participatory monitoring and evaluation at all levels;
5. Decentralisation initiatives should not be prescriptive, but instead take into account the specific contexts (e. g. local cultures).[15] Moreover, a specific framework incentives-focused able to motivate local people should be established.

Notes

1. Report of the Capacity Development Workshop on "Decentralized Governance and Poverty Reduction", organized by UNDP, during the 4th Global Forum on Re-inventing Government - Citizens, Businesses and Governments: Dialogue and partnerships for Development and Democracy, Marrakech, Morocco, 10-13 December 2002, UN, New York 2002. www.unpan.org - www.globalforum.ma
2. UNDP, Human Development Report – 2003, "Millennium Development Goals: A compact among nations to end human poverty", UN, NY, 2003.
3. Report of the workshop on Poverty Alleviation and Decentralisation for ten West African countries, jointly organised by UNDESA and the Government of Senegal, Dakar, July, 2003.
4. Mani, Presentation to the workshop on Poverty Alleviation and Decentralisation for ten West African countries, organised jointly by UNDESA and the Government of Senegal, Dakar, July, 2003.
5. Katsiaouni, Presentation to the workshop on Poverty Alleviation and Decentralisation for ten West African countries, jointly organised by UNDESA and the Government of Senegal, Dakar, July, 2003.
6. Khan and Katsiaouni, Presentation to the workshop on Poverty Alleviation and Decentralisation for ten West African countries, jointly organised by UNDESA and the Government of Senegal, Dakar, July, 2003.
7. Adablah and Mani, Presentation to the workshop on Poverty Alleviation and Decentralisation for ten West African countries, jointly organised by UNDESA and the Government of Senegal, Dakar, July, 2003.
8. Fifth African Governance Forum (AGFV), "Local Governance for Poverty Reduction in Africa", Maputo, Mozambique, 23-25 May 2002.

9. Kemo Conteh and Sheikh E.T Lewis, "Decentralization and Civil Society approaches as means of improving governance and poverty reduction: The Gambia Experience"; and Sao-Kpato Max-Kyne and Abu Brima "Sierra Leone's experience with decentralization as a means to improve governance and combat poverty", 2003.
10. Aliyu Dr. Abdullahi, "Nigerian experience of decentralization as a mean to improve governance and how it contributes to combating poverty", 2003.
11. Adablah, Presentation to the workshop on Poverty Alleviation and Decentralization for ten West African countries, organized jointly by UNDESA and the Government of Senegal, Dakar, July, 2003.
12. Gyan-Baffour Prof. George, "Decentralisation as a means to improve governance and poverty reduction: Experience from Ghana", 2003.
13. Kauzya John-Mary, "Local Governance Capacity Building for Full Range Participation: Concepts, Framewoeks, and Experiences in African Countries"; Background Paper of the 4th. Global Forum on Re-inventing Government - Citizens, Businesses and Governments: Dialogue and partnerships for Development and Democracy, Marrakech, Morocco, 10th.-13th. December, 2002, UN, New York 2002. www.unpan.org - www.globalforum.ma
14. Kauzya John-Mary, idem.
15. Report of the Capacity Development Workshop on "Decentralized Governance and Poverty Reduction", organized by UNDP, during the 4th. Global Forum on Re-inventing Government - Citizens, Businesses and Governments: Dialogue and partnerships for Development and Democracy, Marrakech, Morocco, 10th.-13th. December, 2002, UN, New York 2002. www.unpan.org - www.globalforum.ma

3

FROM e-GOVERNMENT TO e-GOVERNANCE: A PARADIGMATIC SHIFT

3.1. ICTS AS A TOOL FOR DEVELOPMENT

The debate regarding the effectiveness of using ICTs to help achieve development goals arises not only around questions concerning the evidence in support of the relationship between ICTs and development, but also more substantially from inherent doubts about the relevance of ICTs in achieving sustainable development, and fears that investment in ICTs will draw resources away from traditional development goals.

ICTs instead can be a powerful tool for development, both because of their inherent characteristics and the mounting empirical evidence that suggest they can, in fact, contribute a great deal to development goals. They can do so at both micro and national levels by increasing the effectiveness and reach of development interventions, enhancing good governance and lowering the costs of service delivery. Moreover, the right complement of targeted ICTs interventions has the potential to play an even more substantial role in accelerating a sustainable dynamic of social and economic development in developing countries.[1]

Therefore, it should be clear from the outset that ICTs are not a panacea for the problems of the developing world. Social and economic development is dependent upon many factors which should be addressed through an overall development strategy. Factors such as political stability, macroeconomic governance, transparency and accountability of national and local administrations, the rule of law, physical infrastructure (for example, clean water and energy), and basic literacy should also be addressed in an explicit manner, and ICTs should not be seen as a substitute.

However, the integration of ICTs into overall national development strategies can help facilitate implementation, expand scope and coverage and increase the results for most of these factors. Moreover, development goals cannot be achieved by government efforts alone. The involvement of civil society and the private sector is crucial, and ICTs can help the different stakeholders to be aware, provide and exchange information and communicate among each other.

This is much more important if we consider that full and effective participation in the emerging global information network is of fundamental importance for a country that wants to avoid marginalisation from the globalisation process and is essential for the full participation of its citizens in all spheres of life. ICTs can contribute to the integration of developed and developing countries in the world economy, and it can create the conditions for information and knowledge exchange and utilisation. ICTs offer tremendous potential to raise standards of living and enlarge opportunities for individuals, communities, countries and regions. While many in the world still remain directly untouched by the information revolution, one cannot deny the transformative effect they have already had on our global society.

3.2. e-GOVERNMENT: BENEFITS AND RISKS

Conventional use of the prefix "e" suggests that an activity is electronic or digital in nature. By accepting this, e-government would simply refer to the use of electronic information and communications technologies in undertaking all kind of government activities, in education, health, agriculture, governance, customs, etc. However, this does not reflect the value that the use of ICTs can actually add to a government's ability to foster development.

E-government can support broad public sector reforms and good governance through the introduction of innovative and sustainable applications of ICTs both within government administrations, as well as in their interaction with citizens and the private sector.

Therefore, the key word in e-government is not electronic, but government.

E-government should be regarded as an alternative and complementary approach to government administration and service delivery, as well as a means to redefine the way it interacts with citizens and the private sector. Analogous to e-business, which allows businesses to transact with each other more efficiently (B2B) and brings customers closer to businesses (B2C), e-government applications can affect the interaction and transaction between inter-agency government relationships (G2G), government and business enterprises (G2B), and government and citizens (G2C), in a more friendly, convenient, transparent and inexpensive way.[2]

In this sense "e" means:

- **efficiency:** Governments should use ICTs to minimise transaction costs and streamline their bureaucratic procedures, making their operations more efficient, freeing up resources that enable them to deliver services in a better-organised and economical manner.
- **effectiveness:** Governments can achieve better results and meet development goals by using ICTs to increase the relevancy of the policy formulation process through increased participation, improve the process of resource allocation, respond timely to citizens' needs and increase coverage and quality of their services.
- **empowerment:** ICTs can support increased interaction between citizens and their governments, for citizens both to participate in the decision making process and to become more aware of their personal and community development.
- **economic and social development:** Beyond the economic benefits that accrue to government due to efficiency and effectiveness gains, the use of ICTs in government and in its interaction with the business community and citizens can create new businesses, attract investments and generate employment.[3]

The possible impact of some e-government applications can be divided into three main dimensions of policy objectives: the economic dimension, the social dimension and the governance dimension.

On the economic side, these range from reduced transaction costs to better capacity to target services, increased coverage and quality of service delivery, enhanced response capacity to address issues of poverty and increase in revenue. Other benefits, less often considered in selecting applications, include the intended economic spin-offs that e-government may bring to the business sector, which can then become more competitive in the national and international environment. Lower transaction costs and simplified procedures will translate into comparative advantages by the private sector. In the same way, increased interaction or transactionability with government can help create new businesses. Furthermore, economic benefits may also derive from increased accountability and transparency, which may greatly reduce the risk of corruption and raise the perception of good government among citizens. Citizens' trust in their government may have an impact on their willingness to invest and to pay taxes and levies for services.

Social benefits are considerable and range from employment creation in the third sector, to improvements in the education and health system, from better targeting of the government's services, to increased capacity for the provision of safety and security. In the majority of cases these benefits can be evaluated in political terms and quantified in financial terms.[4]

In other words, appropriate e-government initiatives can lead to strengthened conditions for good governance. Development of e-government is therefore not only a technical issue but also a political one.

As e-government applications can differ in the way they have an impact on, and provide benefits to, the society at large, governments should review the alternatives at their disposal to optimise the use of their resources according to the country's priorities. In this view, "e-government is about the transformation of government, and it may well be the biggest transformation since the democratic revolution of the late 18th. century. Nevertheless, as with all revolutions, many outcomes are possible. ICTs are very likely to lead to more efficient service delivery. It is not clear that they will lead to a form of government that is more open, transparent, accountable or democratic than conventional government"[5].

Addressing such issues poses many challenges: meeting them requires leadership that is committed, informed and engaged, especially at the political level. A firm commitment from decision makers to think through the issues and steer the right course is critical, otherwise it risks to be just a wishful claim useful only for political purpose. Providing such leadership might be the single biggest challenge on the horizon. In fact, in one form or another, e-government will come; but what is important is which kind of government it will be in the digital era. This involves a broader vision of government systems which includes and integrates the three major aspects of e-government:

- Improving service delivery;
- Improving information management;
- Improving accessibility and participation of the different stakeholders.

These three aspects of e-government provide a starting point and, in analysing them, it has to be considered that they are interconnected and interdependent. Therefore, it is necessary to think about the integration of ICTs in the government through a holistic approach, considering e-government as an integrated and evolving platform for a management system. A particular aspect, in fact, is related to the interest that different stakeholders have in how ICTs are being used to transform government. There is a growing awareness, also in developing countries, that new ICTs-networks and databases are creating a new public "infrastructure" which is the basis of e-government. They want to be sure that, as the infrastructure develops, their interests will be taken into account. This is more an more evident and enhanced with the increasing use of "peer-to-peer" systems over the Internet such as Web 2.0 applications (web blogs, communities of practices, etc) that creates ad additional communication platform often defined as Citizens to Government (C2G), and also Citizens to Politicians, and Citizens to Citizens (C2C).[6]

However, considering the risks of introducing e-government, it should be underlined that most e-government projects, both in industrialised and developing countries, fail either totally or partially. There are very little data about rates of success and failure of e-government projects, but some baseline estimates indicate that behind the high-tech glamour of these projects lies a dirty reality – the majority of projects are failures.[7] This is due principally to the lack of "e-readiness", and the oversize gaps between project design and on-the-ground reality (known as "design-reality gaps"), meaning the lack of assessment of needs prior to the implementation of a project. These failures come at a high price for the world's poorer countries, and six categories of potential costs of e-government failure have been identified by Richard Heeks (2003):

1. *Direct Financial Costs*: The money invested in equipment, consultants, new facilities, training programmes, etc;

2. *Indirect Financial Costs*: The money invested in the time and effort of public servants involved;
3. *Opportunity Costs*: The better ways in which that money could have been spent, if it had not been spent on the e-government failure;
4. *Political Costs*: The loss of 'face' and loss of image for individuals, organisations and nations involved in failure;
5. *Beneficiary Costs*: The loss of benefits that a successful e-government project would have brought;
6. *Future Costs*: An e-government failure increases the barriers for future e-government projects. It does this in two main ways. Firstly, through the loss of morale of stakeholders, particularly e-government champions, who may 'defect' to the private sector or overseas. Secondly, through the loss of credibility and loss of trust in e-government as an approach to change. This increases risk adversion in some stakeholders and provides support for others with vested interests in the status quo.

A key problem among e-government practitioners and policy-makers is a lack of awareness of these costs. Most costs are intangible; few are ever measured in the event of e-government failure; e-government failures are often hushed up. This may explain why, despite the high costs of failure and the high prevalence of failure, many officials and politicians are still very keen on e-government.[8] Here, though, we must recognise this high cost of failure, and look for ways to reduce risks. We should therefore understand which are the external and internal barriers to e-government[9] and what are the needs and challenges to overcome failures and successfully implement e-government. This will be addressed in the following paragraphs.

3.3. IMPLEMENTING E-GOVERNMENT: NEEDS AND OBSTACLES

There is no single established way, no "best practice" that would lead to successful e-government. Whilst in broad terms the elements for success are already known,[10] their interpretation and application must be invented locally. However, it cannot be stressed strongly enough that if a public administration does cross the "digital divide", it opens endless opportunities that are practically inaccessible by any other means. This is true for all public administrations in the world, regardless of the level of economic development, human capacities, and the social and cultural context prevailing in the community or country concerned[11].

Solutions to development often require changes in government processes. Internally derived objectives for change generally tend to focus on economic benefits and on the improvement of effectiveness and efficiency in the provision of services. On the other hand, increased public demands calling for democratic participation, accountability, transparency and quality and speed of service delivery can be an important driving force for change.

To establish an e-government system countries need to embark upon a significant transformation process, particularly in those nations where aspects of good governance are yet to be strengthened. A genuine commitment from government leaders, the private sector and other institutions of the civil society is required to create leverages, benefit from synergies and sustain this transformation within the national development process. Experience has shown, in fact, that the introduction of e-government was either a consequence of sound public sector reforms, directed towards the improvement of governance conditions, or a catalyst for their introduction.

Institutional capacity development in areas such as policy development, public sector reform, legal and regulatory frameworks, strategic planning and change management, as well as co-ordination of intergovernmental relations will be required to harmonise the transformation process with the existing development objectives and facilitate the exchange of information between the different entities that compose the governance system. Furthermore, building a positive perception about the value of ICTs within government and society at large should be regarded as a priority.

Countries should carefully plan their e-government strategic goals, implementation timeframes and resources, vis-à-vis obstacles and risks to be overcome, to ensure the success of this process. Particularly during the start-up phase, lessons learned by other countries that have been at the forefront of e-government should help avoid the costly trial and error approach.

The following initial steps have been identified to guide countries within the framework in which e-government is carried out:

- Formulation of an environmental analysis (e-government Readiness);
- Elaboration of the long-term vision, including the expected contribution to development foreseen by e-government;
- Formulation of the strategic goals being pursued;
- Identification of the priorities and expected impact.[12]

E-government requires a conducive environment to maximise its potential. Before defining an e-government strategy or plan of action, a thorough analysis of the existing environment in which e-government will be implemented is required. Government can pose itself some key questions in order to assess how strategically prepared it is for e-government.

As indicated before, a country level of "e-readiness" is the degree to which each country is prepared for the introduction of e-government. By assessing the relative advancement in the areas that are most critical for e-government adoption by different key factors, countries would be in a better position to evaluate opportunities and challenges, as well as their own strengths and weaknesses.

However, as uniformity across the border is impossible, the objective of the e-readiness analysis is to identify specific actions for improvements and potential niches for the initial start up of e-government programmes, rather than a positive or negative answer to e-government as a whole. The following areas and key factors should be carefully analysed in order to examine the risks and assess the obstacles that may need to be overcome before entering into e-government.

a) **Political conditions and leadership:** Good governance, as a condition for sustainable development, requires genuine commitment from political leaders, the private sector and organisations of civil society. In the same way, the introduction of e-government in society requires strong political will to see through the transformation process it implies to government both in its internal operations as well as with regard to its interaction with civil society.
b) **Regulatory framework:** A proper regulatory framework is needed in order to enable secure information exchanges within government and between government, citizens and businesses. It is also needed to create the economic conditions for accessible ICTs infrastructures, services and equipment;

c) **Organisational conditions:** International experience shows that the introduction of e-government calls for and causes profound and evolutionary change of the institutional arrangements. To guide this transformation process, appropriate management and co-ordination mechanisms are needed;

d) **Cultural and human resources conditions:** Positive attitudes, knowledge and skills need to be in place – especially within the public sector – to initiate, implement and sustain e-government. Cultural aspects may cause general resistance to change and information-sharing. Inadequate human resource capacity may lead to lack of customer-orientation and overall commitment.

e) **Financial conditions:** The initial costs related to implementing e-government can be considerable and governments may have limited capacity to bridge the period between the initial investment and returns. Proper resource planning and access to innovative financing mechanisms are critical for e-government sustainability.

f) **Communication environment:** in today's world, communicating with citizens is a duty and a necessity for governments. E-government needs to be accepted and understood by all stakeholders to ensure that its benefits flow to the society as a whole.

g) **Technological Infrastructure:** Lack of technologies is a major bottleneck for countries aiming to implement and maintain e-government. Legacy systems may also represent considerable obstacles to change. The demographic and geographic conditions of different areas, accompanied by the distribution of economic activities, may also represent a strong bias in the rollout of ICTs infrastructure if left to the market alone.

h) **Data and information systems:** Management systems, records and work processes must be in place to provide the necessary data to support the move to e-government.

Countries should update the environmental analysis on a regular basis to reassess their readiness against technological progress and ongoing changes in the governance system. At different stages of e-government maturity, the relative importance of environmental areas and key factors may differ. The **stages of e-government maturity** allude to[13]:

a) *full digital data availability*, when all government data processing operations in its multitude of institutions are done in digital form and data can move among different operating platforms;
b) *e-publishing*, when all these institutions are posting their relevant information online, in an organised and easily accessible way to other government agencies, businesses and citizens;
c) *e-interaction*, when all relevant interactions, including participation in policy analysis and formulation, can take place online between government agencies, as well as between government and business and government and citizens;
d) *e-transaction*, when all relevant transactions between government agencies and between these agencies and the private sector businesses and citizens can take place online;
e) *transformed government*, when government has gone through the full transformation process, providing fully integrated services requiring broad organisational change, aligning its organisational set-up with the new capacities it has acquired as a 'digital state'.

The different stages of e-government maturity are closely linked to the successive phases of ICTs implementation at the institutional level. Over time, individual government agencies are expected to go through similar phases.

The speed by which a country will be able to move from one stage of e-government maturity to the other is highly dependent on political leadership and the human and financial resources it can rely on, as well as on the capacity of different institutions to move through their successive phases.

The above does not imply that a country can only move from one phase to the other if all government institutions have met the criteria for that particular phase. On the contrary, to a certain extent, asymmetry will almost by definition occur. Especially in the first phases, individual agencies can move relatively independently although co-operation with an increasing number of other institutions will be required to move into more advanced phases of the e-government process.

Countries should define e-government priorities within the framework of their national policy goals, e-government vision and strategic objectives by evaluating the way different applications draw on scarce available resources and add different value to and impact on the governance process.

E-government tends to be multidimensional, impacting above all on economic, social and governance dimensions. The prioritisation process should focus on these impacts from a people-centred and development-oriented perspective. From the start a participatory approach should therefore be stimulated and guidance provided to ensure that different stakeholders and institutions start discussing the different available options. Experience has also shown that e-government cannot be introduced through a single major initiative but rather through small, achievable components which can build success and credibility. This is what is increasingly be used as the **"Think-big, Start-small, Scale fast" approach** used in many success stories (or claimed to be so).

In this regard, many examples of "Think-big and start small" exist, but there are not many examples of successful "Scale fast" experiences, despite the political claims on this.

In fact, achieving the future as envisaged by the policy-makers necessitates an incremental and modular basis implementation, a building block approach that allows for greater control and flexibility of the process, particularly during the initial phase. The focus could therefore be placed on priorities that could create an enabling environment for successive stages of e-government maturity. For instance, the ability to facilitate communication and co-ordination of activities among major partner institutions could be one of the main deliverables that is sought after. This kind of priority may involve initially very little technology since the focus would be more on reaching agreement on standardisation of key data sets which could enable linking the information bases of individual partners.

Among the most important criteria to determine their set of priorities, countries should include sustainability, the rate of return in terms of social and economic benefits and the potential spin-offs that e-government applications can generate. In fact, understanding the 'market' in which institutions operate, the social and economic impact and the potential spin-offs is of critical importance in determining how the required inputs could be met by and for the individual institutions.

Overall, however, the impact of e-government on the economic, social and governance spheres is still considered the main determining factor in the prioritisation process and in establishing the level of support that governments will provide.

In this regard, it is important that a clear, strategic vision of what a government aims to achieve through e-government will be generated to guide the transformation process. This may encompass a system-wide perspective, for example at the central government level, or be limited to a specific sector of government administration. This vision has to take into account the national and local development needs and opportunities, as well as the conditions facing the government system or specific sectors.

The vision of e-government for development needs to be aligned with national development strategies and plans, in particular with the national ICTs strategy and governance reform goals. As different political contexts and development needs have to be brought together in one vision, leadership should recognise that a consultative process with all stakeholders is necessary to form consensus.

The vision is a medium to long-term statement concerning broad goals, and which provides a road map and general guidance for institutional change, allowing systematic issues to be better understood and more coherently addressed. It provides a framework within which the actions and interests of different stakeholders can be brought together to ensure a common orientation that makes increments of action by various stakeholders consistent and compatible with the desired long-term goal of democracy, good governance and sustainable development.[14]

3.4. e-GOVERNMENT AND e-GOVERNANCE: CHALLENGES AND THREATS

The development of e-government and e-governance takes place in a very specific environment and contextual pressure which we must understand and learn, in order to steer at best. This overall change can be identified as manifold, although producing a composed impact on our lifestyle, level of wealth and relationships, inter-regionally and inter-nationally speaking.

In particular, three main aspects should be stressed, to better understand the phenomenon:

Globalisation, appears as an emerging and constantly reinforcing process. Globalisation is more than just the "mundialisation" identified by previous researchers, from Braudel to Wallerstein, rooted in Middle Age discoveries and expressed through successive expansions, themselves supported by ever more efficient communication means, up to the complete coverage and information production upon, of the planet as the ultimate cognitive object. Globalisation is the effect of this building process in the sense that its overall power relationships (let us think about conflicts or the inequalities of means and performance), but also local initiatives may have an impact instantly or gradually on the rest of the world, thanks to highly interconnected processes and interests. It is, needless to say, that ICTs reinforce this process. Globalisation can be perceived as a source of opportunities, as the scale for any activity tends to take place in a much broader arena than before, but also as a constant pressure, with positive and negative consequences.

Economic competition, as a result of the previous phenomenon, became pervasive and almost a safeguard free paradigm, with significant consequences in terms of energy and material output, nature transformation and technology mastering, but also social and knowledge divides as well as damage at various scales and severe environmental threats ahead; economic competition is believed to benefit the customer, encourage innovation at all levels and, as a consequence, generate a better society. It also generates local shifts and undesired effects, with economic, social and cultural dimensions, to which remedies must be found. Public policy and more significantly political elites and leaders in major OECD countries have set up a framework for developing competition which goes even further, changing the rules of politico-economic regimes in a serious programme trend called liberalisation.

State transformation, in this context, reinforced local means to express needs, projects and alliances in separate terms are growing in parallel with the pressure of globalisation and transnational forms of economic competitiveness; it is therefore no surprise to see the state entering a phase of redefinition. Sovereignty is often at the core of the discussion, but fundamentally, what seem to be essential state prerogatives in most regions of the globe, are being rearranged: public service delivery can often be delegated, with the necessary reinforcement of policy making and regulation capabilities towards more efficient, ethically consistent supervision of services. It is of course particularly the case in industries traditionally owned by the state in many countries (telecommunications, energy industries, transport, health, etc.), but also of more specific administrative services (let us think of geographical information systems for instance).

In fact, the numerous e-activities, e-products, and e-services which are currently being displayed in the public sector cannot be fully understood, appreciated and assessed if they are not placed within the much broader framework of state transformation[15].

However, it is important to stress why. Indeed, the transformation of the state's status encompasses changes in three separate dimensions, namely:

- the growing emergence of non-state actors, basically transnational corporations (TNCs) and non-governmental organisations (NGOs). Increasingly, the state has to share its power with these non-state actors. Such power sharing is most pronounced at the supra- and at the infra-national levels.
- The growing emergence of levels of managing public affairs, other than the nation-state level. I refer here in particular of the emergence of supra-national levels (EU, global), as well as of infra-national levels (local, regions).
- The growing differentiation of the state's three main functions, namely the service delivery function, the rule-making function and the regulatory function. These three functions can be increasingly treated as being separate from each other and therefore being shifted to the different levels and the different actors.

These three movements are being combined with each other, which leads to the fact that public affairs become more and more fragmented (in terms of functions), diluted (in terms of levels) and outsourced (to non-state actors). There is, in particular, a deficit of cross-functions, seamless operations in which non-state stakeholders can play a proactive role. At the same time, enterprise-based and private individuals' e-activities develop quite freely and increasingly. There is therefore a place for a different type of steering than the one e-government promotes. This is what I defined as governance with, and of, ICTs, or e-governance[16].

But this new concept brings about a number of challenges and threats to be analysed. Some general challenges, as previously evoked are linked to the fact that e-government, just like all e-activities, tends to modify organisational boundaries, statuses and even more, to generate new risks and opportunities that were not part of the pre-Internet landscape. Some of these changes concern the networking capabilities of the organisations, their internal or shared processes, the rationale of the value-chain and even some institutional adjustments. In fact, one could say that the fully-fledged digital transformation of services, with the possible supporting incorporation of several technological innovations, almost certainly lead to institutional redesign, unless some new problems are immediately recreated (let us remember for instance the risk of an increase in the back-office distraction due to exaggeratedly accessible online services).

However, this organisational and institutional dimension of ICTs-induced changes modify in a considerable manner the issue of measuring and comparing achievements as they necessarily involve more complex changes than just efficiency or optimisation effects due to the digitisation of existing administrative services. A whole new domain of what to measure and how to do it is therefore open to exploration, much beyond the rather simple and always difficult to demonstrate reality of the "e-indexes".

Some other issues or challenges are more specific but no less important, when envisaging a more holistic perspective, such as security and identity management, mobility of actors and organisations supported by enhanced technological means and accesses, territorial and data mining-rooted surveillance and private sphere reconsideration, productivity and benefit capturing, using ICTs as a trigger for development, cultural diversity, etc.

In a more generic statement, I see e-government as very heterogeneous and having quite a number of difficulties to evaluate before, during and after projects are undertaken, with effective and sustainable cost-benefit criteria and setting priorities for high impact solutions (vs. quick wins). In addition to this, while e-government initiatives have so far reached, in many cases spectacular inroads in terms of service delivery, especially by digitising the front-office but also that in many cases are just "mirroring" the existing and not always well-restructured back-office, ICTs are so far not being systematically (or at all) used with regard to the other functions of the state (namely, regulatory and policy making). Thus, the potential of ICTs in linking the overall functions of the state and the different levels and actors involved in the governance process, is far from being realised (or in many cases even started).

Combining the above mentioned, general or more specific, challenges that e-government is confronted with, and the necessity to address these issues with a consistent toolbox and in terms of multi-actor, multi-level and multi-sector involvement, we are obliged to ask whether e-government is not forgetting some important "missing masses" in its linear, optimistic and mostly mono-factor type of deployment.

As already said before, I am fully aware that worldwide, at the moment, for most actors, e-governance is a synonym of e-government. Some scholars try to propose a perspective in which e-governance is just e-government extended to non state actors, but still with the state as the leading force in such endeavours.

The definition I proposed here is instead a radically new and fully innovative vision of e-governance where institutional redesign, state transformation, and organisational changes, as well as networking and relationship management are the key features of this new paradigm.

This conceptual framework is based on some "e-governance theses" I developed together with my colleague Pierre Rossel during the redesign and conceptualisation of the Executive Master in e-governance at EPFL (2005, 2006), and that can be summarised as follows[17]:

- There is a growing awareness of the need to improve the quality of public-service delivery, through new mechanisms and forms, including public-private partnerships, externalisation, delegation, etc. and with an attention to the market, the "citizen-user-customer" and the need to manage efficiently and effectively limited resources, in a time of rapid technological change. In this context, e-government is playing an important role in promoting the transformation of the state, but its value-chain, and the market relations between suppliers and providers are demonstrating its limits, and actually even provoke risks, especially in not well established democracies, or in less developed countries. E-government is therefore becoming an "industry" in itself, with a complex system of relationships that need to be managed and governed. But what have to be governed are not only the solutions to collective problems but the manner of collectively constructing the Information Society.

- Rapid technological change induces organisational changes and these result in a continuous "dynamic tension" that generates pressure for institutional change and new needs in the society that cannot always be satisfied, controlled or even followed by the state. These needs of change cannot be governed or decided by a static decision making process and often go beyond the rigid existing regulatory frameworks, but need innovative solutions involving all stakeholders. ICTs add complexity and increase the speed of change. In the same way as governance is about collective problem solving, but unlike the state, not necessarily or not only in a vertical or hierarchical way; e-governance is therefore collective problem-solving not only with the use of ICTs, but also of the ICTs. It is also about innovating, to solve some problems that cannot be solved the usual way and, if necessary, it is finally about changing the institutional rules, processes, configurations or boundaries or even inventing new ones, e-governance is also a new form of social engineering. Non-state actors are not just citizens or users of the administration, they are stakeholders of problems that require attention or solutions, these problems are quite diverse and have to cope with many possible industrial domains. Once again, more than just problems (to be solved collectively) they are actors in the building of the Information Society.
- E-governance is more a process about the "how" than the "what". E-governance is a reflective activity in which the way problems are tackled is as important as the result and even to a great extent having an impact on the result. In this sense, accessibility, transparency, evaluation and accountability are features intrinsically marking a robust e-governance process, where e-government is only an instrument for better service delivery (the governance with ICTs). But ICTs, in addition to being used to perform the governance task, are multi-faceted in nature. There is at least a triple aspect to ICTs: as a tool, as a means for producing a structural effect and as a domain, all aspects of which also have to be regulated and governed as they involve many types of stakeholders. ICTs as tools explain to a large extent the governance "with" ICTs aspect of e-governance; the structural effect is largely the consequence of the impact of

the many and rapidly changing technologies of the Information Society. This is difficult to measure and also largely involves policy-making and not just regulatory action; ICTs as domain cross-cut all activities and need to be regulated (e-governance as governance "of" ICTs). Most activities involve two or three of these facets, although most of the time only the first one is taken into account.

- E-governance is also a knowledge creation and management process, but at the same time it is a learning process and, as such, it must be concerned with measurement, evaluation and also fore-sight. The requirement therefore is to build an evaluation system that will be at the same time capable of measuring the impact of the tools (i.e. the use of ICTs or the e-government), but that can be linked to the measurement of the e-governance. This means considering the capacity of the various stakeholders points of view to appraise processes, new services or business models, and the capacity to incorporate values, diversity, openness and multi-level perspective to embed any significance, as well as foresighting about long-term impacts, rather than just the short term immediate results of introducing ICTs in a specific process. E-governance is therefore about maintaining, beyond the problem solving actions and taking into consideration what exists, the necessity to open new avenues of how to do things among stakeholders.

These theses are intended to dismiss the naïve perspective of valuing the connective aspect of the Internet as if we were from now on only part of one network. There are many networks, of different kinds, social, organisational, technological-infrastructural, and they partially interconnect, they also oppose one another and e-governance is also the negotiations, intermediations, compromises taking place and the crafting of ad hoc organisational and institutional forms to allow or maintain such half-way solutions.

Convergence of the first order, making it possible for the same type of data to flow through various channels or at least to be captured and managed as such at key points of the infrastructure networks does not make enough in terms of networking: discontinuities are essential to explain the generation of a solution, much more than the presence of connective tools.

Society, in fact, is not harmonious and just saying that e-governance, like governance, is about the transactional aspect of inter-actor life would not account for the complexity of what really takes place, it is also confrontational. Stakeholders have to muddle their way through even when they are not fundamentally friends, inter-industry-wise and inter-level-wise. This is why e-governance can be seen as the expression of a dynamic tension. As mentioned before (see Definition of e-governance) there is although a basic asymmetry between the two side of the coin that define e-governance (governance with and of): where "with" means basically "bureauatic", web-based and connective type of technologies and applications or rather the said mediation-supportive technologies and applications; whereas governance of ICTs means dealing in terms of innovation and regulation with all the technologies of the Information society.

3.5. FROM e-GOVERNMENT TO e-GOVERNANCE: THE WAY TOWARDS A KNOWLEDGE SOCIETY

The need to respond to changing pressures resulting from globalisation, fiscal demands, evolving societies and citizens' expectations has meant a continuing process of public administration reform to enhance performance, both in industrialised and developing countries, notwithstanding significant changes over the last two decades. Reforms have addressed (and are addressing, especially under the guidance of the UN MDGs) the full range of good governance objectives. In many areas, ICTs have been an important enabling tool for reform. While the pursuit of efficiency gains and the effective delivery of programme outcomes have been main drivers of ICTs use in government, governments are now confronted with a new reality and changed imperatives as a result of the diffusion of ICTs throughout the world and within their nations. The focus has turned more recently to other good governance objectives, such as facilitating consultation and public engagement to respond to standards of accountability, transparency and participatory governance as critical elements for democracy and state legitimacy.[18]

In this framework, ICTs allow a government's internal and external communication to gain speed, precision, simplicity, outreach and networking capacity. This can be converted into cost reductions and increased effectiveness – two desired features of all government operations, but especially of public services. It can also be converted into 24 hour 7 days a week usefulness, transparency and accountability, networked structures of public administration, information management and eventually knowledge creation.

But what is now becoming more important is that, in addition to this, ICTs can equip people for genuine participation in an inclusive political process that can produce well-informed public consent, the ever more prevalent basis for the legitimacy of governments.[19]

This demands a fundamental change in the way the state acts internally and interacts with its citizenry, particularly in its function of promoting good governance as a condition for sustainable development. E-government can transform the existing government structure and consolidate the establishment of an inclusive governance system, through digital means, that is capable of exercising its powers and functions efficiently and effectively. It can produce a governance system that is committed to working with civil society in a transparent and accountable way to reduce poverty, safeguard the environment, redress inequality, foster security and fulfill social, economic, cultural, civic and political rights.[20] In other words, governance, in combination with ICTs, is making its way towards "e-governance", where - as we have seen before - the concept of e-governance further encompasses the concept of e-government. E-governance, in fact, involves not only the use of ICTs, but also a new way of looking at, and attitude to, governing and managing ICTs, where participation and efficiency are required of all the partners linked in a network[21].

While e-government may be understood as the performance of the governance systems via the electronic medium in order to facilitate an efficient, speedy and transparent process of disseminating information to the public and other agencies, and for performing government administration activities, e-governance is generally considered as a wider concept than e-government, since it can bring about a change in the way citizens relate to governments and to each other. For someone, the idea of adopting ICTs in governance is to move beyond passive information-giving to active citizen involvement in the decision making process[22].

The purpose of implementing e-governance, is seen not only to enhance good governance, but to take advantage of the recent advances in ICTs, and especially the Internet, to provide opportunities to transform the relationship between governments and citizens in a new way, bringing forth new concepts of citizenship, both in terms of citizen needs and responsibilities. The use of ICTs, in fact, can increase the broad involvement of citizens in the process of governance at all levels by providing the possibility of online discussion groups and by enhancing the rapid development and effectiveness of pressure groups. The government should gain in that through the provision of better service in terms of time it makes governance more efficient and more effective. In addition, the transaction costs can be lowered and government services become more accessible, while it can engage, enable and empower the citizen.

However, for this to be a reality, it is required not only to define new ways of organising and delivering information and services, but a new style of leadership, new ways of debating and deciding policy and investment, new ways of accessing education, new ways of listening to citizens, and at the same time providing adequate and innovative regulatory frameworks.

Within this context, e-governance is also necessarily about the improvement of the performance of civil servants to provide better services to citizens. In principle, it has the potential to enhance decentralisation, accountability and transparency, and can thereby improve the position of developing countries in the global political economy.

However, recent studies have found vast differences between countries in the maturity of their e-government efforts. Perhaps the key findings, is that even the most mature countries have tapped less than 20% of the potential.[23] Furthermore, the results of the UN Global e-government Survey 2003, identify that: "only very few governments have opted to use e-government applications for transactional services or networking; and even fewer governments use it to support the genuine participation of citizens in politics. Those who do, in most cases, apply it at a very rudimentary level".

On the other hand, one of the main findings of the UN Global e-government Survey 2003 was that: "No country or group of countries in the world owns the monopoly on imagination, wisdom and commitment or political will for use of e-government for the delivery of the public value of human development. Original, advanced content of e-government applications finds a home in the geographic and developmental South, as it does in the North".

Analogous to the development of e-commerce in the private sector (which has evolved already through several stages: from publishing, through interactivity, completing transactions, and delivery, and it has now been overtaken, at least in some areas, by the so called "e-conomy", that involves the creation and use of "e-marketplace" instead of e-procurement relations) e-government has so far centred its activity on publishing, but, in many cases, it is evolving quickly through the different stages of e-government maturity. Thus, if we consider the same analogy, and having in mind what was underlined by the Human Development Report (2001) "*.....technology networks are transforming the traditional map of development, expanding people's horizons and creating the potential to realise in a decade progress that required generations in the past.....*"[24] developing countries could benefit from the progress made in the sector of ICTs application to accomplish government tasks and service delivery, and reaching the "e-marketplace" solution immediately, without passing through the "e-procurement" applications, in a sort of "leapfrogging" paradigm, still far to be effectively realised, despite the potential and the political discourses about it.

Obviously, this new participatory approach in running governance affairs has to be developed - and not only in the developing countries - considering the barriers and threats to its implementation, being viewed as a complex process, articulated over time, embracing the overall system in which governments operate and interact with individuals, organisations and communities to perform their functions, achieving public ends by digital means[25].

In general terms, the debate regarding e-governance is most often polarised between those who feel that the new ICTs will enhance participation by the citizen in the government policy decision making process and those who feel that it will simply be business as usual via a new medium. The arguments range from a promise that the new ICTs will completely revitalise democracy, giving more power to the citizen, to the opposite position that it will do nothing more than enhance the existing mechanisms to deliver government services in a more efficient manner.

But, as the subjects of e-government and e-governance (with the related issues of e-Participation and e-Democracy) are in their nascent stages, there is still very little empirical data to support either side of these arguments[26].

In spite of the criticism of technocracy, those who believe in the success of e-governance argue that further development of information systems will contribute to overcoming bureaucratic contradictions within government[27]. At the same time, this will also allow the enhancement of the economic performance of developing countries, more through the creation/strengthening of an ICTs industry, than through the easier access of the private sector to crucial public sector information, and the increase of "capacity for public service delivery of basic social services, public administration reform, integrated planning, increased citizen participation in decision making, decentralisation, transparency, accountability and combating corruption".[28]

Despite this optimistic approach, somewhat induced by an ICTs-driven positivistic philosophy, as I have already underlined before, and in this comforted by the evidence of fieldwork and analysis that try to go beyond the "supply side" indicators available in the front-office, entering into the back-office and looking at the "demand-side" indicators, the potential for e-government and e-governance in both industrialized and developing countries, remains largely unexploited[29]. This is perhaps because of the difficulty in achieving the revised organizational structures and skills; degree of decentralization of decision making; new forms of leadership; transformation toward public-private partnerships; and effective involvement of stakeholders, that is required. Moreover, local governance is in general given little attention within national e-government policies and strategies. In this regard, the broad assumption that the use of ICTs can greatly increase good governance has yet to be proven. To date there is little empirical evidence of the "multidimensional" effects of ICTs on governance, which can in turn inform national e-government policies.

Furthermore, and more important, if we consider the large amount of money wasted for e-government for Development initiatives that, in some cases, have been criticized to be a new form of market acquisition for national industries from the so called developed countries, or even new forms of "e-Colonialism..."[30], I want to stress here the risks beside the opportunities of introducing ICTs in different contexts, and the need to look at the issue of development considering that, based on the conceptual framework I presented here, it is not sufficient to just introduce ICTs into Government operations to solve the problems of today's world, or even worst just transferring "best practices", as unfortunately many policymakers seems to believe.

So far, the main effort in e-government has been dedicated to the digitization of existing information and procedures, addressing in a hopefully more efficient way a variety of administrative functions and service delivery options. We have to recognise the value of this ongoing achievement. At the same time, the underpinning assumptions, methods and philosophical biases that have been used to support that type of change (that we call change I, see after) bear some cost and to some extent, prevent an easy move towards more ambitious transformation, such as suggested by the higher stages of the maturity model in particular and in any case by an effective local development involving grass-root motivations and projects. One of the reasons behind this paradoxical barrier is the success and productivity of the process-minded approach.

In this regard, the Business Process Reengineering phenomenon (or simply BPR), which has been highly fashionable throughout the nineties, was heavily convoked, directly or indirectly, to address the issue of transforming administrations with ICTs toolsets. In my opinion, however, it did so in a rather simplistic manner (although technically it can be quite sophisticated). It has been necessary to adapt the process re-engineering rationale to the characteristics of the particular process analysed, taking into consideration the peculiarities of the public sector. The challenge was to identify the different sub-processes (stages) that take place within the public sector, in particular with regard to the linkages with politics and the role of the different "clients": citizens, users, customers, other administrations and agencies, private sector, etc. and decide which process re-engineering concepts can be beneficially used in their analysis.

In fact, BPR[31] is about redefining the complexity of organizations on the basis of linear and interrelated threads of action called processes, with regard to specific human resources as well as infrastructure use, hopefully leading to customers' satisfaction. The problem is that the solution is immediately perceptible and impacting the organization, but at the same time it narrows down the vision of its scope, place and options in a wider framework of inter-organizational, market or governance-minded considerations. It therefore tends to close down to similar practices, self-rewarding indicators and short-term results. In its lower-end version, BPR may have meant nothing more than some very partial process reformulation and a general excuse for undertaking severe organizational restructuring. Today new concepts have taken the relay, including more "network-minded" substance (ICTs mean more and more the involvement of the Internet in and out) than BPR, which was organization-centered, namely Service-Oriented Architecture (SOA) and the notion of ICTs/business process "alignment".

In this context, it has to be considered in fact that, especially in developing countries, the public sector is increasingly seen as the main engine to bridge the digital divide at country level. Public agencies can start acting as model users of ICTs and be catalysts for others to follow. The public sector tends to be the biggest provider of local content and it can nurture and foster the further development of the local ICTs industry. For this reason, the enhancement and/or building of the capacity of public bodies and government agencies in the use of e-government applications, promoting at the same time the accessibility of businesses and citizens to internet and government services online, can improve availability of information and eventually produce knowledge.

The debate is therefore now turning towards the discussion of the role of information and knowledge in public sector reform, and the role of the public sector in developing and implementing the Knowledge Society as a whole, through national policies. The role of knowledge development and governance is certainly not new. However, it has to be recognised that knowledge has taken on an even greater degree of relevance and a different shape with the advent and deepening of the knowledge economy and society. There are multiple drivers of this phenomenon, one of them being the way in which society is becoming more complex and unpredictable in both positive and challenging ways. One can point to: globalisation, the economic value of ideas, global production chains, demographics of youth, challenges to political systems and rapid development in science and technology, including ICTs as examples of this change. These new imperatives demand responses that are more creative, innovative and smarter and more active in their use of knowledge. Yet while there is an abundance of information there is a deficit of knowledge, or at least a deficit in the ability of the public sector to create, use and apply it meaningfully.

The UN Millennium Declaration, in addition to detailing a number of socio-economic and governance goals, also takes note of the importance of innovation, science and technology and knowledge as tools for meeting the Declaration's objectives. Capacity building towards these ends is called for. Guided by this philosophy, it becomes necessary to seek to determine those knowledge related activities and policy decisions that add public value and result in the meaningful utilisation of knowledge throughout the whole society. For this purpose, there is a recognisable need to translate these general goals and recommendations into more concise – though flexible – conceptual frameworks, implementable policy and concrete actions, especially taking into consideration the lessons learned to date by those around the world seeking to realise the potential of the Knowledge Society.

While the precise role of the public sector in developing national knowledge systems may be the subject of debate, there is a clear role for the public sector in enhancing its own generation, dissemination and use of knowledge and in the gathering of knowledge through public debate and citizen participation in policy making and implementation. This goes beyond mere e-government policies and seeks to place knowledge as an essential factor in improving quality, effectiveness, collaboration, multidisciplinary programmes and meaningful government reform. As such, it is important to focus not only on the tools for knowledge management, but also on the content and use of knowledge as it is found in various forms in the public sector[32].

However, as I have already mentioned, access to information, while an important component of acquiring knowledge, does not in itself constitute learning[33]. Information is not knowledge or competence. As a matter of fact, information access and sharing, as well as expert data handling, necessitates having a lot of knowledge. Information is not the first stage towards, nor the pre-condition of knowledge, it is quite the opposite. From the same perspective, the increase of participation in the usage of ICTs is no automatic and linear step towards deep, effective, sustainable or democratic evidence. Just the opposite, one has to stress that to carry out collective learning of some significance through ICTs, more horizontal processes, empowerment and trial and error linked with experience sharing must somehow take place "upstream" or at least considered quite early on in an ICTs-based project to constitute a democratic enhancement chance.

As a matter of fact, the Internet, e-government, e-learning, etc..., do not lead in a straightforward manner to better chances and awareness among practitioners. Altogether, particularly if mishandled, wrongly put into perspective or simply shortsightedly tied with short-term, low impact efficiency goals of substituting actual processes with a digital equivalent without any further analysis of the organisation, ICTs may not be always necessarily profitable, nor e-government in all cases, lead to improvement of administration performance or service to the citizen.

The pitfall suggested above, that involves a mere digital translation of existing services, with all the technological solutions outsourced and no particular change induced in the value chain, we (Misuraca, Rossel, see op. cit.)[34] call **"Change I type"**.

The e-governance type of interactions and collective problem solving negotiation, which may involve state agencies and requires some redesign to fit the new assignments, experiments or opportunities of alliances and partnerships, we call **"Change II type"**.

Change I is ICTs driven, Change II is basically the art of reconfiguring processes, tasks, roles and, if necessary, institutions in order to make better use of ICTs. Change I is mainly a substitution operation, Change II a new deal to enhance each stakeholder's chances. Change I is mostly an administration-focussed preoccupation, rhetorically concerned with improving the servicing of customers or users. Change II is often multi-actor, multi-level and multi-sector.

Based upon this conceptual framework and considering that any complex issue will quite quickly bring complex issues to deal with, some key areas of concern for e-governance can be identified such as: Public security development and regulation, Identity management, Risk management, not only technological, but also economic, political and social; Sustaining the motivation for innovation beyond the best or good practice trend (which aims at not always re-inventing the wheel, a goal quite noble in itself); Developing new mobility schemes for individuals and organisations, with the kind of knowledge and environments which will enable them; Cross-border applications and projects; Cross-function learning beyond the boundaries of the various network industries in which e-activities are deployed (telecoms, post, transport, energy, health, education, etc.); Territorial management for development; The various types of digital divides to be taken care of, etc.

For all these problems and, of course, many more to be identified and documented, which most of the time do not occur separately but in conjunction (the above listing in reality must be regarded as a matrix of issues), there is a need for new competence, leadership and combined efforts and learning patterns, first in projects, experiments, knowledge sharing and benchmarking as in practice up to now, but also in knowledge management and neo-institutional skills[35].

E-governance is therefore first of all an open area for innovation and solution pooling, which presently seem only to be in its infancy. A lot remains to be done to really harness ICTs as tools as they should be, instead of being steered by them, as unfortunately happens too often. This appears the only way to achieve a knowledgeable and inclusive society, taking advantage of ICTs, and managing the risks deriving from them in the best way possible.

3.6. e-GOVERNANCE IN AFRICA: CHALLENGES AHEAD

Africa's experience with ICTs has unfortunately, and for the most part, taken a different path from most of the world. Poor ICTs infrastructure, combined with weak policy and regulatory frameworks, low technological penetration and unimpressive human and institutional capacity, have led to inadequate access to affordable telephones, broadcasting, computers, the Internet and efficient postal services. This has hampered the continent's ability to capitalise on ICTs as a central tool in creating new business opportunities. The combined constraints have also played a key role in creating rifts within and between nations, between sub-regional African markets, isolating them from global markets.

The contexts and institutional frameworks within African countries are changing rapidly, reflecting their commitment to the Information Society. Many reforms have been introduced and measures have been taken by policy makers and telecommunications operators. Despite these reforms, telecommunications costs are still relatively high, particularly at the local level; whereas international communications costs are relatively cheaper. This is evidence that telecommunications policies still favour international rather than national communications. Significant progress has indeed been made in the ICTs sector, and a number of African countries have embarked on policy reforms that have introduced competition and improved policy and regulatory frameworks. In fact, since 1990, approximately forty countries have initiated programmes to separate postal functions from telecommunications. Over twenty have privatised their state-owned national telephone companies. Thirty have liberalised their markets and opened up to private cellular services, and over twenty have revised their regulatory frameworks to facilitate more effective private investment. Over forty-five have at least one cellular services provider, and at least forty have achieved some level of connectivity and the presence of local full-service dialup Internet Services Providers (ISPs), even though Internet service and other advanced services are limited by scarce bandwidth.[36] These developments reflect a growing belief that Africans are realising the enormous potential of ICTs as a key driver for social and economic development and poverty reduction, particularly as reforming countries are reaping the benefits through improved infrastructure, increased applications and better accessibility and affordability of ICTs infrastructure, equipment and services.

But although the foundations of integration into the Information Society have been laid, integration into the information economy remains the responsibility of the policy makers and the different development actors. In fact, in many African countries, a systematic and consistent policy to integrate ICTs into all aspects of economic and social life is yet to be formulated. The development of the telecommunications sector is far from being integrated into the overall macroeconomic framework, and it continues to reflect a sectoral approach to telecommunications policy. Even then, most of the reforms have been done without much co-ordination at the sub-regional level. The region as a whole does not have a consistent strategy to attract larger and higher quality, local and foreign capital and other resources for investment, or to remove the many barriers in order to accelerate development. In addition, one of the major developmental challenges confronting Africa is to develop the capacities, strategies, and mechanisms necessary to take full advantage of the opportunities for development offered by ICTs. Given the potential for ICTs to induce changes, many development analysts -and I am among them- believe that these instruments can play an important role in the development process.

For example, the recent trend and developments of mobile technologies, fits within this claim, obeying the principles of the underpinning approach and earlier mentioned characteristics of e-governance (generating at the same time opportunities, resources and nuisances, durable problems, which we shall examine further), but somehow now opening to new service and user-involvement perspectives (see for that Rossel, Finger and Misuraca, 2005).

Besides describing concrete trials to make e-governance real, in Africa, it is generally admitted that ICTs have the potential to help poor communities to find new ways of accelerating their development process. But this is an implicit hypothesis based upon the fact that because development is neither a linear nor unitary process, the transforming nature of ICTs can be used to catalyse rapid and sustainable economic and social development. ICTs-enabled developed countries have been able to take maximum advantage of the opportunities that these tools can offer. Therefore, poor countries and communities should be able to take advantage of these new tools to improve their capacities to create wealth and reach an improved level of development.

The fact that ICTs are increasingly integrated into the development programmes of African countries is confirmed by their prominent position in the New Partnership for Africa's Development (NEPAD). Steps are being taken to gradually institutionalise ICTs tools in the economic and social system of African countries to promote more rapid integration of these countries into the global economy. However, these steps are still limited and general strategies or policies that integrate ICTs into the overall macroeconomic framework of African countries are lacking. Integration of African nations into the Information Society will require far-reaching actions that will affect all aspects of economic and social life. However, the potential exists for ICTs to be used in all fields of activity if the constraints limiting their transforming effects can be lifted. ICTs can make this contribution by helping to meet the dynamic and changing expectations of Africans for access to information on such subjects as agriculture, education, and governance, for example. As people become familiar with ICTs they discover the opportunities that these tools can offer and express their needs on the basis of the anticipated usefulness of these technologies. In other words, they anticipate the capacity of ICTs to deliver information that will solve the practical and concrete problems they face.[37]

Some countries and local communities have undergone substantial changes in their effort to appropriate the tools. The changes, which have occurred at the individual level and within community organisations, include capacity building, acquisition of new skills, more efficiency in community activities, and better integration of previously marginalised groups.

Therefore, it is urgent to take far-reaching actions to meet not only expectations but also to consolidate the advances that have been made in ICTs appropriation by these African communities. Challenges and problems are generally common to the whole of Africa. As identified by the e-Africa Commission of NEPAD, the main challenges for integrating ICTs in Africa can be summarised as follows[38]:

Leadership: Need for a Clear e-Vision; Capacity and will to lead change; Management and accountability structures;

People: Appropriate skills and attitudes available at all levels; Availability of training programmes; Entrenching a culture of increased information access and transparency; Commitment to high level teamwork; Support for public service wide collaboration; Change management initiatives.

Policy: Liberalised telecommunications sector and effective regulation; Policy environment supportive of growth of ICTs adoption and use; Policy frameworks that secure freedom of information, privacy, security, intellectual property and copyright; Arresting the "brain drain".

Processes: Identification and improvement of critical processes; Process adaptable, integrated and open to innovation; Monitoring and evaluation; Identification and adoption of best practices.

Technology: Access to ICTs networks, services and equipment; Development of local content in local languages; Ensuring that programmes drive ICTs; Standard approaches to ICTs infrastructure, to ensure scalability and interoperability; Privacy and data sharing; Authentication; Building user trust.

Stakeholders and Access: Support for the need for "e"; Ownership across the board; Making information widely available to citizens; Utilising a variety of channels, including those owned and managed by the commercial and voluntary sectors (such as Kiosks and Call centres); Consideration of people with disabilities; Ensuring that any new channel live up to high consistent standards of trust, confidentiality, security and accountability (PCs, interactive TV, cell phones, telephones/mail, etc.).

A number of initiatives and projects on ICTs for development in Africa are already under way[39]. However, many of the projects on ICTs for development led by International Organisations focus on financing technological infrastructure and providing assistance oriented to lower tariffs. New approaches aim to incorporate socio-cultural dimensions "placing the individual at the centre of development objectives"[40]. Increasingly, initiatives focussed on enhancing "local dynamics" and creativity, are being implemented, especially in rural and remote areas of the world. This is required also in order to address what has been defined the "dynamic digital divide", that is given considering not only the national "e-Readiness" capacity at a certain point in time, and how it evolves in a specific timeframe, but instead it considers various components of the digital divide, within a given context, and how they evolve in relation to the local and the global conditions[41].

In this context, the centrality and importance of strengthening the political and administrative frameworks in African countries is therefore pivotal. Recent developments in ICTs have however opened up Africa to exciting possibilities for public administration, in particular, and governance in general. The appropriate use of ICTs in managing public services and governing state affairs has therefore become a necessity. This is well recognised by the New Partnership for Africa's Development (NEPAD) and in particular by African Ministers with responsibility for the public services. The establishment of the e-Africa Commission of NEPAD, focussing on a range of areas pertinent to ICTs implementation, from policy to e-applications, as well as the identification of good governance as a focus area for capacity-building within NEPAD, reflect the importance given to building the capacity of African states to function more effectively through the use of ICTs.

But, of course, the scenario for integrating ICTs in Africa's governance is difficult and there are some technological and human barriers that threaten the exploitation of ICTs. In short, the barriers against such initiatives are summarised by the weakness of the ICTs infrastructure in Africa and the low rate of ICTs penetration in administration. Africa ranks at the bottom of world statistics not only regarding ICTs penetration, but also for other telecommunications technologies such as television and broadband. Regarding ICTs penetration in general, according to the NUA Survey, Africa has only 3.11 million users, that is miniscule as a proportion of its population. When compared with the world's other regions the digital gap is even more evident, where Asia/Pacific has 104.88, Europe 113.14, Canada and USA 167.12. The number of users in Latin America is growing, and is now at 16.45. Only the Middle East, with 2.40 millions users is in as bad a situation as Africa, although with a smaller population[42]. A specific barrier is also related to the weakness and marginalised role of parliaments in Africa, as highlighted by the UNECA Report on "Striving for Good Governance"[43].

However, despite the many indicators showing Africa at a disadvantage, the potential for growth through integrating ICTs in the governance systems is encouraging. In particular, the key issue is how to build capacity to move towards an African knowledge-based society that will allow enhancement of the economic performance of governments and the public sector. African countries can enormously benefit from the use of ICTs for their effective development. In addition to faster management and analysis of the execution of decisions, ICTs can especially support, in the best instances, how each public administration intends to implement its activities in relation to budget allocation, and how it thinks it ought to manage performance. The introduction of digital, knowledge-based economy in Africa would have a strong impact on the life of all citizens. It can be a powerful engine for growth, competitiveness and jobs, while at the same time improving citizens' quality of life.

However, the central issue behind ICTs utilisation in Africa is not a matter of technology transfer. It has everything to do with people's empowerment and society's ability to use the technology as a facilitator for democracy, a tool for universal access to services, opportunities and resources. "Market forces or financial superpowers alone cannot solve these questions. They must be engineered within the framework of social movements' thirst for freedom, genuine development and social justice"[44].

Notes

1. Khan Sarbuland, "ICTs as an instrument to Leverage the Millennium Development Goals", in ICTs for African Development, Edited by Okpaku Joseph Sr, PhD, UN ICTs Task Force, New York, 2003
2. World Bank, www.worldbank.org
3. UNDESA, Government of Italy, Ministry for Innovation and Technologies, Plan of Action – e-government for Development, 2002, www.palermoconference2002.org www.unpan.org
4. A Comprehensive System of Indicators for Monitoring and Evaluation of e-government is being developed within the framework of the e-government for Development Initiative of UNDESA and the Italian Government www.unpan.org
5. Lenihan Donald, "Realigning Governance: from e-government to e-Democracy", Crossing Boundaries Paper, Changing Government, Volume 6, Centre for Collaborative Government, Canada
6. Web 2.0 and peer-to-per communication mechanisms are still in their infancy but are growing fast. For more about this see, among others, Glassey Olivier, (2005; 2006).
7. Estimates indicate a rate of 70-80% of e-government Projects as total or partial failure (see Heeks, R., 2003).
8. Heeks Richard, "Most eGovernment-for-Development Projects Fail: How Can Risks be Reduced?", in iGovernment Working Paper Series, No 14, eGovernment for Development Information Exchange project, co-ordinated by the University of Manchester's IDPM, funded and managed by the Commonwealth Telecommunications Organisation as part of the UK Department for International Development's "Building Digital Opportunities" programme. http://www.egov4dev.org/ or http://www.e-devexchange.org/eGov/topic1.htm
9. On this issue see also: Breaking Barriers to eGovernment, anEU-funded project led by the Oxford Internet Institute, implemented in collaboration with Gov3 ltd and the University of Namur.
10. In this regard, both OECD and United Nations compiled a list of "Guiding Principles for Successful e-government". See OECD, e-government Studies, "The e-government Imperative", 2003, www.oecd.org (pag. 19); and United Nations, "World Public Sector Report 2003: e-government at the Crossroads", New York, 2003, www.unpan.org, (Box 3, pag. 8 and 9).
11. In this regard, see also the Results of the UN Global e-government Survey, 2003, www.unpan.org

12. Many of the operational indications reported in this paragraph are the results of activities conducted within the framework of the UNDESA, Government of Italy, Ministry for Innovation and Technologies, Plan of Action – e-government for Development Initiative, 2002, www.palermoconference2002.org www.unpan.org
13. UNDESA, Government of Italy, Ministry for Innovation and Technologies, Plan of Action – e-government for Development, 2002, www.palermoconference2002.org. See also Gartner, from 2000; and European Commission, from 2001.
14. UNDESA, Government of Italy, Ministry for Innovation and Technologies, Plan of Action – e-government for Development, 2002, www.palermoconference2002.org
15. On this see, Fingeret et al ii. (2004; 2005).
16. Matthias Finger, Gianluca Misuraca and Pierre Rossel, "Governance with and of ICTs: the need for new institutional design in a changing world", egov magazine, Volume II – Issue 5
17. For the e-governance theses see: Rossel, Misuraca, "Triggering the governance perspective of e-government projects: beyond mere digitization of administration services; or the Change I to Change II shift issue", Lausanne, CDM-EPFL Working Paper, 2006 (forthcoming); and also "Rossel, Finger, Misuraca, "Assessing and steering mobile e-government options: findings and indication proposals", ECEG, 2006.
18. See the United Nations Millennium Declaration, section 'Human rights, democracy and good governance'; the Monterrey Consensus, which states that 'good governance is essential for sustainable development' (Section II); and, the World Bank Development Report 2002, Chapter 5 reports that 'Good governance matters for growth and poverty reduction'.
19. United Nations, "World Public Sector Report 2003: e-government at the Crossroads", New York, 2003, www.unpan.org
20. UNDESA, Government of Italy, Ministry for Innovation and Technologies, Plan of Action – e-government for Development, 2002, www.palermoconference2002.org
21. Misuraca Gianluca, "From e-government to e-governance: the e-Africa initiative for good governance", paper presented to the International Conferene on e-government, SITEXPO 2004, Casablanca, Morocco, 18th.-21st. February, 2004, *not published*.
22. www.portal-unesco.org
23. World Bank, 2002, www.worldbank.org which reports a Study by Accenture, www.accenture.com

24. UNDP, Human Development Report 2001 "Making New Technologies Work for Human Development"
25. CAFRAD, "e-Africa: Elements and Principles for a Strategic Plan of Action" - Draft Working Paper, not published, edited with the technical assistance of Gianluca Misuraca.
26. Gilbert Riley Cathia, "The Changing Role of Citizen in the e-governance & e-Democracy Equation", CceG, 2003, www.electronicgov.net
27. IDEA, Conference on "Democracy and the Information Revolution, Stockholm, June 2001, www.idea.int
28. UN Road map to good governance and democracy
29. An interesting research in this area has been carried out by RSO-Spa, LUISS Management on behalf of the European Commission within the framework of the "eGEP Project – eGovernment Economics Impact Project, see www.rso.com
30. On this see for example, Andrea Di Maio, 2002, www.gartner.com
31. It is somehow unsatisfactory to embrace all BPR approaches with one single label. Business Process Re-engineering (BPR) has provided the business world with several complementing approaches (Davenport, 1993), (Glykas, 1994), (Harrington, 1991), (Hammer, 1993), (Morris, 1993), (Ould, 1992), most of which follow five generic steps in the process of redesign (Valiris and Glykas, 1999). Starting from the original analysis of Davenport, Stoddard, Hammer and Champy applied to the private sector and being then "translated" into the public sector, BPR became a sort of discipline in its own, with several different applications and "schools". According to Kettinger, Teng and Guha (1997), there are at least 25 different BPR Methodologies, 72 Methods and 102 Tools. Different perspectives of process modelling are suggested, such as functional, behavioral, organizational and informational, pointing out the notions of agent, role and artefact (resource, transaction) as basic process modelling constructs (Curtis et al, 1992). Some of these approaches are closer to beyond-process options and stakeholder involvement than others.
32. Bertucci Guido, "Opening Remarks to the UN Ad Hoc Expert Group Meeting on Knowledge Systems for Development", UN New York, 4th.-5th. September, 2003, www.unpan.org
33. Okpaku Joseph, E-Culture, Human Culture and In-Between: Meeting the Challenges of the 21st. Century Digital World - An Address to the ITU Conference on Creating New Leaders for E-Culture, Coventry, UK, August, 2001
34. Rossel, Misuraca, "Triggering the governance perspective of e-government projects: beyond mere digitisation of administration services; or

the Change I to Change II shift issue", Lausanne, CDM-EPFL Working Paper, 2006 (forthcoming).

35. An effort in this area is the Executive Master in e-governance of EPFL, crafted exactly to undertake a continuous "learning journey" around the Governance "with and of" ICTs. (http://egov.epfl.ch/)
36. Olekambainei Emmanuel and Sintim-Misa Mavis Ampah, "Info-communication for Development in Africa", UN ICTs Task Force Series 2, ICTs for African Development, UN, NY 2003.
37. Molo Thioune Ramata, (Edited by) Information and Communication Technologies for Development in Africa: Opportunities and Challenges for Community Development, CODESRIA/IDRC, 2003.
38. NEPAD e-Africa Commission, www.nepad.org
39. The most recent and accurate overview of ongoing initiatives with regard to ICTs for development in Africa is included as an annexe to this book.
40. UNESCO's medium term strategy 2002-2007, 31 C/4: Chapter on "The contribution of ICTs to the development of education, science and culture and the construction of a knowledge society" - pp.53-56.
41. See Rossel Pierre, Cooperation at EPFL, 2002, Bridging digital divide
42. www.nua.com/surveys/how_many_online/index.html
43. United Nations Economic Commission for Africa, Striving for Good Governance in Africa, 2004.
44. Sy, J. Habib, "Critical and Prospective Views on ICTs and Governance in Africa", in "Africa Networking: Development Information ICTs and Governance, United Nations Economic Commission for Africa, UNECA, Addis Ababa, 2004

4

ICTs FOR LOCAL GOVERNANCE IN AFRICA

4.1 LOCAL e-GOVERNMENT AND e-LOCAL GOVERNANCE: BENEFITS AND LIMITS

If we consider the "basic e-government equations: G2C, G2B and G2G", these are exponentially reproduced at local level. Local governments, in fact, are in the front line of government in their service delivery to the citizen (LG2C) and to business (LG2B), while at the same time, ICTs can improve co-ordination and communication within government agencies at different levels ($LG2G^n$) (where n = levels of government in a specific institutional setting). This is particularly true in the strengthening of financial systems and accountability, by reducing the risk of corruption through minimising the face-to-face relationships.

Local governments, in addition to being close to citizens and business, constitute for many of them the main (or even unique) representation of government. The relationship of citizens and local authorities tends to be one based on proximity as the interests at stake for both parties are clearly entwined concerning issues such as public services, urban development, school planning, environmental concerns and local politics. It is at the local level that the impact of ICTs on the relationship between governments and citizens, can be most effective.

Traditionally, the interaction between a citizen or business and a government agency took place in a government office. Utilising ICTs it is possible to locate service centres closer to the "clients" (e.g. citizens and businesses). Such centres may consist of an unattended kiosk in the government agency, a service kiosk located close to the client, or the use of a personal computer in the home or office. In this regard, it has to be underlined that the potential for ICTs to have a positive impact on the lives of citizens in a variety of ways (especially in marginalised and rural areas) is being widely recognised. In fact, cities and local authorities play key roles in the Information Society and are fully involved in the process of the World Summit on Information Society (WSIS).

The Declaration of the World Summit of Cities and Local Authorities on the Information Society (Lyon, 5 December 2003), was the result of observations carried out throughout 2003 at the preparatory meetings of Bilbao, Shanghai, Curitiba and Nouakchott. It used as reference points other declarations and works carried out by many organisations in this field, such as the "Charter of citizens' rights in the Information Society", taking into account that "half of the world's population lives in cities and urban areas, whereas the other half relies increasingly on cities for their economic survival and very existence". Also being aware of the fact that, "by relying on the heritage and vitality of cities and regions, there is the increasing need to build a society of inclusive cities whose wealth is founded on their diversity, cultures and languages rather than a society of impersonal and uniform information", observing, among other conclusions and recommendations, that "cities and regions are often at the forefront regarding the transformations brought about by ICTs in areas as diverse as universal access, education and training, housing, culture sustainable economic development, water, sanitary conditions, social cohesion, etc.. it was therefore determined "to totally fulfil the role that befalls in developing the Information Society, being eager to provide new local and regional dynamism in its development, with the aim of improving the quality of life in local communities and answering the needs of citizens".[1] For this purpose the United Cities and Local Governments (UCLG), was also established in Paris, in May 2004, and the second phase of the World Summit of Cities and Local Authorities on the Information Society took place in Bilbao in November 2005.

But why should we focus on the local/municipal level when introducing ICTs in government operations?

At the local level (urban and rural municipalities), it is recognised that the appropriate use and integration of ICTs in the community can enhance and support social and economic development, particularly in empowering officials and community representatives; ensuring linkages, networking and community cohesion; providing timely, efficient, transparent and accountable services; improving the management of the services and operations; facilitating planning and policy making processes; monitoring and recording physical and social changes in the municipalities.

Moreover, the integration of ICTs into the local/municipal governance can lead to informed populations being the basis of effective participatory governance and a knowledgeable community. The challenge remains, however, on how the use of ICTs in the municipalities can be beneficiary to all the stakeholders while avoiding, at the same time, a digital divide between members of the municipality itself.

A particular and important aspect of the application of ICTs at the local level is related to the recognition of the governance system as an integrated combination of several actors other than the government and considering the potential in all the services that the government is to provide.

In fact, the developmental impact of ICTs at local level is twofold. The first consists of the benefits of enhancement of the infrastructure and applications to users of information and communication services who can be distinguished according to whether they use these services as an everyday tool for production, distribution or consumption, and for their day-to-day activities. The second consists of the benefits derived by the economy from changes in the production, supply and operation of communications infrastructure, facilities, equipment, services and applications, or more generally what we called: ICTs or info-communications (see before). [2]

Improvements in ICTs lower the cost of information and knowledge exchange, the cost of dealing with others in the market (such as suppliers and customers), and the cost of business start-ups and of delivering social economic services, including governmental services. Through these processes, transaction costs in society drop which improves overall efficiency and growth. In many instances, the additional and more reliable information that becomes accessible will contribute to the expansion of markets, assisting, for example, producers to move from local/rural into regional and national markets, and from domestic to international markets. Access (or the lack of it) to cheap and sufficient information is an important determinant of the competitive advantage of firms, sectors and countries. Furthermore, the efficient and easy access by citizens to up-to-date information on their local and central governments, NGOs and other civil society institutions, and even corporate enterprises, improves interaction, mutual trust, confidence and participation. These, in turn, could enhance empowerment, unity, democracy, peace and stability.

But although there are many examples on the nature of the linkages between ICTs and local governments, there is no evidence that unequivocally proves that there is a direct causal connection between ICTs and innovations in local governance, ultimately, to support local economic development.

If we look at the experiences of integrating ICTs in local governance worldwide, there is a growing effort in providing connectivity and accessibility at a local level, but there is not yet enough on monitoring and evaluating the real impact of projects and programmes on effective social and economic development of local communities.

Most local governments in the USA have already met the recommendation by the Kettl Commission that all local governments serving populations of more than 25,000 have web sites by June 30th., 2002. Only 2 out of 71 local governments with this population did not have web sites in 2005. In this context there are also some interesting examples of "participatory e-governance at local level" or "e-participation", such as the City of St. Paul, in Minnesota, or Menlo Park, in California[3], but some people argue that instead of increasing, "democracy is reducing in the United States, with people overloaded with false, misleading, corrupt or politically tainted information".[4]

The e-Europe Strategy[5] focusses on "connectivity" at local level: schools, home-access, with national/local indicators and rewards for local governments and, within this framework at national level, there are many examples of particular interest in terms of e-participation, such as the National Strategy for local e-government of the British Government[6], or the Italian National e-government strategy with Regional Plans[7], and the new French national e-Administration strategy ADELE[8] (just to mention a few). But the economy and especially the integration of ICTs in the day-to-day life of citizens and government is still lagging behind in many regions in Europe, especially in the south and marginalised areas.

The Canadian Government has been a pioneer in developing services "far-reaching" connecting communities and local governments with citizens, allowing their participation, even in control of the decision making process.[9] But how much did the government spend to achieve these results? In Japan, the e-Japan Strategy emphasises the development of local e-governance schemes, including self-evaluation of online government services, allowing citizens' feedback and participation.[10] However in the instance of Japan, as well as in the previous examples, we are talking about the richest regions of the world, and in particular some of the G8 countries.

In Australia, a "best practice" example is represented by the City of Brisbane[11], the capital city of the State of Queensland. It is the third largest city in Australia with a growing economy. The Brisbane City Council's development of electronic government started in 1994 with the Customer Service Integration Project that introduced advanced technology and electronic business into Brisbane's Contact Centre environment. This Centre currently handles over 1.6 million calls per annum, providing information and action on more than 3000 separate Council services. The next major step was in 1996 when the Council released corporate information to Brisbane via the Internet at www.brisbane.qld.gov.au , at the same time as starting internal knowledge management through an extensive intranet known as CityWeb. A number of projects followed including public information kiosks, Internet applications and a telecommunications infrastructure review of the city. The Council then launched the first "Ourbrisbane.com Strategy" in late 2000. This has been an eight initiative programme which has included pro-active support for assisting communities and businesses online; the ourbrisbane.com Portal at www.ourbrisbane.com which connects the city's people with information and other people to encourage participation in the global information revolution and the city's life; affordable access strategies to address the "digital divide"; and further work on the telecommunications infrastructure. Successes to date include the doubling of community and business access to the Internet with 300 community organisations online covering sporting, environmental and seniors groups; more than 3000 businesses connected to each other via the eBIG user group and 7 online business networks; a successful city Portal; over 500 "Green PCs " (refurbished PCs at affordable prices) distributed; Internet training for nearly 50,000 people; free Internet offered through the extensive Library network and a city-wide telecommunications infrastructure plan. The next stage of the Strategy includes targets of: increasing weekly Internet usage by

Brisbane people from 59% to 75% by December 2004; broadening the range of everyday uses for which Brisbane people use the Internet; and increasing the percentage of Brisbane business trading on the Internet. But is Brisbane the rule in Australia, or just an exception?

Some emerging countries have also pointed out the importance of strengthening local governance using ICTs. For example, in Mexico, the "Agenda Presidencial de Buen Gobierno", puts particular stress on Innovation & Quality of Local Governments[12].

In Malaysia, the National ICTs Policy Planning and Strategic Intervention, is centred on the efficient provision of online services by the government at all levels, to improve the economic and social development of the country.[13]

The Indian case is recognised worldwide as an example, considering the several "good practices" on local e-governance development, often created with a "bottom-up" approach and the involvement of the civil society organisations, often led by young people. One of the most popular experiences is the e-Seva Centre in Andhra Pradesh.[14] Following this example, many other initiatives have been started involving local communities in their own self-development.

In South-East Asia, the progress achieved by countries in the last few years bears witness to the effective potential of ICTs for development and how ICTs can lead the economy in a positive way in developing countries.

Looking at the municipal level, the "First Study on Digital Governance in Municipalities Worldwide"[15] ranked Seoul, the City States of Hong Kong and Singapore, New York, and Shanghai as the Top Five Cities of 100 Large Cities Worldwide, even if New York City was ranked no.1 worldwide in terms of content. Rome, Auckland, Jerusalem, Tokyo and Toronto rank respectively in the 6th to 10th positions. Among the top 20 cities, three are from emerging countries: Tallinn (Estonia) 14th., Dubai (United Arab Emirates) 18th., and Jakarta (Indonesia) 20th. This survey was the first research effort to evaluate digital governance in municipalities throughout the world by examining the largest city in each of 98 countries with the highest percentage of Internet users, including Hong Kong and Macao. The research evaluated the official Web sites of each city in their native languages, by using 92 measures over five core areas (Security and Privacy, Usability, Content, Services, Citizen Participation), developing an index which was considered "culture neutral". The research identified a digital divide between developed and less developed countries. Although the average score for all cities is 28.10 out of 100, the average score in OECD countries is 36.34; while the average score in non-OECD countries is only 24.26. In addition, 67% of cities selected in Africa have not established official city websites, whereas only 3% in Europe have no city Web sites.

The results of this survey are highlighted from many examples of projects and experiences of innovative applications of ICTs at local level. Some of particular interest in developed countries are the project of e-Participation in the City of Tampere, Finland[16]; the Personalised Information and email notification system, in the United Kingdom[17]; the Iperbole Internet Civic Network, in Bologna, Italy[18]; the e-Democracy experience of the City of Issy-les-Moulineaux, France,[19] and the M.O.R.E. – Member Organised Resource Exchange, in St. Louis, Missouri, USA.[20] Some interesting examples of projects and experiences in developing countries are, for instance, the Citizen Service Centres, in Bahia, Brazil[21], the Seoul Anti Corruption - OPEN System, in South Korea[22] and the TOM Portal for e-Democracy in Estonia[23].

But are we sure that all these experiences are successful and are really increasing the participation of citizens, and especially the poor and marginalised people ?

A recent report of UNCRD, Japan, evaluates the cases of Singapore and Naga City (Philippines) underlining that, "while these cities are making major contributions to their country's economy and house populations who are participating in the information revolution, large sections of their populations (50% or more), live in poverty, are located in slums, and engaged in informal sector activities, being therefore seriously threatened by human development"[24]. What about their needs and voices?

This situation can lead to an increased "domestic digital divide" (DDD Factor). In fact, according to Bridges.org Report (2004), "there is an overall trend of growing disparities in access to and use of ICTs between countries (the international digital divide), and between groups within countries (the domestic digital divide)"[25]. In addition to this, the constraints are aggravated in most countries by other factors, such as: class and age (intergenerational digital divide), ethnics and gender inequalities and discriminations, and race (digital apartheid).[26]

Of particular importance at local level is moreover what can be defined the "language divide". In fact, most of the applications and the content of ICTs (especially the Internet) is in English. Thus, millions of people are not in a position to benefit from ICTs because of the language barrier.

An important aspect to be considered is that, in introducing ICTs in governmental operations, there is the risk that large amounts of funds are being spent on creating infrastructure to enable people to have access to ICTs in developing countries. However, if we fail to recognise that access is necessary, but not the only condition for creating impact, and ignores capacity-building, citizens' participation and content development, then much of this funding will be wasted (Cost Factor).

In this connection, many of the ICTs applications that are deemed to be successful on anecdotal evidence, are, in practice, only partially successful: early recognition blinds the project managers to possible shortcomings, which remain unattended to and which can lead to failure. In particular, it is apparent that solutions that work in developed countries cannot simply be transplanted to developing country environments: solutions must be based on an understanding of local needs and conditions. (Contextualisation Factor).

Furthermore the, let us say, "natural" limits that are connected to local governance systems, such as the lack of capacity both in terms of human and financial resources, the difficulties related to the geographical position of local communities (distance from cities and lack of access to infra and info structure) have to be considered. Last, but not least, the need to communicate in local languages, respecting and in keeping with the local cultural heritage and traditional systems of governance; this includes the important role to be played by women and young people, and their connection with the hierarchical and chieftaincy organisation of local societies. This is the Cultural Factor, that is of course directly linked to the degree of "readiness" of the community for the introduction of ICTs and innovation in general. (Readiness Factor).

Therefore, if we consider the factors of risk (or success) identified above, enumerating them in a logical order, such as: Readiness; Contextualisation; Cultural/Language; Cost and Domestic Digital Divide factors, we will have a complex equation that will never have the same solution.

Introducing ICTs in local governance is not at all a simple issue; it has to deal not only with the "physical" access problem, but with the lost opportunity of people who are unable to effectively use ICTs either because they do not know how to use them or do not understand how ICTs can be relevant to their lives. It is fundamental to look at the social issues like basic literacy, poverty and healthcare and how ICTs can become part of the solution to these critical problems.

Given this fact, the key to success in introducing ICTs in local governance, are political will, community leadership and ownership. In addition, accurate strategic planning, effective monitoring and critical evaluation are indispensable in the identification of factors that inhibit impact and ensure sustainability. The development of such a policy framework cannot be done without considering the "local" component and community development and how these integrate and use ICTs, in order to create the concept of "**e-Local Governance**", that can be defined as:

> *the application of ICTs to transform the business of government and to enable the broad inclusion of citizens in public management, public service delivery and democratic participation at the local level"*
> *(LOG-IN Africa Project Proposal to IDRC by G. Misuraca on behalf of CAFRAD, November 2005).*

4.2. SOME EXPERIENCES OF USING ICTs AT LOCAL GOVERNMENT LEVEL IN AFRICA

In Africa, many countries are developing National ICTs Strategies that, in some cases, are already producing positive results and are leading (or can lead) to success. Some examples are: Egypt, Ghana, Kenya, Mauritius, Morocco, Nigeria, South Africa and Tunisia. Many other countries are embarking on National ICTs Strategies and Programmes, often "mixed" with Administrative Reforms, Good Governance Strategies, or Decentralisation Programmes.

At the same time, there are many examples of interesting projects, often supported by international donors and agencies, that are focussing on innovative applications of ICTs in local governance in countries lacking of ICTs infrastructure, through the use of hand held devices, touch screens and keyboard access in local languages. Some of these projects were presented to the "Workshop on Innovative Applications of ICTs for Local Governance in Africa", jointly organised by the International Development Research Centre (IDRC), the United Nations Capital Development Fund (UNCDF) and the United Nations Economic Commission for Africa (UNECA) in Addis Ababa, between 7th. and 9th. June, 2004.[27] Among the several presentations of case studies, programmes and projects, of particular interest was the Project of "Application of Hand-held Computers in the Delivery of Health Services in Uganda", managed by the Uganda Health Information Network (UHIN) and funded by IDRC. This project aims at determining cost-effective ways of enhancing access, sharing and communication of critical health and medical information in a timely and efficient manner for the benefit of health care providers, managers and planners, in the Ugandan technological and institutional context. Successful examples of the application of ICTs at local level are represented by the case of the Mangaung Local Municipality, in South Africa, with the project of "Knowledge Management in the Electronic Delivery of Municipal Services", and the Project of ICTs Application in Local Government in Senegal managed by the NGO "Observatoire de la Gouvernance" (SAFEFOD) and funded by IDRC, on the development of an ICTs based accounting system of control, to prevent corruption.

Other projects of particular relevance for their cultural aspects include the Project of "Capacity Building Support for Local Governments" in Zimbabwe; and the "ICTs and Traditional Governance Project" in Ghana.

Some interesting efforts of strongly introducing ICTs in the governmental strategies, were presented in the "Woreda Study: ICTs Needs in Decentralisation Process" in Ethiopia, as well as the Project on "E-government Applications for Local and Central Governments in Ethiopia", which developed an interface in Amharic through a Multi-lingual Content Management System; the "Utilization of ICTs in the Promotion of Decentralized Governance" in Uganda and the e-government Strategy in the Gambia.

As highlighted in the annexe to this study, many other initiatives, programmes and projects in Africa focus on the application of ICTs for local governance. What is important is that these initiatives are always integrated in the government strategies of decentralisation and to effectively improve the governance systems for better delivery services to citizens and business, and to also increase their participation. But notwithstanding the growing importance of ICTs and local governance, there is a clear recognition of the need to move away from anecdotal analysis of strengthening local governance towards a more rigorous, evidence and outcome-based analysis of developing trends and the implementation of ICTs in local governance in Africa.

Notes

1. Declaration of the World Summit of Cities and Local Authorities on the Information Society (Lyon, 5th. December, 2003).
2. See also, Olekambainei Emmanuel and Sintim-Misa Mavis Ampah, "Info-communication for Development in Africa", UN ICTs Task Force Series 2, ICTs for African Development, UN, NY 2003.
3. www.firstgov.gov
4. Sy, J. Habib, "Critical and Prospective Views on ICTs and Governance in Africa", in "Africa Networking: Development Information ICTs and Governance, United Nations Economic Commission for Africa, UNECA, Addis Ababa, 2004
5. www.europa.eu.int
6. www.localegov.gov.uk
7. www.italia.gov.it
8. www.adele.fr
9. http://www.gc.ca
10. www.kantei.go.jp
11. www.ourbrisbane.com
12. www.presidencia.gob.mx
13. www.gov.my/MyGov
14. www.andhrapradesh.com
15. This survey was conducted jointly by the E-governance Institute of Rutgers University-Newark and the Global e-Policy e-government Institute of Sungkyunkwan University, Korea, and was co-sponsored by the UN Division for Public Administration and Development Management (UNDESA/DPADM)), and the American Society for Public Administration (ASPA). The results of the survey are available on www.unpan.org
16. www.etampere.fi/infocity
17. www.info4local.gov.uk

18. www.comune.bologna.it
19. www.issy.com
20. www.stlouis.missouri.org
21. www.ba.gov.br
22. www.open.metro.seoul.kr
23. tom.riik.ee
24. Regional Development Dialogue, Vol. 23, N° 2, United Nations Centre for Regional Development, UNCRD, Nagoya, Japan, 2002.
25. Bridges.org, "Spanning the Digital Divide: Understanding and tackling the Issues", www.bridges.org
26. USA, Department of Commerce, 2000.
27. www.idrc.org

PART II

CASE STUDIES ON ICTS FOR LOCAL GOVERNANCE

5

THE ROLE OF ICTs IN THE DECENTRALISATION POLICY IN SENEGAL

CASE STUDY OVERVIEW

Location: Senegal

Funding Institution: International Development Research Centre (IDRC)

Executing Institution:

SAFEFOD – African Society of Education and Training for Development

Project Manager: Prof. Yero Sylla, Executive Secretary

Total Budget: 101,276 $ CAD

Project Start Date: 27 December 1997

Project End Date: 9 March 1999

Administrative Information and Contacts:

SAFEFOD: Allées S.N. Tall, Amitié 2, n° 4011,
B.P. 5945, Dakar-Fann, Sénegal
Tel. (221) 8244406 – Fax (221) 8241459,
email: safefod@safefod.org
Web site: www.safefod.org

5.1. CONTEXT AND POLICY

5.1.1. The decentralisation policy in Senegal

Since its independence in 1960, the Republic of Senegal has committed to a comprehensive process of reform of the State. Crucial to this reform is the policy of "progressive" decentralisation that seeks to empower local government and support local development.

This process had been started by the establishment of the "Rural Communities" in 1972, (Law 72-02), and completed in the '90s by the several laws and legal acts that led to the Law 96-06, "Code of Local

Government"[1], and related laws and legal acts. In addition to the Rural Communities, the local governments in Senegal are the "Regions" and the "Communes" (or Municipalities).

The policy of decentralisation is designed in a way that should ensure participation by people and their representatives in the management of public affairs, and this participation should be enhanced as these levels of government become progressively more independent vis-à-vis the central power. Moreover, to implement the decentralisation, in 1998, an Agency for Regional Development (ARD – Agence Régionale de Développement) was established. Its aim is to stimulate regional and local development by supporting the elaboration and implementation of regional and local development plans[2].

At present, there are 441 local governments in Senegal; they are composed of 11 Regions; 110 Communes and 320 Rural Communities. They are supposed to be governed according to the basic principles underpinning the process of decentralisation, which are: free administration, devolution of power and solidarity. It means that, in addition to administrative decentralisation, there is also a strong process of "deconcentration" of functions from central to local level, and a consequent need of resources, both financial and human, to effectively manage the twofold effect of decentralisation policy.

But yet there are many obstacles to the effective transfer of these powers. Most local elected officials have no access to legal texts and they have neither the means nor the capacity to play their roles fully.

These constraints prevent them from clearly understanding the legislation on decentralisation and empowerment of local government and thus acting effectively and according to the capacity of the local government. This situation is of particular concern because the working instruments (codes, regulations, laws, decrees) are in French, the country's official language, while most local officials are illiterate or able to operate only in the dialect of their region, albeit that the new Constitution indicates that all elected representatives should be able to read and write in the national language (i.e. French).

If we consider then the situation of basic equipment and the capacities of managing ICTs, this is even more limited, and in some cases local governments have not even access to basic infrastructures such as electricity or telephony.

5.1.2. The National ICTs Policy and the Senegal ACACIA Strategy (SAS)

The African Communities and the Information Society programme, better known simply as ACACIA, is an IDRC initiative aimed at "promoting the use of ICTs in African communities, in order to prevent them from being increasingly marginalised from the information society, and also to help them achieve their development objectives".

The ACACIA programme seeks to establish a reliable knowledge base by identifying the most appropriate policies, techniques, applications and contents, approaches and methodologies for promoting the appropriation of ICTs by disadvantaged communities, and in particular by young people and women, by providing ready access to these tools and putting them to effective use.

In Senegal, ACACIA has been underway since 1997, in a context that has seen growing empowerment of development players as the state has withdrawn from productive activities.

In this regard, nevertheless, the Senegalese authorities were quick to recognise the importance of ICTs for economic and social development, as confirmed by the Prospective Study: Senegal 2015, which foresaw the emergence of the communication society based on the development of ICTs and which proposed as a strategic objective "strengthening and facilitating access to information and promoting social communication", there was not a coherent framework for introducing ICTs, despite the existence of some of Africa's most highly developed telecommunications infrastructure. In fact, despite the beginnings of what we might call a national policy for ICTs were apparent as early as 1985, with establishment of the National Telecommunications Company (SONATEL), reflecting the determination of the Government of Senegal to give priority to development of the telecommunications sector; and despite the many players involved in the field of ICTs, it was only in 1996 that the government issued its first statement on telecommunications development policy (1996-2000).

Moreover, considering that local governments were taking increasing responsibility, and several policy areas have been transferred to them: education, health, governance, etc., it was pivotal to take into proper consideration the need expressed by local communities in developing strategies and implementing national programmes.

It must also be noted that, despite the interest in ICTs on the part of government and even of the private sector, there was a glaring lack of expertise in this field, particularly when it came to research, while, at the same time, civil society organisations were becoming increasingly active in economic and social life at the local, national and international levels, and through their actions, discrete but often highly visible, there was the clear opportunity to influence the state in its definition of national strategic priorities.

In this context, the process of preparing the Senegal ACACIA Strategy (SAS) was highly participatory, thanks to which the programme has indeed taken account of the needs expressed by the people, but within an overall framework of development priorities identified by the authorities, consistent with the sectoral approach of the country's development strategy. These priorities relate essentially to education, employment and entrepreneurship, natural resource management, governance and health. The Acacia programme therefore reflects the sectoral approach to development in Senegal, through its focus on these key sectors, with due regard of course, to the needs and priorities expressed by the people themselves.

5.1.3. The current framework: the National Programme for Good Governance

Following the previous experiences and considering the different sectoral policies underway, the new Government "Gouvernement de l'Alternance" elected in March 2000, committed itself to strengthen the "good governance" of the country, engaging in a global reform of the state and a modernisation of the public sector.

This commitment, with the support of the development partners, has been institutionalised and designed within the framework of the "National programme for good governance"[3], which is a comprehensive programme coming from the previous "Integrated Programme of Public Sector Reform" (PIRSP), more coherent with the "Strategic Document for Poverty Reduction" (DSRP) and in line with the vision of the New Partnership for Africa's Development (NEPAD) and the orientations identified in the "Economic and Social Development Plan: 2002-2007" (PDES).

Among the strategic lines of the "National programme for good governance", decentralisation is indicated as a central issue for state reform. In fact, it is not only seen with regard to the organisation and execution of local government affairs, but, more generally, with concern about the "functional relations" of power (devolution/transfer of competencies) and the consequent capacity of the state to adapt to evolving society, and the needs of responsibility, proximity and participation of people in the management of public affairs.

The national programme, based on the weaknesses that have been identified in its analysis, indicate three lines of action with regard to local governance: 1) Improving the institutional and organisational framework and the capacity of human resources; 2) Strengthening the co-ordination of activities among different levels of government and development partners; 3) Improving the public finance system at a local level and decentralising the management of public expenditure.

With regard to the role of ICTs, whilst underlining the insufficient and incoherent state of deployment of ICTs in the public administration, it stresses the potential role in supporting the modernisation of the state and the promotion of good governance with a particular focus on providing "quality" information to citizens.

5.1.4. e-Senegal: a Strategic Vision and Action Plan

In January 2002, in an official report, the President of the Republic, H. E. Abdoulaye Wade, expressed the vision of the national e-government, based upon the conviction that ICTs are a great lever for economic development in Africa.

The vision of President Wade for Senegal, is to pass "from Senegal to e-Senegal, that includes the passage from Government to e-government, and from Citizen to e-Citizen".

To manage this transition, in July 2004, the President established the "State Informatics Agency" (ADIE)[4]. This new structure, that followed on from the activity of the previous Direction for State Computerisation ("Direction Informatique de l'Etat"), was created in order to better co-ordinate, monitor and support the implementation of the ambitious programme of computerisation of public administration, and make the national e-government strategy a reality.

In addition to marketing purposes, also being the "champion" of NEPAD's ICTs component, the objectives of e-Senegal were identified and the strategic plan initiated already in 2000, in partnership with the World Bank. In fact, since 2000, the "Programme of modernisation of the Administrative Information Systems" (PMSIA) was launched and implemented according to six action lines: 1) Information Systems Co-ordination, including an ICTs Needs assessment and provision of ICTs necessary equipment; 2) Government ICTs Infrastructure: development of the Government Intranet, including the creation of a "Resource Centre" and an advanced network linking key institutions and Ministries, as well as some applications for communication and management of human resources and material; 3) Computerisation and development of key applications of the Ministry of Economics and Finance; this included the provision of equipment and the development of specific applications and support of already existing systems; 4) Computerisation of a main public service: the Postal Service; 5) Computerisation of a main Academic Centre: the University "Gaston Berger"; 6) Modernisation of the structure of the Ministry of the Interior.

This last action line was directly connected to the process of decentralisation and strengthening of local governance systems. The Ministry of the Interior was already providing basic equipment to the "Prefecture" (local delegations) and supported the establishment of Regional Units of Informatics for Development (Unités Régionales d'Informatiques pour le Développement – URID).

More generally, as underlined during the inauguration of the "Intranet of the Government", held in Dakar, 15th. March 2005, in the presence of H.E. the President of the Republic[5], the objective of the Government was to expand the communication system to link all the different levels of government with a particular focus on remote and disadvantaged areas.

It was clear to the government, in fact, that the success of the e-Senegal strategy would be based upon the effective and efficient utilisation of ICTs to support local governance systems.

5.1.5. The way forward

In this context the Government now considered the revision of the National Programme for Good Governance, in order to strengthen the component related to local governance and its relation with ICTs. A national workshop on "ICTs for local governance" to provide input to the "Roundtable of development partner" was held in June 2005 to revise the PNBG[6].

This is also connected to the renewed role and mission that the government was giving to the competent authorities at central level, which are the Ministry of Decentralisation and Local Government and the Ministry of Regional Planning and Decentralised Co-operation.

It is clear to all the actors of development in Senegal that despite the availability of financial and technical resources and the strong leadership and commitment by the Government, there was a lack of co-ordination and a weak strategic plan with regard to the issue of local governance, and in particular how to make best use of ICTs for local development.

5.2. SAFEFOD'S PROJECT ON "THE ROLE OF ICTS IN DECENTRALISATION POLICY"

5.2.1. Background and Justification

The strategic justification of the Senegal ACACIA Strategy (SAS), preparation of which started in October 1996 and which was completed in March 1997, was the decision to make ICTs available to communities, in particular poor communities, and to see how these ICTs could contribute to their development.

The SAS sought to foster co-ordinated activity in policymaking, infrastructure, technologies, and applications and contents in order to promote a true national strategy for using ICTs for development. The objective was to encourage establishment of an independent framework for concerted action in the field of ICTs, a framework that would provide the political authorities with a solid basis for their ICTs policy. This was based essentially on a series of experimental demonstration projects. These pilot projects were undertaken in order to verify the hypotheses underlying the Acacia programme, as well as to derive lessons that could be applied on a broader scale, and that would be of use to policy-makers.

For this purpose, the preparation of the programme was made with the participation of various institutions, national and local, representing government and civil society, researchers, and development players. This consultation process included, in addition to a Permanent Secretariat and some horizontal and co-ordinating committees, five sectoral working groups (health, education and training, employment and income generation, natural resource management and governance).

These were standing fora for consideration and discussion among agencies and individuals: each group was supposed to oversee the research priorities in its respective field.

An important point to be considered is the profile of the members of the various SAS structures. These members come from different key sectors of the country (universities, private sector, NGOs, civil society) and are involved in research, the economy, health, governance etc. These are supposed to be people who have the capacity to exert direct or indirect influence on policies, or who are aware of the usefulness of ICTs for development.

Therefore, considering the increasing importance of the role of local governments, and the great potential of ICTs in improving the performances of any modern administration, the Working Group on Governance which was co-ordinated by Prof. Yero Sylla, identified the role of ICTs in decentralisation policy as one of the priority areas to be explored.

In fact, despite the, at that time, recent advent of the Internet and of high-capacity processing and storage technologies, it was clear to the working group that ICTs could enormously support the needs of management of local governments, as well as the potential for increasing the participation of citizens in decision making with regard to public affairs at local level. At the same time, this could support local economic development. But the situation of local governments, and in particular the awareness and capacities of elected representatives was negligible and, in the majority of local governments, there was a lack of basic infrastructure and conditions (such as electricity for instance) for the introduction of ICTs at local level. Specific tools to support management of local government were also non-existent.

In the face of this situation, the SAS Working Group on Governance proposed to launch a research project, to raise awareness about the potential of ICTs for local governance, and to develop and test some pilot applications to sustain the daily management of local authorities.

It was proposed that the project be co-ordinated by SAFEFOD (African Society of Education and Training for Development) with financial support from IDRC/ACACIA.

5.2.2. Strategy and Objectives

The global objective of the project was to inform and sensitise local officials, elected representatives and the government about the role and impact of ICTs on decentralisation policy, and, at the same time, create the enabling environment for the implementation of an "Observatory of Decentralisation and Local Governance".

To attain this goal, the specific objectives of the project were to:

a) Build a partnership between the government, the local elected representatives and the civil society;
b) Assess the "state of the art" of ICTs integration in local government operations;
c) Establish a "research-laboratory" to develop and test ICTs applications to support local government operations;
d) Disseminate the results of research and laboratory tests through a National Campaign of awareness and communication on the role of ICTs for local governance;
e) Study the feasibility of the "Observatory of Decentralisation and Local Governance".

The project was expected to increase the awareness of the "actors of decentralisation" on the possibilities and potential of ICTs to support local governance and sustain the decentralisation process, as well as establishing a permanent mechanism for consultation among all the stakeholders involved in this policy.

To achieve this result, the methodology to be followed implied a strong participatory approach, in order to effectively involve all the necessary experts and representatives of governmental and non-governmental authorities and bodies concerned.

Moreover, in order to provide a strong demonstrator effect, it was decided to give high visibility to the output of the research by organising practical demonstrations for the benefit of all interested stakeholders, both at local and central level.

5.2.3. Rationale and Structure

Before the implementation of the project, during the activities of the SAS working group on governance, a preliminary analysis of the main problems related to the introduction of ICTs at local government level, was carried out.

This preliminary activity, mainly based on the experience of the members of the Working Group, was further reinforced during the first phase of activity of the project.

The main elements identified as weaknesses for local governments, can be summarised by the following:

- Many local governments have no access to basic infrastructures, including electricity and telephones, so that the potential of using ICTs cannot possibly even be considered;
- Even where possible, there is a very limited use of basic ICTs in the management of local governments. This is due to several reasons, including financial limitations, limited management skills and in particular a weak capacity in the management of ICTs.
- In addition to these factors, there are other important issues that emerged in analysing the situation, such as the fact that there was a very limited awareness of the capacities of ICTs, and consequently a potential reluctance to innovate, as well as more concrete constraints due to the comparison of this issue with the other priorities of the different communities.
- Moreover, following the introduction of the new law of decentralisation that foresaw a different administrative organisation and devolution of important functions and power to the local governments, there were no effective changes to support its operational implementation. In particular, notwithstanding the complexity of the management of the local government, and especially considering the new functions to be executed, all activities were performed in a traditional way, with very little use (if any) of ICTs.

Based upon the above mentioned preliminary analysis and the strategic options identified, the project was structured around a period of one year, with a number of activities to be conducted in parallel. These activities included the following timetable (the number representing the month):

1. Launch of the project and establishment of the institutional partnership;
2. Launch of the study on ICTs and decentralisation;

3. Establishment of the laboratory;
4. Conclusion of the study on ICTs and decentralisation;
5. Analysis and exploitation of the results and data acquired with the study;
6. Preliminary test of basic products in the laboratory;
7. Test and demonstration of basic products with other experts and partners;
8. Inclusion of feed-back of the demonstration and comments by other experts and partners;
9. Preliminary presentation of results and products among key stakeholders;
10. Dissemination of results and public demonstrations of products;
11. Study of feasibility of the Observatory of local governance and decentralisation;
12. Final Report and Evaluation.

The structure of the project shows that the process that the research had been designed to undertake could not be fulfilled without the active participation by the representatives of all the stakeholders, directly or indirectly, involved in decentralisation.

For this reason, particular importance was given to the involvement of experts coming from different institutions in the analysis of priorities and the development of the products, as well as to the dissemination of results and the public demonstration that was supposed to coincide, during the ninth month of the project, with the electoral campaign for the regional and local elections.

The principal players involved during the project were:

- Associations of local elected representatives: Association of Rural Community Presidents, Association of Mayors of Senegal, Association of Regional Council Presidents;
- Central Administration: Ministry of Local Governments; Directorate for State Registry Management; Ministry of Research and Technological Development; Ministry of ICTs; Prime Minister's Office; Presidency of the Republic;
- Local Administrations: some local governments and municipalities, and the Association of Municipality Development (ADM);

- University and other Civil Society Organisations;
- Resource Persons and Experts recognised at national level, including the IDRC/SAS Working Group on Governance.

Active involvement of these players was expected to result in the appropriation of the approach and the outputs of the project, with a view to improving implementation of the decentralisation policy.

5.2.4. Organisation and Management Arrangements

Given the specific objectives attained by the project, and considering its conception within the framework of the SAS working group on governance, it was decided that the project would be executed by SAFEFOD (African Society of Education and Training for Development).

SAFEFOD, in fact, is a Senegalese non-governmental organisation with an tradition of experience in local development and governance. It was created in 1991 with the aim of promoting a democratic and developed society in Senegal, but also with a pan-African horizon.

It is apolitical and non-profit making and, during the years of activity it developed and tested an integrated and participative model for Local Governance centred on education and training, communication and development support.

The target of the activities of SAFEFOD has always been the grassroots communities, including the local elected representatives. But to make good governance emerge, there is the need that governments, both at local and at central level, and civil society, play their roles fully, and in partnership with each other.

The model of local governance instituted by SAFEFOD is based upon the assistance of the three partners of local development (state, local governments and grassroots communities/civil society) to face the major challenges constituting impediments to good governance: poverty, illiteracy and lack of communication.

To achieve this, the SAFEFOD model of local governance, tested in the field since the early 90,s, consists of three main strategies:

- Training and Capacity Building;
- Dynamic Interactions and communication;
- Development Support.

As indicated by Prof. Yero Sylla, Executive Secretary of SAFEFOD, "the originality of this model derives from the fact that it views the "dynamization" of people and institutions through the deliberative organs of the local governments. Indeed, these entities are rarely taken into account, least of all involved, by the various intervening parties of the civil society. Yet they constitute the link between the state and the citizens, since they are the most decentralized politico-administrative centre from which it is possible to stimulate a purposeful and a behaviour likely to give thrust to lasting development at the grassroots". [7]

Early in the development of the "local governance model", it appeared clear that ICTs could play an important role in reaching the objectives assigned to local governments, as well as sustaining their achievements, and so SAFEFOD decided to integrate ICTs in the centre of the model itself. Thus, the project on "The role of ICTs in decentralisation policy", gave SAFEFOD the opportunity to achieve this option, as early as in 1997 in Africa.

Since the project was a research activity, and also considering the preliminary, and perhaps even too advanced subject of research identified, it was decided to invest a relatively small amount of financial resources, that is, a total budget of 101,276 Canadian Dollars ($CAD). The resources were distributed as indicated in the following table.

SAFEFOD's Project The Role of ICTs in decentralisation policy – Budget:

Description	Cost (in $ CAD)
Workshops and communication	9,000
Consultants	23,200
Research Expenses	34,073
Technical Assistance	6,980
Equipment	28,023
TOTAL	**101,276**

Source: IDRC, Dossier n.97-8153-01.

The project was therefore conducted with a reasonable investment in computer hardware and the participation of local human resources. In particular, in addition to its Project Manager, Prof. Yero Sylla, Executive Secretary of SAFEFOD, two principal and experienced consultants were hired to conduct the studies on ICTs and decentralisation, and to present their findings to a national workshop to launch the project. Moreover, other technical consultants were hired to develop the specific products and organise the research and tests in the laboratory. At the same time, to support the research activities and also as a way to improve the research capacity in this area, it was decided to hire some young researchers as trainees, from the University.

In addition to the principal consultants specifically hired for the project, other resources were dedicated to the project among SAFEFOD's staff. This was in particular with the objective to develop a sustainable laboratory of research usable after the end of the IDRC's funded project, and to utilise the "network" of contacts and presence that SAFEFOD already had in the field, to test the products output of the research and to disseminate the results and findings of the project.

Thus, the project, notwithstanding that much of the research was developed in the laboratory, also involved a continuous contact with representatives of the central and local administrations and institutions identified, as well as many tests and demonstrations in the field.

With regard to the timing of the project's activities, it should be noted that, as the phase of preparation, started in July 1997, lasted longer than expected, the project itself started officially only in December 1997, therefore becoming effectively operational in January 1998.

In the same way, since the release of the outputs of the research were not immediately successful, the dissemination of results and demonstration of the products, as well as its update and improvement, continued also after the end of the project (the final workshop was held in March 1999, with three months of delay) as a self-sustained activity by SAFEFOD. In this regard, it should also be underlined that the human resources dedicated to the project, and especially to its follow-up, have been changed from a more researchers profile to the team that is now taking care of the results of the research and is much more market-oriented (see the next section).

Finally, with regard to monitoring and evaluation of the Project, IDRC established a Committee for monitoring the progress of the project, also aiming at supporting the executing agency in its activities. In many cases, IDRC supported the activity of disseminating the results of the project, by inviting SAFEFOD to demonstrate the products in workshops, organised by IDRC, which were not part of the project's budget[8].

Figure 1. SAFEFOD's stand at an International Fair in Dakar, 1999

5.2.5. Activities and Results

a) The Study on ICTs and decentralisation and the "Partnership-Workshop"

The activities of the project followed the structure proposed in the project document and attained all the achievements and expected output of the research.

In the first phase of the project, a more detailed and in-depth research of the "state of the art" and the situation of ICTs and decentralisation in the field was undertaken, in the period January-February 1998, by the two principal consultants. The two consultants focussed their analysis on not only the general theory of decentralisation and ICTs, but also on the practice and concrete application at the local level, also providing some comparisons and examples from other cases at the international level.

Next, the study, in two different reports, was presented to the "Partnership-Workshop on the role of ICTs in the implementation of decentralisation policy in Senegal", organised by SAFEFOD and IDRC on the 25th. February, 1998 at the Savana Hotel in Dakar.

The workshop was attended by all the stakeholders (actors in the decentralisation), including representatives of the Central and Local governments, of the local elected representatives; media and civil society organisations. To mark the importance of the event, the workshop was opened by the Minister of Decentralisation who observed that the workshop was "a fundamental step for the implementation of an observatory of decentralisation and local governance".

After presenting the objectives of the project and launching it officially, the findings of the two studies on Decentralisation and ICTs were presented. In particular, they underlined the three-fold relationship between participation, local management/administration and responsibility and the functional relationship that exists between decentralisation-policy and ICTs in the governance arena.

Having this relationship in mind, the objectives of the workshop were to highlight the relations of causality, interdependence and complementarity existing between the problems faced by the policy of decentralisation and the management of local governments, and the solutions that ICTs can provide to them. For this reason, the working activities of the workshop were divided into three working groups, each of them focussing on the specific aspects faced by the different categories of Local Government: Regions, Municipalities/Communes; Rural Communities.

The conclusions of the workshop helped the project management team to better identify the matrix of problems, infrastructures and roles of actors in the management of local government; to elaborate the Questionnaire for the survey; orientate the laboratory tests; and enable the implementation of the Observatory for local governance and decentralisation.

In this connection, once the laboratory was established and exploited the findings and data acquired with the studies, the following phase of the project focussed on the research in the laboratory and the preliminary test of basic products was developed. In this regard, given the results of the studies and the conclusions of the workshop, the research identified priorities and conducted the following experiments and activities:

1. Design of a Web Site;
2. Development of two software applications for
    a. management of the budget and
    b. the management of the registry system;
3. Conception of an interactive multi-language vocal server.

Figure 2. Partnership-Workshop

From left to right : MM. Cheikh Sadibou Fall, Association of Mayors of Senegal (AMS), Moussé Daby Diagne, Association of Regional Council Presidents (APR), Pr Yèro Sylla, Executive Secretary of SAFEFOD, Macky Sall, Minister in charge of Ministry of Local Government and Decentralisation, Djilali Benmouffok, Representative of IDRC and Aly Lô, President of the Association of Rural Community Presidents.

b) The output of the laboratory research:

1. The Web Site - Observatory on Local Governance:

The designed website is bilingual (French and English) and provides information about decentralisation laws and legal and administrative acts; as well as information on local governments and their councils, and a press review on decentralisation policy.

The Web site also contains several publications, including the summary of each issue of the "Journal of Local Governance", edited in French by SAFEFOD[9].

Of course, if we look at the web site today, it may appear to be not a great innovation, but if we consider that the idea of using Internet technology was conceived in a project for local governance in Africa in 1996, and the web site designed and developed in 1997/98, when the Internet was still a new technology not yet widely diffused even in industrialised countries, then the innovative role of this activity is quite obvious.

The web site has been operational since 1998 and it has been continuously updated and managed by local resources at SAFEFOD. Its address is: www.safefod.org

2. Management software applications for local governments:

The software applications designed and developed during the research project were focussing on two basic operations executed by local government, and which were not yet computerised: the management of the budget; and the management of the civil registry.

Therefore, the technological solutions adopted as software at the beginning were based on simple existing, proprietary systems, such as Microsoft Excel and, in a second version, Microsoft Access. The preliminary versions also had a low level of security and resulted in some problems of management and sustainability. After several revisions, tests, demonstrations, and advanced releases, and especially after the update undertaken in partnership with a private company, in 2004 the software was revised completely in order to have improved performance and taking into account users' requirements with regard to security and "user-friendliness". From a technical perspective, the systems are designed with up-to-date IT tools, involving relational database manager programmes (Microsoft SQL, Access or Oracle), and the applications can be installed on Stand Alone Systems or Local Area Networks (LAN).

The functionalities of the software, in their current version, are the following:

a. CAURI: Budget Management Software;

The software allows the management of the entire administrative accounting system for local governments, providing the possibility of supporting the preparation and execution of the budget in accordance with the prevailing regulations and, at the same time, to produce the Administrative Account Statement as required by the authorities. In this regard, it also allows recording, but without the possibility of modifying, the approved budgets of the previous years. It is therefore a statistical analysis tool which provides performance indicators indispensable for decision-making.

b. CIVIS: Civil Registry Management Software:

The software includes all the functionalities required for the management of a registration centre, providing the necessary functionality for the management of the registries of births, deaths and marriages, including marginal notes and explanations. It also provides for the possibility of editing all registration forms, in different versions, as required by the regulations and to produce statistics and reports. Integrating a large number of parameters to be adapted to all the cases evoked by the regulations regarding the registration systems, the application is flexible and secure, since it includes an advanced system to manage users' accounts allowing different and specific functionalities based on groups of users.

3. Vocal server:

The Vocal server was designed and programmed to be multilingual, with the possibility of using French, English and six local languages spoken in Senegal: Fula, Wolof, Joola, Sereer, Mandinka and Soninke).

The vocal server was designed to provide information about decentralisation, local governments, civil society organisations and donor agencies, available anytime and from anywhere in Senegal and throughout the world, by only a telephone call at the server number. The server provides a voice mail message system to allow communication between the different "actors of decentralisation" (state, local governments, civil society organisations, donors, etc.). The vocal server was tested successfully at the end of the project, and it is still available, but its implementation was not continued after the project due to the high cost of implementing its content and the limited response by the potential users.

c) Demonstration activities and Dissemination of results:

Once the products output of the research in the laboratory were developed, the project started the phase of demonstration to disseminate the results of the research, verify the usefulness of the products and, with particular regard to the management software, to test their applicability to local governments. For this purpose, in addition to a number of communication activities which also included many press-releases about the project and its results, a Final National workshop to present the results of the research was organised by SAFEFOD and IDRC, on 9th. March, 1999.

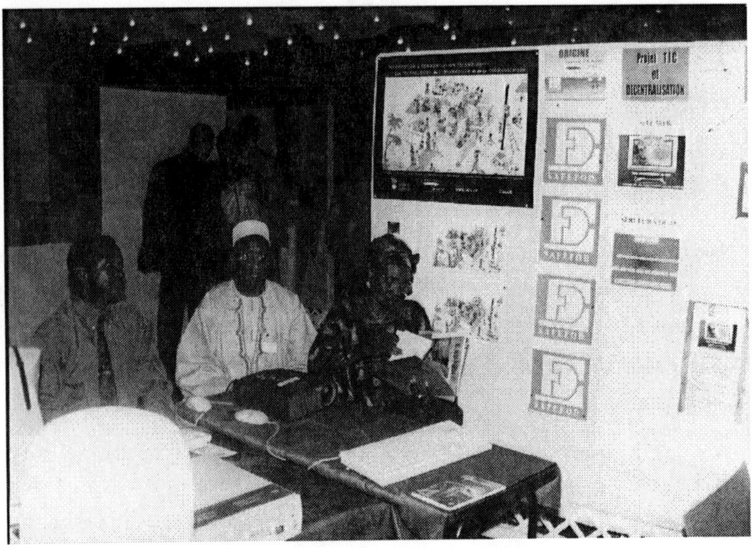

Figure 3. Final National Workshop

The workshop was attended by many practitioners and representatives of all the different stakeholders involved in the process of decentralisation.

Many other public demonstrations were also organised in the following months, including presentations to the President of the Republic Abdou Diouf, many Ministers, and other high level personalities and representatives of authorities at local, central and international level.

Among the different activities, the output of the project was also presented as a case of success of the ACACIA Programme, to the former Prime Minister of Canada, Jean Chrétien, accompanied by the former Prime Minister of Senegal, Mr. Mamadou Lamine Loum, during a visit to Senegal on 9th. November, 1999, to participate in an event organised by IDRC/ACACIA.

Finally, as a result of the research project, what cannot be forgotten is the high awareness raised about the potential of ICTs for local governance, as well as the needs and challenges to face in successfully implementing the decentralisation policy. As a consequence of this, the main objective of the project, to establish an Observatory of local governance and decentralisation, in addition to being a result of the research, was necessarily also identified as a required mechanism to

Figure 4. Demonstration to the President of the Republic Abdou Diouf

The former President of the Republic of Senegal M. Abdou Diouf visit the stand of SAFEFOD for a demonstration during the exposiion organised beside the General Assembly of the Association of Mayors of Senegal (AMS), 22nd and 23rd July 1999, Hôtel Méridien Président (Dakar)

be further developed and monitored continuously by all the different stakeholders, but in particular by the civil society.

5.3. CONCLUSIONS

5.3.1. Impact on decentralisation policy

As indicated by the project manager, Prof. Yero Sylla, "the research project was designed in a way to provide the local authorities with instruments for managing local government. But it was up to these authorities to decide how to use these instruments". An example might be a government decision to adopt the tools (budget and civil registry software) developed by the project for local government management. The project manager believes that with this strategy, the decentralisation policy would have become more effective over time, because those responsible for implementing it would be better equipped.

Figure 5. Demonstration to the Prime Minister of Canada M. Jean Chrétien, and Prime Minister of Senegal, Mr. Mamadou Lamine Loum,

IDRC/ACACIA Exposition on ICTs and decentralisation, 7th 9th November 1999, Dakar

According to the Acacia programme officer at that time, Mr Alioune Camara, "the project's objective was not to amend the decentralisation law, but to show how ICTs can help improve its implementation, through partnership between the government and the various players".

This was confirmed by the project manager, "the project was not intended to influence decentralisation policy directly, but to develop tools that, if used by local officials, could lead to changes in that policy, specifically through transparent management of local budgets, and through access to official documents on decentralisation".

Nevertheless, we may say that, even if the project was not intended to influence decentralisation policy directly, it has produced tools that, if put to use, could improve its implementation, something that is a strategic development objective of the government.

As indicated in the evaluation report of the SAS, three major mechanisms were included in the project for influencing decentralisation policy:

1. Capacity building:

This involved producing knowledge, by developing applications to meet different management and organisational needs generated by decentralisation (software for local government management, local budget management, civil registry management, etc.); publicising the results and outputs of the project among local officials; and undertaking a study on implementing the observatory on local governance and decentralisation.

2. Broadening the project's influence:

This was done essentially by publicising information and documentation on decentralisation by posting online the major legislation and regulations governing decentralisation, and information on the field of local government.

3. Sensitisation and information for local officials, elected representatives and citizens:

In this connection, the project provided information about the major laws and regulations governing decentralisation, translated them into national languages and posted them online. Moreover, the results were highly disseminated by demonstrating the products to organisations and potential users.

All these activities were conducted during the last phase of the project and continued afterward. But, the products and results of the project have not been used with any noticeable impact on public policies at the local level, reflecting in part, according to Mr. Lô, at that time National President of the Rural Community Presidents' Association, and one of the key players in decentralisation policy, and currently President of the Association of Local Elected Representatives, "the communications gap, and the absence of public activities for disseminating those results and products".

5.3.2. Obstacles and challenges from Research to Practice

But in reality, as we have seen, the project has involved, since its conception, various players in the decentralisation policy and many authorities have been in contact with the products developed by the project, nationally and even internationally, on the occasions of visits, tests and demonstrations. Moreover, numbers of players and political authorities have used the voice server or have consulted the project's web site. All of these authorities and policymakers found the project's products to be useful.

In particular, following several presentations of the products and a successful test in the Records Automation Division, the Minister of the Interior, at the time, proposed the use of the civil registry software. In the words of the Director of Local Government at the time, Mr. Mamadou Diouf, "the civil registry software is a good product that should be made available to the communes". But no steps have been taken as yet, however, to follow through with this initiative.

At the same time, with respect to the software on budget management, the Associations of local officials welcomed the products. Therefore, the Agency for Municipal Development (ADM) invited SAFEFOD to test the software in three municipalities of different sizes: Dakar, Joal-Fadhiout and Kaffrine. The tests were conducted successfully with the Agency experts, and they decided to acquire the product. Being supported by the World Bank, ADM asked its donor to authorise the purchase of the budget software for the communes. But this recommendation has not been followed up.

After that, another international donor was contacted by SAFEFOD and was ready to provide all the municipalities/communes with basic computer equipment and the budget management software. However, a request from the President of the National Association of Mayors was required. According to the Project Manager, the President of the Association did not want to sign the request, apparently without any specific reason for not doing so.

With regard, to the vocal server, the then chief of staff of the Minister of Scientific and Technical Research, noting that it could be used to access a database with administrative, economic, political and cultural information on various local governments, went so far as to ask that SAFEFOD products be incorporated into the government's "voice and data" project in late 1999.

But none of this happened, why? Which are the main obstacles that, although national and local decision makers were informed of the applications developed during the project and some of them attended the demonstration sessions and showed their interest, impede the products of the project to be systematically used in the daily activities of local governments?

Why, although the results of the research were considered successful, the output, and in particular the management software, were not applied?

From analysis of the interviews and discussion with the key actors involved in the project and in the decentralisation policy at large, it emerged that the unsuccessful transition from research to action was in part because of the changes that happened in the political regime in 2000.

In fact, in 2000, after national elections, the so called "alternance era" in Senegal arrived and a new government was established. This of course caused, as in many cases when there is a change of government, a delay in reorganising all policies, as well as a change of orientations and the will to start everything from zero.

Therefore, SAFEFOD, changed its approach and established a "joint venture" with a private company (namely OCTIS) to have a more market-oriented strategy and to negotiate commercial agreements with the key Ministries involved in the decentralisation process.

Yet during the interviews with representatives of the current Government and the newly established Association of Local Elected Representatives (that associates the representatives of the Association of Rural Community Presidents, Association of Mayors of Senegal, and Association of Regional Council Presidents), they expressed an interest in examining these products to see how useful they might be for local governments.

In fact, to date, there is still no concrete advance in the use of ICTs at local government level. A recent survey conducted by the SAFEFOD/OCTIS joint-venture in 43 municipalities in the main region of Dakar shows that none of them uses a computer to manage the registry system, and there is no specialised software used for the budget management (only a minority of them use Excel software). The results of this survey confirm the same conclusions that were reached by the IDRC SAS in 1997. This is also a confirmation of the difficulty of applying the results of research, especially if innovative due to the context, to produce concrete changes in the governance system.

In the light of its results, SAFEFOD's project can definitely be considered "pioneeristic", and in fact, the needs that were explored during the research phase are still required today.

There are some attempts to fill the gap, but still a lot needs to be done, especially the following of an integrated and co-ordinated policy. For example, according to Mr Mohamadou Kabir Sow, the new Director-General of the Agency for Municipality Development (ADM), following the demonstrations of SAFEFOD's products, the ADM decided to develop its own software in-house, and at present, with the support of the World Bank, it is installing basic computer equipment in all the 110 municipalities in Senegal. After being equipped, at least with a Personal Computer, the ADM intends also to provide the budget management software currently under testing and revision. It was in fact developed from an existing product in MS-DOS.

This is witness to the fact that, according to Mr Cheickhou Amadou Diop, Senior Financial Analyst Expert of ADM, thanks to ACACIA and SAFEFOD's Project, the not yet clearly expressed needs of local governments were taken into effective account, and the possibility of providing a solution by developing ICTs tools was analysed as a concrete option.

If we consider that, even and especially at local level, governance is a highly information-intensive practice, notwithstanding the limitation of government structures, ICTs can be highly beneficial, providing a service to local administration by making management simpler and more transparent.

In this regard, one of the issues that is not easily discussed, but that is clearly part of the problem under analysis, is the fact that, especially at local level, there is a widespread bad practice of "charging" users for normally due administrative services, or just to facilitate a procedure.

This abuse, would of course be more difficult to do in the presence of automised and transparent ICTs tools. But, according to the majority of the interviewees, the so called by some "collateral costs" on public management, are not the main obstacles to introduce ICTs in government at local level. In fact, it seems that, even if this practice is still a "rule" in many cases, there is less and less resistance to change and, actually, there is a growing awareness by local elected representatives of the benefits that ICTs can bring to support local development.

5.3.3. Lessons Learned

The main objective of this project was to explore how ICTs could help local officials improve local government management and to broadcast the results of this research. It is a clear and necessary goal especially if we consider the products that have been developed. They are very simple but extremely useful software products to help manage daily procedures. As indicated by a statement by Prof. Sylla, "they represent *les fundamentaux*....(the fundamentals) for any public management. And that was the starting point for SAFEFOD's Project".

"How can you govern any administration if you cannot manage correctly and in time the budget, or you don't even know what is the population? Which is the civil status of citizens, and so on?"

But, as it emerged in the analysis of this case, in many local governments, there are many other issues that may be considered more important, and so introducing ICTs cannot be considered a "priority among priorities". This is especially true where financial resources are limited and the purchase of ICTs, even if basic, would at the beginning bring more problems than solutions. Who will use it? How will people be trained? What about the costs and time of maintenance and repair if there are problems? How fast do these ICTs become obsolete? What about the cost of replacement?

All these questions pose the problem of the return on investment on ICTs that each local administrator has to face when making a decision and, at the same time, facing the consensus of the population that, in many cases, has other more concrete difficulties to solve.

In addition to this, these local governments, it must be remembered, are answerable to the central government and must apply policy measures decided at the national level. Moreover, the local level must adapt these policy measures to the conditions in the communities they represent. And as we have already underlined, in many cases there is a lack of basic infrastructures and therefore the decision of the local government to buy computer equipment could be seen as a nonsense.

In this regard, moreover, there is another psychological or cultural aspect to take into consideration. As in many other developing countries, Senegal in particular, benefits from a large amount of aid for development. Going around Dakar you can see a representation of almost all the development agencies and donors, from Canada to the

Grand-Duchy of Luxembourg.... As well as many local governments from industrialised countries that are willing to participate in decentralised-co-operation initiatives. This situation, according to some of the interviewees, could hide a sort of "culture of assistance"... thus making administrators or elected representatives, especially at local level, looking for aid instead of investing in their own future. And in the case of ICTs, in particular, it is rare to find a local government that purchases its own equipment instead of waiting for a donation or the intervention of the central government.

All this of course is enormously delaying the process of integration of ICTs into local governments, although, according to the majority of interviewees, it seems that local governments and their populations are "ready" to introduce and use ICTs.

Of course it is a readiness in terms of not being reluctant, but there is still not readiness in terms of capacity to manage the ICTs, and especially the changes that ICTs bring about. In this regard, it still requires a lot of training, not only at the technical level, but also with regard to reorganisation and communication skills. For this reason, a specific Unit of Technical Assistance to the National Association of Local Elected Representatives (CAEL) has been established and, according to its Director, Ms Sall, many activities are now underway to build the capacities of Local Elected Representatives and support the transition into the Information Society.

At the same time, this project that was based essentially on creating applications and contents which could be used by decision makers at the local level, thus helping to bridge the communication gap and provide access to useful information, was not aimed directly at changing policies. But, as we have seen, the use and adoption of its products could help local decision makers to take better account of the needs of their voters, particularly in terms of sound planning.

There is therefore a great potential impact of this kind of activity for local governance development and in particular in making policy-makers aware and capable of better managing public affairs, with an increase in transparency, accountability and participation of the citizens, thus strengthening public sector efficiency and democracy.

In particular, ranked within the category of policy-makers, we can differentiate between politicians or officials, in the light of the degree of their involvement in the policy preparation process. The present case indicates clearly that the successful introduction of ICTs in governance, at local level, needs the clear commitment and involvement of both categories. A strong leadership at the political level is required, to champion and take the correct decisions, but at the same time, the participation of the administrator, both in developing the applications and contents in the phase of research, and in managing the transition from research to practice is fundamental.

Without this mixed approach the difficulties that we have seen in this case, in solidly implementing the solution, can be experienced. In addition to this, and to better face the obvious problem of resistance to change that is implicitly connected to any innovation, there is the need of an effective and strong communication policy to disseminate the results of the research and immediately apply, if useful and agreed. Otherwise, there is the risk that too many research activities remained "locked in the drawers" and the potential benefit for communities is not exploited as it should be.

In this connection, a clear recommendation that emerged from analysis of the interview, and in particular discussing the issue with representatives of the Delegation on Public Management, of the Presidency of the Republic, Mr Tidiane Sow, Adviser in Management, and Mr Amadou Sadio, Advisor in Organisation and also Mayor of Thionck-Essyl, is the need of a more effective coordination of the activities related to decentralisation and local governance, especially when it comes to a significant investment such as the introduction of ICTs.

In fact, the role of ICTs for local governance being well established, the issue is now how to efficiently manage this process in a cost-effective manner, and how to integrate and coordinate the efforts of all the different stakeholders involved in the implementation of the decentralisation policy. In this regard, even if it resulted in being not completely successful, the project under analysis demonstrated an interesting approach, where participation and discussion were open and a mechanism of partnership was established to share experiences and ideas and find common solutions. A possibility for the successful implementation of the decentralisation policy in Senegal, as well as in many other African countries, should definitely take into consideration this recommendation.

As for the technical aspects of the project, it should be noteworthy to emphasise the local-based development of contents and applications, and the importance given to the "language-divide". Often, in fact, solutions are just imported from elsewhere and they result in not being in line with local requirements or not at all compatible with the technical systems in place. The issue of language and the capacity to access (accessibility), including the costs, are important factors that, if not solved, can prevent any introduction of ICTs at local level. They should be considered as a "pre" condition for any local governance activity.

5.3.4. Towards a local governance observatory

The long-term objective of the IDRC's funded project was the institution of the "Observatory on Local Governance and Decentralisation". After its establishment, and despite all the difficulties that we mentioned before in relation to the concrete application of the products developed during the research, in the years that followed, SAFEFOD continued working on the development of the observatory, monitoring the implementation of the decentralisation-policy in Senegal and supporting some of the activities undertaken at local level, especially in the rural communities, in partnership with the local and central governments and the civil society, trying to adopt its "model of local governance" which it had developed.

Moreover, during the elaboration and first investigations of this "model of local governance", it appeared that what could not be ignored were the realities of development problems and which are of concern to all the actors involved. It is for this reason that the model, while giving priority to training, needed to take into consideration the necessary contribution to removing certain institutional and material obstacles at the level of deconcentrated structures (deputy prefects) and decentralised structures (local representatives) and community organisations, for a more effective development, which is sine-qua-non for the smooth running of governance.

Development support, which goes with training in project conception and implementation, targets not only these institutional constraints, but also productive investments, women groups and youth organisations, as well as various programmes such as health and the registry system.

In this regard, according to Ms. Soukeyna Ndiaye Ba, Minister of Decentralised Co-operation and Regional Planning "we still have to improve communication in all directions (grass-roots communities, government, development partners), educate local elected officials (literacy problems), associate ICTs with traditional means of communication".

Yet, Prof. Sylla and SAFEFOD's team are confident that the potential effects of the project on public policies should become evident with a further communication campaign to inform the new local leaders elected in 2001, who would be more open to innovation, especially through instituting the civil registry software in all municipalities in Senegal.

In addition to this, and thanks to OXFAM/America, SAFEFOD established in 2003 the first antenna of the observatory implementing a project in the rural community of Barkedji, in the Louga Region in Senegal. This first "pilot" of a local observatory on local governance was aimed at ensuring the follow-up of experiences and strengthening the capacities of decentralised authorities and the civil society with a view to effectively promoting good governance through an optimal use of ICTs and media channels.

In the long-term, the observatory on local governance was intended to develop and manage data bases on decentralisation and local governance, on the basis of an exhaustive collection of the most pertinent information on decentralisation in general and the management of renewable natural resources and services, in particular local democracy, the functioning of local institutions, budget management, reports and decisions of local bodies, local development plans, etc. This information would be e-processed, translated into the national dialects and appropriately stored, with a view to circulating it widely to grassroots actors, policymakers and other national and international partners. This would be done through adapted and appropriate information products and services (reviews, films, soundtracks, interactive CD-Rom, etc.). In the pilot experience in Barkedji, a newspaper, called "Eerango", was published in the Fula language.

At the same time, the observatory was intended to accompany the process of ICTs appropriation by local governments, and disseminate information and sharing experiences, through organising fora in which all stakeholders could exchange their views, ideas and practices.

In this way, the intention of establishing an observatory bolstered by the civil society was to ensure the setting up of an information system on local governance that would support local governance development and strengthen local democracy.

Notes

1. Loi n° 96-06 du 22 mars 1996 portant code des collectivités locales.
2. The programming documents are the following: Plan Régional de Développement Integrée (PRDI); Plan d'Investissements Communaux (PIC); Plan Locaux de Développement (PLD).
3. Le Programme national de Bonne Gouvernance (PNBG), Délégation au Management Public, Secrétariat Général de la Présidence de la République, Janvier 2003.
4. L'Agence De l'Informatique de l'Etat (ADIE), established by Presidential «décret: n° 2004-1038 du 23 juillet».
5. Inauguration de l'Intranet Gouvernemental, Projet Intranet Gouvernemental (PING), Dakar, 15 mars 2005.
6. This workshop was jointly organized by the Presidency of the Republic, Delegation on Public Management, Ministry of Local Government and Decentralisation, and the SAFEFOD Project and recommendations for incorporating its results into the PNBG were presented by G. Misuraca.
7. Prof. Yero Sylla, Executive Secretary SAFEFOD, "ICTs and Local Governance in Senegal: a Challenge to Civil Society Organizations", Presentation to the IDRC/UNECA Workshop on "Innovative applications of ICTs for local governance in Africa", Addis Ababa, 7th.-9th. June, 2004; and Interviews by Gianluca Misuraca.
8. A specific evaluation of the overall ACACIA activities in Senegal was conducted by IDRC in January 2003, while a more detailed study of the impact of SAS was got under way by an independent consultant and was to be available before the end of 2005.
9. La Revue de la Gouvernance Locale, published every three months by SAFEFOD.

References

CRDI/IDRC, Working papers of the ACACIA Working group in Governance, 1997;

CRDI/IDRC, Introductory Note of the President of the ACACIA Working group in Governance, Prof. Yero Sylla, 1997;

CRDI/IDRC, Document de Projet n. 65199/97-8153-01, «Le rôle des technologies de l'Information et de la communication dans la mise en ouvre de la politique de décentralisation au Sénégal», 1997;

CRDI/IDRC, Fiche de Projet 97-8153-01, Rôle des TIC dans la mise en oeuvre de la politique de décentralisation au Sénégal 1997;

CRDI/IDRC, Financial and Monitoring Reports of the Project n. 65199/97-8153-01, «Le rôle des technologies de l'Information et de la communication dans la mise en ouvre de la politique de décentralisation au Sénégal», 1998;

CRDI/IDRC, Senegal Strategic Assessment, The policy influence of projects financed by IDRC's Acacia program: The Case of Senegal, by Mr. Khamathe Sene, and Ms. Ramata Thioune, January 2003;

République du Sénégal, Loi n° 96-06 du 22 mars 1996 portant code des collectivités locales;

République du Sénégal, Délégation au Management Public, Secrétariat Général de la Présidence de la République, Programme national de Bonne Gouvernance (PNBG), Janvier 2003;

République du Sénégal, Présidence de la République, Décret: n° 2004-1038 du 23 juillet sur l'Agence De l'Informatique de l'Etat (ADIE);

République du Sénégal, Présidence de la République, l'Agence De l'Informatique de l'Etat (ADIE), Présentation de l'INTRANET Gouvernemental, pendant l'Inauguration du Projet Intranet Gouvernemental (PING), Dakar, 15 mars 2005;

République du Sénégal, Discours Inaugural sur l'INTRANET Gouvernemental, de S.E. Maître Abdoulaye Wade, Président de la République du Sénégal, Dakar, 15 mars 2005;

République du Sénégal, Ministère de la Co-opération Décentralisée et de la Planification Régionale, Plan d'Action, 2005;

SAFEFOD, Cahier des charges pour le laboratoire de gouvernance locale, document de travail, Projet n. 65199/97-8153-01, «Le rôle des technologies de l'Information et de la communication dans la mise en ouvre de la politique de décentralisation au Sénégal», Octobre 1998;

SAFEFOD, Rapport du Séminaire de Partenariat organisée par la SAFEFOD et le CRDI sur le rôle des technologies de l'Information et de la communication dans la mise en ouvre de la politique de décentralisation au Sénégal, 25 février 1999;

SAFEFOD, Press Review, 1998-2000;

SAFEFOD/OCTIS, Présentations des logiciels CAURI, CIVIS, GESTEC et MERCES, 2004;

SAFEFOD/OXFAM-America, "Décentralisation, Gouvernance Démocratique et Participation en milieu rural", 2003, 2004;

Sylla Prof. Yero, Executive Secretary SAFEFOD, "ICTs and Local Governance in Senegal: a Challenge to Civil Society Organizations", Presentation to the IDRC/UNECA Workshop on "Innovative applications of ICTs for local governance in Africa", Addis Ababa, 7-9 June 2004;

Union des Associations d'Elus Locaux, Cellule d'Appui aux Elus Locaux, «Rapport Annuel 2003-2004» et présentation, 2004;

6

ICTs AND TRADITIONAL GOVERNANCE IN GHANA

CASE STUDY OVERVIEW

Location: Ghana

Funding Institution: Open Society Initiative for Western Africa (OSIWA)

Executing Institution: Centre on Governance, Culture and Development / University of Ghana, Legon, Accra,

Project Manager: Prof. Irene K. Odotei

Total Budget: $US150,000.00

Project Start Date: May 2003

Project End Date: May 2004

Administrative Information and Contacts:

Centre on Governance, Culture and Development,
Department on Chieftaincy, Governance, Culture and Development,
Institute of African Studies, University of Ghana, Legon, Accra, Ghana
Tel. (+233) 21513389/504030 – Fax (+233) 21 502 397
email: irenekodotei@Chieftaincy.org
Web site: www.chieftai

6.1. CONTEXT AND POLICY

6.1.1. Modern versus Traditional authority: implications on Governance

A major challenge for most of Africa is the quest for good governance. This quest must take into consideration the dual "mixed" nature of the system of governance that is inherent in African local culture and due to its historical evolution.

On the one hand, is the western or European model of governance that has been "imported" with colonisation. On the other hand, is the traditional or indigenous form of governance, which evolved out of the history, tradition and culture of the people. Furthermore, the traditional or indigenous institutions, within which context traditional governance operates, are defined and linked to diverse ethnic identities, and to the perception of governance held by various ethnic groups.

Ghana has more than 40 ethnic groups and within these groups is a variety of forms and institutions. These include priestly authority, female traditional authority in the forms of Queen Mothers, female Chiefs and priestesses, traditional military companies, indigenous health delivery, agriculture and commercial authority. At the apex of these structures of governance is the institution of Chieftaincy, which permeates through all the 40 or so ethnic groups, limited only in power and influence by the history, tradition and culture of the various communities where the authority is exercised.

In pre-colonial times, traditional institutions were entirely responsible for governance, and Chiefs played a crucial and leading role in most municipalities in Africa. The advent of colonial rule introduced western forms of governance that, today, with their accompanying political and administrative structures, dominate at the national and regional levels. However, at the district and community levels they share the responsibility of governance with traditional authority, mainly that of the Chiefs. In rural communities, for example, inadequate infrastructure and poverty hamper access to modern or state agencies of security, justice and health. In such a situation, the chief assumes a very central role to the people, being therefore a vital and strategic partner for development. Under colonial rule and post-colonial governments, traditional institutions of governance suffered erosion of their authority. Now that the government, Chiefs and the people were rising to the challenges of modernisation, democratisation and the role of the chief as an agent of development, a new initiative was needed to facilitate and accelerate growth of a system of governance sensitive to the culture and history of Ghana. This may provide the answers for stability, alternative dispute resolution, peace-building, poverty alleviation and wealth generation.

But while western institutions of governance have been able to adjust to some of the challenges brought by modernisation, traditional forms of governance have been slow to respond to change.

The pressure due to globalisation and the democratisation process blowing through Africa is now strongly addressing the need to consider the duality of the mixed nature of the system of governance in Africa.

Chiefs have been asking for integration of the traditional system into mainstream governance, and at the same time, the role of indigenous institutions, in relation to the modern state, was receiving increasing attention and has been the subject of seminars, conferences, workshops and publications. In this context, it has also to be considered that Chiefs are now transforming their role, being often young and well educated people, able to fully grasp the advantages of Information and Communication Technologies (ICTs) and global knowledge.

6.1.2. Traditional Governance and its role for Democratic Consolidation

The significance of traditional governance in Ghana has been such that the various constitutions of the country have guaranteed its existence and operation. The Chieftaincy Act of 1971, for example, sets out the guidelines for the functioning of the various Houses of Chiefs and mandates the National House of Chiefs to undertake the progressive study, interpretation and codification of customary laws. The 1992 Constitution of the Republic of Ghana continues to recognise and guarantee the institution, although it bans Chiefs from participating in partisan politics.

To facilitate the administration of the diverse traditional authorities and units and as evidence of the importance attached to the institutions of traditional governance, the Government of Ghana has been maintaining a regulatory unit in charge of Chieftaincy Affairs at the national level, referred to as the "Chieftaincy Secretariat". It is in effect the Chieftaincy Division of the Office of the President, thus part of the Presidency and under the seat of the Government. In addition to the Secretariat, there is a National House of Chiefs, ten Regional Houses of Chiefs (representing each region of the country) and 165 Traditional Councils, representing each traditional area. The 1992 Constitution paid special attention to Chieftaincy, guaranteeing its protection. Moreover, in 2003, the President of the Republic John Agyekum Kuffour, set up a special Presidential Commission of Chieftaincy Affairs.

The constitutional guarantees reflect the relevance of traditional governance in modern democratic governance and clearly justified the inclusion of the institution in any discourse on nation building and development. That the inability of the central government to follow through on its policies and development agenda in the remotest parts of the country has created a leadership and authority vacuum is indisputable. For instance, in rural communities, as a consequence of this, most people living in the rural areas of the country resort to the chief's palace in matters of dispute pertaining to domestic and non-domestic conflict situations, rather than to the law courts or the police station, which either do not exist or do not enjoy the confidence and trust of the people.

Moreover, research on the subject revealed that Ghanaian perception of Chieftaincy is positive. There is no doubt that traditional governance has a lot to offer. Its incorporation into mainstream governance can maximise the utilisation of traditional leadership, which represents a rich human resource, bringing into focus the broader issues and links between governance, culture and development.

The traditional authorities, as custodians of the land and other natural resources, play a critical role in the economic activities of the people, such as farming, mining, construction, etc. Traditional leaders, as guardians of the history and culture of the people, are thus regarded as one of the crucial echelons of leadership through which the Ghanaian development agenda of poverty reduction and wealth creation could be achieved.

A survey in 2001 covering all the regions of Ghana, indicated that there was considerable goodwill towards the institution of Chieftaincy among the majority of Ghanaians. Indeed they claim that the institution needs support from the state.

Of course, any attempt to incorporate traditional governance into mainstream constitutional rule required some preparation and capacity building for the incumbents and the counterparts (executive, judiciary, legislative, civil society and other stakeholders).

6.1.3. The Ghana ICTs for Accelerated Development Policy (ICT4AD)

In line with the worldwide recognition of the developmental opportunities and the challenges emerging from the "information age", Ghana, was exploring ways of facilitating its development process through the deployment and exploitation of ICTs within its economy and society.

The Ghana ICT4AD Policy charted a roadmap for the nation's development in the emerging knowledge-based economy , representing the Vision for Ghana in the Information Society.

The Policy Statement is based on an extensively researched framework document that analysed and crystallised the challenges facing the country and made a case for an ICTs-led socio-economic development agenda for the country.

The Strategic Policy was designed to aid Ghana's development process by contributing to addressing the nation's key developmental challenges, with the aim of transforming the country in a middle income, information-rich, knowledge based and technology-driven economy and society by 2022. To facilitate this process, 14 priority areas constituting the pillars of the policy were identified as targets and, for each of those, objectives and strategies were stated.

To implement the policy several 4-year rolling plans were envisaged, as well as periodic revisions and the establishment of co-ordinating agencies and co-operating mechanisms.

In fact, despite the consistent strategic document highlighting in detail the policy goals and objectives, and the broad strategic lines of interventions, as well as the key drivers and focus areas, the process is still at the beginning and a concrete implementation policy would require a much committed and disruptive intervention to realise the potential of the strategic document.

The document also briefly analyses the current situation, and it is clear that Ghana is characterised by a weak policy, infrastructural and regulatory framework of ICTs, as well as the general challenges/opportunities in developing countries, such as in particular the educational and human capacity level, with regard to the demographic indicators: Ghana has a relatively high population growth rate (2,5%); relatively youthful (60% under 25 years); with an illiteracy rate of about 40% and only 3% of population with tertiary level education; with a high school drop-out rate and about 50% of junior secondary school leavers. In general, close to 40% of Ghanaians currently live below the poverty line of less than 1$ per day, with an unequal geographic distribution, where five out of ten of the country's regions have a much higher percentage of their population living in poverty.

If we look at the economic indicators, moreover, the Ghanaian economy has not experienced a major structural transformation since independence, and the majority of the working population (60%) is still actively involved in agriculture, with only 13% in industry and 28% in services. These sectors are still narrow and underdeveloped. The informal private sector is by far the largest employment sector. Job creation in the economy is extremely low with only 15% of employment in public and private sector organisations, while 68% of the population with jobs are self-employed. There is also a general human resource problem in the lack of technical and managerial skills, especially in the area of ICTs, and academic and R&D capacity is limited. Finally, the national debt is a major impediment to economic development, exceeding the annual average gross national income per capita, that is 340US$, lower than the average for Sub-Saharan African countries.

Therefore, the aspiration to accelerate Ghana's socio-economic development will require a double figure growth rate, thus an extraordinary effort, to transform the economic trend.

However, it is worth noting that the development of this policy was based on an extensive nationwide consultation with stakeholders from the public and private sectors, the academic community as well as civil society, including members of various political parties.

In this context, a specific role has been given to the Chieftaincy Institutions that, albeit at the beginning were not fully involved, and thanks to the growing debate around the role of Chiefs as "agents for local development", have now been integrated, on a national level, in the process of the development of the ICT4AD Policy and its Strategic implementation.

In this regard, the publication in 2003 and dissemination in 2004 (also using CD-Rom) of the ICT4AD Policy was a strong signal of the Government's commitment to ICTs deployment to cover all sectors of the economy and a starting point for implementation.

Following the massive consultation and the effort of co-ordination of strategies and policies at central level, to address the challenges identified in the policy document steps were initiated in 2004 to develop strategies, especially in commerce and trade, education, agriculture, governance, health and gender. In September 2004, all sector Ministries and Regional Consultative Councils validated their ICTs Policies to enable them to focus on priority development areas where ICTs solutions could be applied to allow sectors to carve out a niche in the digital landscape and also create a greater interaction with citizenry. During 2005 it was expected to consolidate the strategy frameworks through stakeholders discussions to facilitate the development of a National ICTs Plan, for the period 2005-2008.

Some of the indicative programmes and action lines identified include the following:

- developing the requisite capacity in ICTs skills to promote the rapid deployment of ICTs;
- establishing the Ghana ICTs Directorate (GICTeD) to serve as an operational body to promote a cohesive and structured strategy for e-governance and other e-initiatives, part of ICT4AD;
- implementing the Ghana Multimedia Centre to promote ICTs as a driver of Private Sector development, facilitating integration and use of ICTs in business development;
- developing a Technology Park to promote a comprehensive framework for ICTs integrated services and collaboration between the Private Sector and Research Centres;
- liberalising the telecommunications sector in order to revitalise it and make it effective and competitive. In this regard, the transformation of the National Communication Authority is also pursued in order to make it more independent in its operations;
- facilitating the integration of disparate communications infrastructure into a common backbone, in order to open up the entire country and indeed the sub-regions, to receive access to telecoms, especially promoting Public Private Partnerships (PPPs);
- enhancing the teledensity, by increasing the number and penetration of fixed and mobile lines. From December 2003, in one year, the penetration rate growth of over 100%: from 4% (800,000 people given a population of 20 million) to 9,1% (1,835,000 people). In 2005 it was expected to achieve 15% penetration rate;
- make access available to all Secondary Schools (then connectivity was available in about 50% of the towns with secondary schools

and training colleges); also developing financial mechanisms for "last mile coverage";

- creating the Ghana Investment Fund for Telecommunications (GIFTEL) to generate funds to support the development of infrastructure in the underserved areas;
- promoting the universal service obligation of the postal sector and transforming the Meteorological Services Department into a semi-autonomous Agency;

Finally, with specific regard to the theme under discussion, the Ministry of Communications was to introduce Community Information Centres (CICs) in all 230 electoral constituencies across the country. They will provide the communities with direct access to ICTs facilities, thus supporting development in remote and rural areas.

6.1.4. The National Decentralisation Action Plan (NDAP)

Decentralisation, as a policy option, has been on Ghana's political agenda since independence. The Government of Ghana embarked upon the implementation of a comprehensive Decentralisation Policy and local government reform programme in 1988, aiming at establishing efficient, decentralised, government machinery as a means to providing strong support for participatory development. The process of decentralisation in Ghana involved a mixture of political devolution enshrined in the constitution, as well as administrative and technical de-concentration of key service delivery institutions which were in part backed by law and in the main reflecting conventional practices.

However, the smooth implementation of the policy has been constrained by inadequate resources, ineffective collaboration and the lack of well-focussed programmes for the short, medium and long term. While the institutional and legal framework for decentralisation have made modest progress since the establishment of the District Assemblies and the operation of the District Assembly Common Fund in 1992, support to deepen and institutionalise the efforts of the government have been incoherent, in part due to several uncoordinated projects and the divergent approaches used for their implementation.

Analysis of the current situation, in fact, highlights the existence of two competing concepts of decentralisation operating in Ghana. The first is the devolution of major political and administrative responsibilities from Central Government to District Assemblies, comprising partially elected bodies with the mandate for local government and community development. The second, running parallel to devolution intentions is the process of administrative and technical de-concentration practised by Ministries, Departments and Agencies, that plan and deliver specific services to communities. Devolution has far-reaching implications for political, administrative and technical set-up, proposing to restructure institutions and mandates for service delivery. De-concentration, on the other hand, in Ghana has involved the rearrangement simply of the locations of key personnel and where their functions are delivered.

At the centre of the debate there is of course the issue of accountability, both of government and service providers to citizens, in particular the poor and disadvantaged communities.

In this connection, the commitment to decentralisation has received renewed attention since the completion of the Poverty Reduction and Growth Strategy in 2001, (GPRS).

As the implementation of this strategy and its associated programmes commenced, a National Decentralisation Action Plan (NDAP) has been developed under the Ministry of Local Government and Rural Development leadership. It aimed at re-invigorating national policy and institutions for decentralisation, guiding the strategic targeting of resources to poverty reduction efforts at the local level and promoting greater participation of key private sector, civil society and traditional authorities in the process of governance and development at the local level.

To begin this process, an Action Plan had been developed to reflect realistic goals agreed by key stakeholders and serve as a framework to shape detailed programming in the near future.

To guide the implementation of the Action plan four main programme areas were formulated:

1. Policy and Institutional Arrangements for Decentralisation Implementation;
2. District Development Funding Facility;
3. Capacity Building and Human Resources Development;
4. Partnership and Participation for Accountable Local Governance.

As part of the process of developing the strategic actions and framework for programming, the Ministry of Local Government and Rural Development established a Decentralisation Secretariat and supported the formation of an Inter-Sectoral Working Group, comprising members from various Ministries, Departments and Agencies to support the implementation of the plan.

An important aspect of the implementation of the programme was the specific role given to civil society organisations, NGOs and the private sector, as well as traditional authorities, to collaborate in the development of partnership and participate in decentralisation efforts. But is it correct to give traditional institutions the same role of civil society organisations?

The domain of Chiefs is unquestionably local governance. In recognition of this, the 1957, 1960, and 1969 Constitutions of the Republic of Ghana provided for the institutional representation of Chiefs in local government structures. As we have seen, the 1992 Constitution did not. However, Art. 242 of the Constitution provides that the Chiefs can serve on District Assemblies only where they are nominated by the President.

This situation resulted in a distinction between the activities of the political heads of the districts in the modern and traditional systems of governance (i.e. District Chief Executives and Chiefs).

Some District Chief Executives in fact, do not consider consultation with Chiefs in the performance of their duties. Neither do some members of District Assemblies consult Chiefs in decision making. In consequence, Chiefs who were closest to their people at the local level were sometimes marginalised in the socio-political decision making process.

The debate was open and very controversial. It was advocated that Chiefs should be institutionally represented in District Assemblies and that the Act 370 of the Chieftaincy Act should be amended, to provide for District Houses of Chiefs. At central government level, it was also proposed to constitute an Upper House of Parliament consisting of Chiefs, following the British model of the House of Lords. On the other side, there were arguments for the exclusion of Chiefs from local institutions, for the reason that the Chiefs have not always conducted themselves well, not administering justice impartially and not being conscientious with regard to the management of resources. Furthermore, inclusion in local government structures was seen as undemocratic, because Chiefs are not popularly elected and, even though outwardly neutral, they invariably aligned themselves with political parties and have exhibited partisan tendencies, thus risking the inclusion of partisanship in local government structures. Considering that Chieftaincy institutions have been affected by endless litigation, this could be transferred into local government management, also there would be the chance that as Chiefs they may look to their own interests and not those of the people. In fact, one of the main reasons against the inclusion of Chiefs was that, where Chiefs conduct themselves well, their contribution to local level development could still be made outside statutory local government structures.

It was evident, in fact, that Chiefs, by their position, are the leaders of their people. They have naturally therefore been part of local governance, for example by mobilising people at the grassroots level for development. Thus, even though Chiefs are not popularly elected, their inclusion in local government structures can be seen as not incompatible with democratic practices, exactly because this would enhance popular participation. In fact, Chiefs, as the local managers of their lands, have ultimate responsibility for the local development. Subjects still look up to Chiefs for direction and leadership, and invariably judge the performance of Chiefs by the development projects that they initiate. In this regard, "Modern Chiefs" also started exploiting marketing solutions to provide information about their achievements[1].

6.1.4.1. The "Modern Chief" and the potential of ICTs for Traditional Governance

In a communiqué issued in Accra, in January 2003, at an international conference on "Chieftaincy in Africa: Culture, Governance and Development", it was stated that:

- The Chieftaincy institution be assisted to enhance its profile as an integral and viable component of the contemporary socio-political structure in Ghana;
- The Chieftaincy institution be seen as a critical and indispensable partner in governance at the local level (Metropolitan, Municipal and District Assemblies) and that the Constitution be amended to allow for institutional participation of Chiefs in Metropolitan, Municipal and District Assemblies;

- The judicial functions of Chiefs be recognised, properly defined and enhanced;
- The Chieftaincy institution being central to the nation's cultural heritage notes the importance of culture in development and calls for the urgent promulgation of a cultural policy;
- It was also requested that the Chieftaincy institutions be adequately resourced from the consolidated fund of the Government, and that their capacity building efforts be supported financially.

In respect of these calls for support, the enhancement of the active role of traditional leaders in governance was however far from being unanimous. There were in fact dissenting voices which pointed to the anachronistic nature of the institutions of traditional authorities, underlining that:

- The military role of traditional leaders has been taken over by a modern national army;
- The judicial functions of traditional leaders have been rendered superfluous by the extension of the modern judicial system into the traditional areas;
- Traditional leaders have lost their administrative functions, given the emergence of new local government structures in the traditional areas;
- Traditional leaders' legislative functions have become redundant with the establishment of the Parliament and District Assemblies which are respectively empowered to make laws for the nation as a whole and for the District;
- The economic resources once available to traditional leaders for the promotion of prosperity in their areas of authority are now no longer available to them;
- The institution of traditional leadership is bedevilled with conflict and disputes in connection with land and succession.

Despite these detractions, the potential of Chieftaincy for effective leadership was not in doubt, even if they seemed to operate in parallel, and in some cases in contradiction to the governance agenda of the central government. The reason is that Ghanaian society is still predominantly traditional in spite of the ongoing transition to modernity. Given that only a mere 30% of the population is in fact really "modernised", the remaining 70% is predominantly traditional, still looking upon Chiefs as performing important religious and civil functions. In addition to this, central government has relied (and still does) on Chiefs as important links between them and people in rural and remote areas, and have utilised their offices in reaching out to the rural communities. Some Chiefs serve on Statutory Boards, others mediate in areas of conflict and disputes on behalf of government and generally act as cultural ambassadors for Ghana.

Moreover, in view of the lack of accessibility for the majority of Ghanaians to the regular judicial courts, the Chief's tribunal is often the only way to discuss disputes and litigations.

It was proposed to re-introduce the Chief's tribunal as part of the judicial system of Ghana, however, Chiefs must be introduced to new techniques in adjudication and conflict resolution, to the finer principles of the rule of law and the equality of everybody before the law and including some education in judicial process so that they can record and sign their decisions.

Given the above, it is clear that there was a clamour for a critical assessment of the aspects of the constitution dealing with traditional leadership. There is now a strong debate about the appropriate roles to be played by traditional leaders in the management of local and national resources, the mobilisation and involvement of communities as partners and stakeholders in development, the search for strategies for containment and resolution of conflict and creation of harmony and peace.

However, the general feeling was that the rather residual functions given to traditional leadership did not afford Chiefs the opportunity to play an effective role in modern governance. There was a need to redefine the roles that a traditional leader could play in order to make him/her an integral part of the modern governance paradigm. Chiefs must consider the opportune time for them to review traditional governance from within, to critique themselves and rid the institution of certain excess and aberrations, repair damages done to the image of the institution and to build its capacity towards integration into mainstream modern governance systems.

In this context, of great importance is the fact that the education background and profile of Chiefs in the modern era have improved considerably, while, at the same time, a regrettable trend in this encouraging development is the emergence of the phenomenon of the "absentee chief", which poses a great challenge to traditional governance.

Taken as a whole, in the diversity of the structures of traditional governance institutions and the different phenomena that characterise their development, there was the need for establishing a framework that would open and facilitate information flow and knowledge sharing. Key components of this framework, that would allow empowerment of Chief institutions, maximising their efficiency, in the light of the recognition as the embodiment of Ghanaian culture, and as a potential catalyst for development, are ICTs.

In fact, the Chief in his duties as the chief executive of his people, needs ICTs to carry out his day-to-day administrative responsibilities. Correspondence, memos to sub-Chiefs, registrars, secretaries and proceedings of meetings, accounts and all the features of modern bureaucracy are relevant to the modern day Chieftaincy. In their responsibility as development partners, Chiefs needed management supporting tools and baseline data on their locality and on the available human and material resources. Even when such information exists with the central "modern" government, it is invariably inaccessible to the Chief, and yet this is basic to the generation of revenue and attraction of investors.

Moreover, possibly even more important, is the fact that, the vast majority of local communities in Ghana are not "connected". In many cases there are not even fixed telephone lines and roads and transportation are very difficult, especially during the rainy season. It is therefore very complicated to travel and communicate, where sending a simple message could take some days to be delivered and at a high cost. The potential of introducing ICTs in this context would be of great advantage both in terms of cost savings and effectiveness.

In addition to this, much of Ghana's land is vested in the hands of Chiefs and traditional councils. The ownership of land and the way it is used have a far-reaching impact on communities, making traditional governance an important arena for economic development. Chiefs are involved with the exchange of land between persons and groups, thus the palace of the Chief must be able to record such transactions, and, of course, it is clear that there is the need and the potential support of the computerisation of archival records to preserve and disseminate information.

6.2. PROJECT ON "ICTS IN SUPPORT OF TRADITIONAL GOVERNANCE IN GHANA"

6.2.1. Background and Justification

In view of the role of Chieftaincy as a traditional institution, with pre-colonial roots, but that continues to occupy politico-social and cultural spaces in Ghana, as well as in many other African countries, and considering that it shares that space with modern state structures and the pan-ethnic institutions that came into existence in the colonial era, it was important to give room, especially after the Constitution of 1992, to different perspectives on the matter.

The need for a systematic study of the interface between Chieftaincy, governance and culture for a full exploitation of the potentials for development in Africa has long been acknowledged. This need has become all the more urgent with the gradual withdrawal of the state from several spheres of national life and the increasing promotion of civil society, community organisations and traditional forms of governance as ways for enhancing local level administration and popular participation in development.

For this reason, already in the nineties, continuing a tradition started many years before, in the University of Ghana, Legon, particularly the Institute of African Studies, there rose the challenge of integrating traditional and modern governance systems, studying and analysing new ways and tools to support traditional governance and culture for local development.

This "pioneeristic" attitude was, in particular that of Prof. Irene K. Odotei who, many years before the advent of the "knowledge society", was already using innovative technologies (such as recording and video) to record customs and disseminate the culture of the traditional systems.

To sustain and support the systematisation of these efforts, and considering the difficulties and sensitivity that are connected to the subject, in the late nineties, the Ford Foundation funded a project on "Chieftaincy, Governance and Development". The project aimed at research and documentation of the institution of Chieftaincy and its role in the general system of governance in the midst of rapid modernisation and globalisation. Its main objectives were the following:

- Conducting research into Chieftaincy and other complementary institutions;
- Integrating the best practice of Chieftaincy into mainstream modern democratic governance to achieve good governance;
- Integrating the studies of Chieftaincy into the academic programmes of the University;
- Capacity building and advocacy for the institutions of Chieftaincy;
- Running of workshops, seminars and short courses that affect good governance, leadership and development;
- Preservation of the intangible cultural heritage through computerisation of archival records in all the houses of Chiefs and traditional councils;
- Educating the public through exhibitions, the media, documentaries and other programmes.

The project started in 2000 with a piece of research on "Perceptions on Chieftaincy in Ghana", and was concluded with an International Conference on "Chieftaincy in Africa: Culture, Governance and Development", held in Accra in January 2003. The conference, organised with the support of other developmental partners in addition to the Ford Foundation, aimed at making the results of the project available to the international community and also to share in the researches that had been undertaken elsewhere in Africa. It brought together an impressive collection of Ghanaian and international intellectuals, academics, researchers, senior civil and public servants, Chiefs, queenmothers and their courtiers.

6.2.2. Strategy and Objectives

With the knowledge gained from the project on "Chieftaincy, Governance and Development", and other projects[2], researches and studies, in May 2003, a new project on "Governance, Culture and Development" funded by the Open Society Initiative of West Africa (OSIWA) was initiated, to further implement various processes started in connection with the endeavour to modernise Traditional Governance with a more consistent introduction and use of ICTs.

In fact, already in the previous activities undertaken, it was clearly understood how record keeping for Chiefs and their councils is important, as it is their responsibility to implement decisions on behalf of the community. Beyond that, the Chief must document the decisions and reasons underpinning his choices for posterity. Indeed, it is the right of posterity to know the path that the community has taken and the reasons underlying a particular decision.

The value of archival records is now fully appreciated by Chiefs, their subjects and the public. Visits to archives to find information on decided cases that establish legitimacy to the office, statuses, ownership to land or the position of boundaries have become a common feature. Where such records exist, evidence is easily available, even if sometimes and notwithstanding that the records exist litigants have developed the habit of pulling out evidence from the files or planting "evidence" created by themselves to help them win the case.

Having realised the importance of records and the risk of deterioration they are subjected to, both manmade and environmental, the project focussed on enhancing the capacities of institutions of traditional governance to enable them to participate effectively in mainstream national governance.

Critical to this capacity building effort was the introduction of Chiefs and other key players in the Chieftaincy institution to the use of ICTs as tools for modernisation and effective governance. The global objective of the project was therefore to strengthen traditional governance institutions through the introduction of ICTs in their setting and in their operations.

To attain this goal, the specific objectives of the projects were as follows:

a) Use ICTs in the institutionalisation of the Chieftaincy and traditional governance institutions to help strengthen the inter-relations between them and citizens, between traditional governance institutions and central and local governance, thereby closing the democratic gap;
b) Use ICTs for capacity building for Chiefs, traditional governance institutions and their support staff. Their ability to provide documentation, effectively manage information serves as a crucial step towards cultural heritage preservation and knowledge building;

c) Use ICTs to generate greater awareness on traditional governance issues, thereby enabling citizens to gain access to such information in an accessible and user-friendly fashion;
d) Using information to prevent conflict and tension situations, usually due to land rights, because of the absence of systematic records that are not in the public domain.

The project also dealt with the critical interfacing of governance-related cultural issues of concern in Africa, namely: democracy; accountability and transparency; collective responsibility for peace, security and stability; indigenous knowledge; intellectual property rights; cultural preservation as well as the mandatory involvement and active participation of civil society in Africa's development process. To realise these policy concerns, however, there was obviously a need for greater creative research, training support and advocacy than is currently offered by a limited portion of the African academic community.

6.2.3. Rationale and Structure

The reasons underpinning the project were the overall constraints in terms of local economic development and the cultural traditions, and especially the nature of the transmission of indigenous knowledge, based on oral tradition, personal observation and experience, which leaves room for argument and disputes leading sometimes to litigation, armed conflict, death and destruction. An example of this is the crisis in the traditional state of Dagbon, in the Northern Region of Ghana, where as a result of factional fighting the King was beheaded, his palace burned and it costs the government a substantial amount of resources to keep the peace.

The ICTs support for traditional governance is thus an effort aimed at building the capacity of indigenous political institutions, to participate in modern governance, have access to information and knowledge as well as to share experiences among themselves and with other stakeholders.

Towards the achievement of these objectives, the activities of the project were decided using plans drawn up as a result of surveys conducted previously for the "Chieftaincy Governance and Development Project". There was a clear connection, in fact, between the research that was conducted in the previous activity, and the attempt to apply and implement solutions that were identified as having a potential positive impact, and using alternative technologies.

For this reason, the project was divided into two major areas of activities:

1) Training; and
2) Infrastructural Support for the Houses of Chiefs.

Training included, in particular, capacity building seminars for Chiefs, registrars and other staff on basic computer skills. This was an important task, as the registrars and support staff are mainly documentalists, record keepers and information managers in an otherwise oral society.

At the same time, their capacity to "produce" information was intended to make the process of traditional governance more accountable and transparent, and to "open the palace" to the general public.

With regard to the partnership between the traditional institutions and the modern state institutions, the introduction and use of ICTs was definitely seen as an effective tool for better co-operation and communication, in order to more effectively sustain local economic development.

In general, of course, all this aimed at solving disputes and preventing conflicts because in the absence of peace it is not possible to have any development.

On the other side, the need for equipment and a communications facility was a consequence of the pursuance of the global objective, in fact, to mention the obvious: "you cannot learn to drive without driving... and to drive you need a car....".

In all this process, what is worthy of note is that the Centre of Governance, Culture and Development of the University of Ghana, which was in charge of Project Management, in collaboration with the Culture, Education and Technology Network, CETNET, established specifically to take care of the ICTs part of the project, tried to ensure that all possible support was given to the stakeholders involved.

6.2.4. Organisation and Management Arrangements

Given the previous "multidisciplinary" experience of the University of Ghana in executing the Project on "Chieftaincy, Governance and Development", and in particular the Institute of African Studies and the Departments of History, Sociology, Political Sciences and Religion, the Project Management was assigned to the University itself.

In one way, it was considered to be a continuation, with a specific focus on ICTs, of the researches and activities that were started within the framework of studying and researching on traditional governance in the modern era.

The project, in fact, started in May 2003, only a few months after the presentation of the results of the previous project in the International Conference mentioned above. But, differently from other activities, in this case the project was based on a relatively small grant of a hundred and fifty thousand United States Dollars ($US 150,000.00) provided from the Open Society Initiative of West Africa (OSIWA) and required specific technical expertise and consulting in the area of ICTs. Given its limited budget and duration, one year, the project was intended to be a "pilot" initiative, mainly devoted to identifying the training needs and experiments on the applicability of some technical solutions, as well as defining the content of training and building capacity.

The resources of the Project were allocated as follows:

GDC, University of Ghana's Project "ICTs & Traditional Governance" – Budget:

Description	Cost (in US$)
Training	40,000
Research and Consulting	40,000
ICTs Infrastructures and Equipment	60,000
Administrative costs	10,000
TOTAL	150,00

Source: University of Ghana, Project Document

The team of researchers from the University of Ghana, identified to manage the programme was composed of the following experts:

1. Project Director: Prof. Irene Odotei;
2. Project Consultant: Prof. R. Addo-Fening;

3. Researchers: Prof. Albert Awedoba and Dr. Kofi Baku;
4. Project Assistant: Mr. Ebenezer Ayesu;
5. ICTs Consultant: Mr Saluji Nana Salluji, Nana Adu-Kwado I.

The team, led by Prof. Odotei, a researcher in culture and traditional governance in Ghana and a renowned historian, made an incredible effort in developing solutions and disseminating information about the activities of the project, often being "in-the-field", notwithstanding the sometimes prohibitive conditions for travelling and communicating.

To facilitate the exchange of data and communication among the people involved in the project, and to disseminate information about its activities, a sort of "Virtual Network" and a web site were established, under www.Chieftaincy.org

An evaluation of the project was also conducted and it reported the positive expression of the opinions of the administrators of the Houses of Chiefs on the project.

In this connection, the uniqueness of the project was especially in the management of activities, since it brought together two major developmental partners, academia through the University of Ghana and the traditional leadership institutions, in an endeavour to improve the quality of management and preserve the national cultural heritage through the use of ICTs.

This partnership has heightened the mutual benefit that the two institutions can draw from each other in their contribution to good governance and development and, at the same time, it also enhanced the image of the University of Ghana as an institution that reached out to share its knowledge and expertise and resources with another institution that needed to be modernised for good governance. For example, the Vice-Chancellor of the University proudly mentioned the project as an outreach programme among the achievements of the University in his annual Congregation speech. So also the president of the National House of Chiefs praised the project and OSIWA as valued partners in the development efforts of traditional governance.

What should also be underlined is the foresight of OSIWA and its dynamic leadership in supporting this project which can definitely be considered a beginning towards the full modernisation of the governance structure in Ghana and, in general, in Africa.

6.2.5. Activities and Results

1. Computer-Assisted Training Programme

A computer-assisted training programme was introduced to promote effective records management in the key Chieftaincy and traditional governance institutions, leading to the computerisation and automation of records from the Houses of Chiefs. Training and workshops on records management to sharpen knowledge of this subject, particularly through the use of computers in each of the regions of the country, were embraced by the Houses of Chiefs.

The project adopted a two-pronged approach: Preventive and Curative. Three major training workshops and two interactive seminars were held to teach staff about the importance of the records and to ensure diligent care of them, and to develop ICTs skills.

The beneficiaries of the training workshops were:

a) Secretaries from The Chieftaincy Secretariat, Central, Brong Ahafo, Northern, Upper East and Upper West Regional Houses of Chiefs;
b) Registrars of the National House of Chiefs, the Chieftaincy Secretariat and the various Regional Houses of Chiefs;
c) Registrars from 25 selected Traditional Councils.

After assessing and identifying the needs of different target groups, the content of the training focussed mainly on an introduction to computers, Internet, records management, preservation and intellectual property rights.

Interactive seminars were held for the following groups of Chiefs:

a) Chiefs in the Greater Accra Region;
b) Chiefs in the National House of Chiefs.

They were aimed at sensitising Chiefs on the potential of ICTs and on intellectual property rights. It was also a means of involving them to ensure success and sustainability for the project.

There is no doubt that the workshops had a positive impact on participants. Indeed, "a sizeable percentage admitted freely that they had never touched a computer before this training programme". Moreover, by the completion of the workshops, each of the participants had acquired an official email address within the domain: yourname@Chieftaincy.org

This was intended to be a means for improving communication and exchange of documentation through the establishment of a **"Traditional Governance and Information System (TGIS)".**

Below are shown some pictures of the different training sessions:

Computer Assisted Training Programme

2. Digitisation of records and establishment of a central database

An important aspect of the project was the digitisation of the Records of the Houses of Chiefs, to be available for the public domain and to enable citizens' to access information and records more easily. These included records and data of critical importance to the history and development of the local communities and the country overall, such as information on indigenous knowledge, political philosophy, traditional laws, constitution and the customs and values of the people. Given the fact that they were generally in a deplorable state, and considering that today's ICTs made it possible to store and preserve records in ingenious ways, affording institutions and organisations a memory bank from which information is accessed and used, as and when required, it was decided not to preclude the institution of Traditional Councils from this great opportunity of knowledge packaging, storage and dissemination.

The process of digitisation initiated also entailed further capacity-building activities for the record keepers and support staff of these institutions.

The digitisation of records increased access to research resources for the people, the Chiefs, the academic community and other researchers, as well as prolonging the life of the original records. This is because important historical records were perishing and were in danger of being lost, due to inadequate storage facilities. The records which were in this poor state prevented easy access to relevant information that could help resolve for instance, the rampant land disputes which were plaguing and threatening the stability of the country and which could escalate into intra-ethnic or inter-ethnic conflicts.

Computers were therefore installed in the National House of Chiefs and the ten Regional Houses of Chiefs as well as in Traditional Councils so that automation and digitisation of records could begin. Given the very large amount of data and records, the project focussed in particular on the digitisation of the judgement books of the judicial committees and proceedings of the standing committees and the full houses. In fact, the management, preservation and dissemination of these data are of fundamental importance in boosting the efforts of Traditional Councils to reduce conflicts associated with traditional governance and culture.

For this purpose, due to the fact that the House of Chiefs undertakes judicial responsibilities, their records needed to be kept in databases for future reference in the interests of transparency and accountability via the Internet.

Under this activity a central database was created to initiate the smooth integration of systems across the regions to enable the various institutions to share the wealth of information available between themselves and the world at large besides ensuring the preservation of important historical data.

These are essential in the development of databases which would contribute to brokerage services for the traditional institutions to be treated by a multi-disciplinary team, and in order to generate discussions and produce publications on the primary material collected. This was intended to be an important resource in conflict situations and claims to land.

In this regard, as a result of these activities, the University of Ghana also provided information brokerage services to the general public as well as to serve the needs of Chiefs and the Houses of Chiefs. This was based on the fact that not all the Chiefs and Council Members would have access to computers and to the information stored in them so there was a need for the provision of such services as they dispense their duties in traditional justice cases.

3. Infrastructural support: the Traditional Governance and Information System (TGIS) (ICTs Equipment, Web Site and Wide Area Network System - WAN)

The most technological part of the research project focussed on investigating the possibilities of using alternative technologies for establishing a communications system among the traditional governance institutions, using new and affordable technologies, namely the Internet and Satellite communication, especially due to the poor accessibility in the remote areas of the country.

For this purpose, the possibility of creating a WAN (Wide Area Network) using a VSAT connection to offer interoperability among the various institutions across the WAN to the central database (server based at the University of Ghana) was investigated.

At the same time, a project website (www.Chieftaincy.org) was created to enhance networking and promote dialogue among traditional governance institutions in the country, as well as to stimulate academic research on governance, culture and development in the country, the rest of Africa and the world.

In terms of ICTs equipment support, the project acquired a customised server, equipped with a SCSI Ultra-Wide platform, a RAID system and utilising state-of-the-art Intel XEON processors to serve the impending network needs. The system unit is bundled with a redundant UPS and runs on the Microsoft Windows NT platform.

Customised Server running LINUX and a Presentation of ICT Equipment in a Regional House

All official permits covering Administrator and 15-Client licences have been acquired alongside the very stable UNIX platform, LINUX Redhat operating system to serve concurrently.

Six DELL Pc's platform, Pentium IV with standard packages inclusive of UPS and Printers, were purchased to serve the Chieftaincy Secretariat, the Central, Brong Ahafo, Northern, Upper East and Upper West Regional Houses of Chiefs.

The project also provided Flatbed, Pen Scanners and other equipment to the National House of Chiefs and the various regional offices. This was a key aspect of the project since it was essential that practical knowledge be applied in daily activities, in order to reach the targeted goal of making the beneficiaries computer literate, while enhancing the productivity base of these institutions of traditional governance. Finally three sets of VSAT equipment equipped with 2.4m dish, LNB, Bandwidth, Ku-Band, Direct Satellite technology were also purchased.

The idea behind the infrastructural support was that of pushing through a "revolution" of the traditional governance system in Ghana, placing information that millions of ordinary Ghanaians depended upon in the public domain. Furthermore, the use of a VSAT afforded those institutions without access to telephone lines to also tap into the system.

Regarding the installation of the ICTs infrastructure and equipment to establish the **Traditional Governance and Information System (TGIS)**, a preliminary research activity of three months was carried out in order to design the Wide Area Network. It was followed by an intensive digitisation process across the regions to facilitate the smooth implementation of the central database, and on 25th. November 2003, a pilot scheme for preliminary connectivity utilising dial-up-Internet-connectivity was initiated within the National House of Chiefs, the ten Regional Houses of Chiefs including the Greater Accra Regional House of Chiefs, the Presidential Commission on Chieftaincy and the Chieftaincy Secretariat.

The **National House of Chiefs** was the first to be connected to the Internet. The equipment that was earlier provided to the House by the Chieftaincy Governance and Development Project funded by the Ford Foundation was in a deplorable state. After troubleshooting procedures had been performed, the system was therefore upgraded with the requisite software. The setting up of the network to Chieftaincy.org, via dial-up Internet involved replacement of some suitable electronic parts and supported by the Microsoft Windows XP operating system and compatible with the V.92 technology which is ideal for long-distance dial-up connections.

A presentation was made to the National House of Chiefs in the presence of 50 prominent traditional rulers from all the ten Regional Houses of Chiefs. It highlighted the project's commitment to the capacity-building of stakeholders and the preservation of materials bordering on indigenous knowledge and also on the Traditional Governance and Information System (TGIS) which included the project's unique e-mail system for traditional institutions and Chiefs.

Following the first installation, the project team visited all the ten Regional House of Chiefs to provide ICTs equipment, support the installation or repair materials, and configure local systems to connect to the Chieftaincy.org/TGIS via dial-up connection. They also solved technical problems or identified alternative solutions for connectivity. But of course, there were difficulties in connection due to the different resources available, technical problems and the capacity of the people in the various regions.

Shots of the road layout to some of the regions reached by the Project's staff

Vegetation along some of the routes to the project sites

After the first attempt to implement the Network using the dial-up connectivity, it was realised that the national communications setup was not efficient enough to accommodate the Internet connectivity that would ultimately lead to the creation of a WAN (Wide Area Network).

This was due to the fact that the telephone network within some of the regions was in a deplorable state and in some cases cables had suffered from wear and tear. Also, most of the regions had systematically connected one telephone line and extended it to cover up to five or more line extensions which in turn led to disruption of the dial–up connectivity. Some of the regional capitals closer to Accra were able to connect and utilise the service while in many other cases the connect time was too long and the strength of connection just too weak.

Technicians installing the VSAT

Another problem that was common to all the regions was the issue of financing huge telephone bills due to many hours of use of the Internet. This made the people responsible quite apprehensive.

Efforts were made to find solutions to these problems and concerns and for this reason, the possibility of using a VSAT solution was explored.

The proposed Wide Area Network (WAN) spanning all the 10 Regional Houses, the National House, Chieftaincy secretariat and the project office was intended to offer total data sharing amongst these institutions, serving as a communications backbone that was independent of the national grid and provided interoperability.

In order to achieve this flexible communications network and provide optimum performance amongst these institutions, whilst minimising the demand on the national communications grid, a VSAT–Broadband solution was chosen. This choice was based upon the advantages that it has over the national communications infrastructure and its practicality in worldwide application in the resonance of networking.

But, unfortunately, and especially at the time of the installation, VSAT technology, despite its numerous advantages and reliability, was not cheap. The project managed to locate a foreign IT company with representatives in Ghana, offering VSAT solutions at a relatively affordable price. However, it was possible to purchase only two VSAT pieces of equipment which have been installed in the Project Office (at the University of Ghana); and at the Chieftaincy Secretariat. The speed of connectivity through the basic bandwidth more than out-performed the dial-up connection previously used, but the objective of putting in place the Traditional Governance and Information System (TGIS) among all the traditional institutions was yet to be realised, since the other sites had not yet received their VSAT.

6.3. CONCLUSIONS

6.3.1. Impact on good governance and community development

According to the assessment of the project and the opinions expressed by the interviewees, the project was successful, especially in terms of raising awareness of the need to systematise the role and functions of traditional institutions vis-à-vis the modern governance system.

Of particular importance, in fact, was the dissemination and institutional building efforts provided that culminated in an enhancement of the awareness and capacity of the Chieftaincy institutions and their staff with regard to the potential and use of ICTs to manage their daily activities and, in particular, to preserve records and data. As a consequence of this, there is in fact, a growing demand for the active involvement of traditional leaders in Central government operations, due to the recognition of the importance of their role in supporting good governance at the local level. A clear example of this is the integration of the Chieftaincy institutions as partners within the "National Governance Programme of the Government". In particular, to state the importance of their opinion, and to promote and better manage the "partnership for development" in Ghana, the 7th. National Governance Workshop, held in Kumasi in October 2004, focussed on "Traditional Authority and Good Governance: implications for Democratic Consolidation". The workshop was organised by the government in collaboration with the National House of Chiefs under the sponsorship of the United Nations Development Programme (UNDP) and the technical input came from Prof. Irene K. Odotei, Project Manager of the "Governance, Culture and Development Project".

This shows how the project, and in general the activities undertaken by the University of Ghana, in particular the Institute of African Studies, were the "initiators" of a process that, although far from being completed, could lead to effective and sustainable development in the country.

In this process the role of ICTs is becoming ever more central. The importance of records of the Chieftaincy institutions is evident for a nation which could have avoided a considerable number of conflicts, associated with traditional governance disputes, if records had been kept properly for posterity. The digitisation and public availability of data will help to create a "memory heritage" from which information can be extracted and used as and when needed. Moreover, it will help to devise and standardise customary tradition and law.

In this sense, many projects, in collaboration with developmental partners, such as UNDP, UNECA, the World Bank, and others, have been initiated to assess the situation and the capacity at local level in order to support the government in better delivering services to the poor at local level, especially in connection with the revitalised process of decentralisation.

As indicated in a recent study of the World Bank Institute, in fact, there is a great confusion about the roles of key actors at local level. This confusion is made worse by the friction between the modern system of governance that the governments superimposed on the traditional institutions, where the weakness comes not from the absence of well defined roles, but from the limitations of the regulatory framework[3]. Therefore, there is an urgent need to make changes in current institutional arrangements so that community members and their traditional leaders can play a more active role in determining their communities' destiny, with the longer term goal of improving governance and local service delivery.

6.3.2. Challenges for integrating ICTs in traditional governance

First of all, the positive opinions and enthusiasm expressed by the participants on the need and the content of the training courses should be underlined. However, due to financial constraints and following the recommendation of the Chiefs, the project concentrated on the administrative staff of the National House of Chiefs, Chieftaincy Secretariat, the ten Regional Houses of Chiefs and selected

Traditional Councils as an initial step. Despite the grant received from OSIWA, which enabled the project to initiate the process, funds are still required to accomplish the task of organising capacity–building workshops and seminars for Chiefs and their support staff in all the ten Regional Houses of Chiefs.

In this sense, it is also important to underline that the project aimed at establishing a sustainable process, where institutional and capacity-building was not only a sporadic activity done "on project", but was in a positive way "institutionalised" within the context of the academic research. For this reason, and also to solve some of the bureaucratic constraints that occurred due to the fact that the project was managed by the central administration of the University, and sometimes delaying the activities of the project, which should have been managed in a flexible way, it was decided to establish a "Centre on Governance, Culture and Development", as a not for profit organisation. This NGO was intended to serve as a scientific and consulting resource centre, to study and provide brokerage and research services on the issue of traditional governance at large.

At the same time, there was the need for specialist skills in ICTs and networking, and those skills were still limited and weak in the academic arena in Ghana. This led to the decision to establish another focussed not-for profit organisation, namely the "Culture, Education and Technology Network-CETNET". It was intended to provide specific services on ICTs and to serve as a complementary player in the modernisation of traditional governance in Ghana and in the continent of Africa.

With regard, more specifically, to ICTs, Ghana has embarked on an ambitious programme in response to the wave of technological transformations that are pervading the world, but due to the still weak infrastructure and the limited resources, it was necessary to focus on alternative affordable solutions and joint efforts to fully grasp the potential of ICTs for local development.

In this respect, the project intended to explore how to best make Internet facilities accessible to the Chieftaincy institutions to avoid them lagging behind in the development process, and so they could contribute to it. The choice made by the project team to utilise VSAT technology was definitely an important and challenging decision. Moreover, the acquisition of VSAT was initially hampered by bureaucratic "bottlenecks" within the National Communications Authority of Ghana (NCA) which regulates the communications infrastructure.

It was important for the project team to consult the NCA due to new regulations requiring that importation into the country of VSAT equipment must satisfy its guidelines and those of the National Frequency Board. After consultations with some leading IT companies in the country, the project team became to the conclusion that it would be most beneficial and cost effective to acquire a dedicated VSAT instead of soliciting the services of these companies.

Due to financial constraints in the purchase of bandwidth and equipment, however, the project outlined a plan of setting up the WAN in phases. It carefully selected the various groups of users, and fitted them into different phases of the project according to current capacity, location and self-sustainability. Unfortunately, it must be said that, at the time of the mission, neither of the two VSAT systems are currently working due to technical difficulties and the high financial cost of operation.

6.3.3. Lessons Learned

One of the objectives achieved by the project was that of raising awareness on the importance of traditional culture and the economic value of information, and the possibilities of using ICTs to support the process of knowledge management, thus improving governance and generating local economic development.

In particular, a specific content of the training dealt with Intellectual Property Rights Protection.

This is important because, in addition to supporting administrative procedure and management of traditional governance systems, the enhanced opportunity for research, publications, codification, and dissemination of information using ICTs and multimedia, (such as production of documentaries for instance) also affords a unique opportunity to re-examine the rich cultural heritage of Ghana from a modern perspective, using ICTs.

It is evident that traditional leaders must acquaint themselves with modern practices of public sector administration and management while building on the traditions and values that command the trust and respect of members of their communities.

This effort is definitely taking place in the context of the government's desire to decentralise power and responsibilities to the communities, and to do so without taking undue risks. For this reason, it is generally believed that "pilot" experiences should provide the proper arena for testing new institutional or organisational arrangements on a reduced scale before lessons can be learned for nationwide application.

The Governance Culture and Development Project, funded by OSIWA has indeed taken a phenomenal step in the modernisation of Traditional Governance Institutions through the use of ICTs. As previously mentioned, other projects and initiatives have begun following this process, and moreover, the interest for the potential of harnessing good governance through reinforcing traditional authority institutions is not limited anymore to few areas and countries. Undoubtedly initiated in Ghana, it is now being recognised in many other African countries, from Cameroon to South Africa, etc.

It is the case that the Kings from different countries are becoming the ambassadors of this renewal of local traditional culture, being invited to meetings in the headquarters of the United Nations or the World Bank, and participating in, for instance, the "Fourth African Development Forum on: Governance for Progressing Africa[4].

With specific regard to the ICTs component of the project, it is clear that the project, especially due to its limited financial budget, was not intended to fully realise the ICTs infrastructure of the Chieftaincy institutions in Ghana. Nevertheless, in addition to equipping some key authorities, the research and exploration of the project highlighted the advantages of VSAT technology. This potential is now increased due to the substantial lowering of prices which has come about as a result of increased experimentation and usage. The reliability is also improving and thus it is possible to say that the technological choice may suggest future positive trends that, if pursued, could lead to the completion of the WAN (Wide Area Network) and this, when completed, should lead to the Traditional Governance Information System (TGIS) in Ghana.

Clearly then, ICTs would provide the critical tools for launching traditional governance into the information age and all the advantages that it offers for development and good governance.

6.3.4. The way forward: towards an e-Traditional governance Network

Considering the fact that the identity of the people of Ghana is rooted in their cultural heritage, as expressed by all the people interviewed and by the Project Management, traditional governance would find a niche in the general governance structure of the people of Africa.

Therefore, this project is not only a project, but a unique attempt to build the capacity of traditional institutions to usher them into the global system of mainstream governance to achieve this objective it is a question of cultural revolution, building on partnerships with NGOs and other institutions who have expertise and similar objectives.

With regard to the specific project initiated under the grant of OSIWA, out of 165 Traditional Councils, the project managed to train one official each from 25 traditional councils. There are therefore still 140 to be trained. Furthermore, two members each have been trained from the 10 Regional Houses of Chiefs, The National House of Chiefs and 3 Institutions related to traditional governance. In effect, only 56-persons so far have been adequately trained.

But, based on the experience gained and the appeal from beneficiaries of the workshops, the University of Ghana, in particular the "Centre of Governance, Culture and Development", in collaboration with the "Culture, Education and Technology Network – CETNET" aims at ensuring that at least one person in all the 165 Traditional Councils would be e-literate in the coming year. Of course this is also a matter of funding, but at the same time it is an issue of correct utilisation of pilot experiences and scale-up of practices.

In this regard, considering that the proliferation of telecommunications centres and cyber cafes, that providing computer and Internet facilities have resulted in the provision of public access to those who do not have access to private ownership due to infrastructural and financial constraints, there is an even more urgent need to acquire basic ICTs skills in order to be part of the long path to follow before Ghana can become a true information and knowledge society.

Joint efforts are needed building on what is already in place.

Therefore, the challenge for Ghana is to find a way to rely on the institutional arrangements for leadership and collective action with which communities feel most comfortable, while adopting universally accepted concepts of good governance. In this "research", the task of the different institutions is to be able to tailor ICTs to support the delicate balance between the past and the future.

Within this framework it is necessary, as part of the overall efforts of integrating tradition and posterity, to blend indigenous and modern forms of governance and to document (in both text and video) salient and positive elements of traditional culture. These will be used as inputs for codifying acknowledged positive patterns of values, ideas, principles and behaviour into written standard rules and practices for constitutional and legislative reforms. They will also serve to prepare policy guidelines for regulating roles, responsibilities, rights and obligations.

In all this, a particular emphasis should be given to the establishment of a network of community e-Traditional Centres where public communications facilities are provided, information is processed and knowledge is produced and made available to the community.

This e-Traditional Network should be done through linking the various initiatives, ongoing or planned, such as the Community Information Centres (CICs); the Community Knowledge Centres (CKCs); or the Village Information and Communication Infrastructure (VICI) and using the traditional leaders and Chieftaincy institutions as promoter and catalyst for innovation and local community development.

Notes

1. World Bank Institute, Delivering Services to the Poor: an assessment of the capacity to deliver Education, Health and Water Services to Local Communities in Ghana, working paper draft for discussion, February 2005.
2. For instance the "History and Development Project", funded by NUFU-Norwegian Cooperation.
3. See for example. "Odwira 2000: 25 years of Sustained Development", Informative brochure, by the Oyeeman Wereko Ampem II, Akuapem Gyasehene and Ohene of Amanokrom
4. Addis Ababa, 11th.-15th. October, 2004, organised by the United Nations Economic Commission for Africa (UNECA).

References

African Training and Research Centre in Administration for Development (CAFRAD), Proceedings and Final report of the CAFRAD, Regional Workshop on e-governance, organized in partnership with ACBF, NEPAD, UNDESA and hosted by the Government of Ghana, Office of the Head of Civil Service, Accra, Ghana, 22-25th. November 2004;

Baku, Kofi, (edited by) "Chieftaincy in Africa: Culture, Governance and Development", Summary of International Conference Proceedings, January 6-10th., 2003, Accra, Ghana;

Odotei K, Irene, Prof., "ICTs in support of Traditional Governance: Chieftaincy and Governance in Ghana", in "Africa Networking: Development Information, ICTs and Governance", United Nations Economic Commission for Africa, 2004;

Odotei K, Irene, Prof., "Technical Report preparatory to the 7th National Governance Workshop on "Traditional Authority and Good Governance: implications for democratic consolidation", Kumasi, Ghana, 27-29th. October 2004;

Oyeeman Wereko Ampem II, Akuapem Gyasehene and Ohene of Amanokrom, "Odwira 2000: 25 years of Sustained Development", Report and brochures, Amanokrom, 2000;

Republic of Ghana, "Constitution of the Republic of Ghana", 1992;

Republic of Ghana, Office of the President of the Republic, National Governance Programme, "Traditional Authority and Good Governance: implications for democratic consolidation", Report of the 7th.National Governance Workshop, Kumasi, Ghana, 27-29th. October 2004;

Republic of Ghana, "The Ghana ICTs for Accelerated Development (ICT4AD) Policy, 2003;

Republic of Ghana, "An integrated ICTs-led Socio-economic Development Policy and Plan Development Framework for Ghana", 2002;

Republic of Ghana, "Vision 2020: Socio-Economic Development Framework", 2002;

Republic of Ghana, "Ghana Poverty Reduction Strategy (GPRS): 2002-2004", 2001;

Republic of Ghana, "Coordinated Programme for Economic and Social Development of Ghana (2003-2012)", 2002;

Republic of Ghana, Ministry of Communications "Community Information Centres (CIC's) in the Age of Information and Communication Technology (ICTs): Ghana's Blueprint for Action", 2004;

Republic of Ghana, Ministry of Communications "Introducing the new Community Information Centres (CIC) in Ghana", 2005;

Republic of Ghana, Ministry of Communications "Draft Paper on ICTs Actions and Development", 2004;

Republic of Ghana, Ministry of Local Government and Rural Development, Decentralisation Secretariat "National Decentralisation Action Plan (NDAP): Towards a Sector-wide approach for decentralisation implementation in Ghana (2003-2005)", September 2004;

University of Ghana, Legon, Institute of African Studies, Working Papers of the Project on "Chieftaincy, Governance and Culture", not published, 2000-2003;

University of Ghana, Legon, Centre on Governance, Culture and Development, Working Papers of the Project on "Governance Culture and Development", not published, 2003-2004;

University of Ghana, Legon, Centre on Governance, Culture and Development, Final Report of the OSIWA funded Project on "Governance Culture and Development", 2004;

University of Ghana, Legon, Ford Foundation, "Perceptions on Chieftaincy in Ghana", Research Report, 2000;

World Bank Institute, "Local Governance Capacity Development", Concept Note, 2004;

World Bank Institute, Delivering Services to the Poor: an assessment of the capacity to deliver Education, Health and Water Services to Local Communities in Ghana, working paper, 2005.

7

DISTRICT ADMINISTRATIVE NETWORK (DISTRICTNET) IN UGANDA

CASE STUDY OVERVIEW

Location: Uganda

Funding Institution: Department for International Development (DFID) through the International Institute for Communication and Development (IICD)

Executing Institution: Ministry of Local Government and Kayunga, Mbale, Mbarara and Lira Districts.

Project Manager: Eng. Steven Dagada, Chairperson of the District of Kayunga and National Project Co-ordinator

Total Budget: 921.839 Ugandan Shillings

Project Start Date: May 2002

Project End Date: May 2005

Administrative Information and Contacts:

Eng. Stephen Dagada,
District Net National Co-ordinator,
Chairperson of the District Council of Kayunga
Tel. 256 77 608784
email: sdagada@yahoo.com
Web site: www.kayunga.go.ug

7.1. CONTEXT AND POLICY

7.1.1. The governance system and the main reforms in Uganda

Uganda, a former British colony, is a sovereign state and a republic. In January 1986, Yoweri Kaguta Museveni became the President of the Republic of Uganda after leading a successful five year liberation struggle. He then introduced the **Movement System of governance,** which theoretically, was a broad-based, inclusive and non-partisan political system (Art 70, 1995 Constitution). In implementing the Movement System, political party activities were suspended, except for operating party offices in the capital city, Kampala.

In July 2005 however, the people of Uganda voted in a referendum to adopt a multi-party political system. The Parliament of Uganda discussed and promulgated a new constitution in July 2005 as a basis for subsequent legal reforms. The new constitution is in the process of being ratified by District Councils as required by law.

The Government of Uganda is comprised of the Executive (headed by the President and assisted by the Vice President, Prime Minister and Cabinet Ministers), Parliament (headed by the Speaker) and the Judiciary (headed by the Chief Justice). Article 176 of the 1995 Constitution further provides that the system of local government in Uganda should be based on the district as a unit under which there should be lower local governments and administrative units. A decentralisation system applies to all levels of local government.

The **Public Service Reform** in Uganda has been going on since the early 1990s. It is spearheaded by the Ministry of Public Service. Key areas of reform include:

i. Restructuring and downsizing.
ii. Introduction of Result Oriented Management (ROM) methodologies, to improve performance in government ministries and departments.
iii. Promoting efficiency and cost reduction in government services by introducing e-government systems, including integrated payroll and pension systems.
iv. The design and implementation of public sector pension reform and the introduction of a self-financing contributory system for future pension obligations, intended to control the growth of pension commitments.

At the same time, the **Law Reform Commission** is completely reviewing the legal system in Uganda to bring it into compliance with the 1995 Constitution (and now with the Uganda Constitution 2005). Some laws are obsolete and create red tape, while others are discriminatory towards the poor. Women's access to justice, in particular, is hindered by discriminatory laws such as land legislation, where inequities in land ownership were not corrected by the Land Act. The Constitutional Court has been instrumental in amending offending legislation including the abolition of corporal punishment and abolishing the inequality of access to divorce between male and female petitioners. Many reforms in the Justice, Law and Order Sector (JLOS) comprising of the Judiciary, Police, Prisons, and Directorate of Public Prosecutions are also under implementation.

7.1.2. The Poverty Eradication Action Plan and economic development

The Government of Uganda has formulated a number of programmes to address the key areas of the Millennium Development Goals (MDGs). Government interventions to this effect included the formulation and implementation of the **Uganda Poverty Eradication Action Plan (PEAP)**, which included elements such as Universal Primary Education (UPE), and the Plan for Modernisation of Agriculture (PMA), Vision 2025 (being revised) and Medium-Term Competitive Strategy for the Private Sector (2000-2005), to mention but a few. The President of Uganda launched the Presidential Investors Roundtable (PIRT), a top-level Business Advisory Council, on 30th. September 2004. This Council has five working groups: Agribusiness, ICTs, Education, Infrastructure and Regulatory Environment. The mandate of the Council is to advise the Government on the steps that should be taken to improve the investment climate and increase Foreign Direct Investment (FDI) inflows to Uganda.

According to the PEAP, which was prepared through a consultative process involving the Central and Local Government, Parliament, Donors and Civil Society, Uganda's overall strategy and goal is aimed at improving the welfare of all Ugandans and the eradication of poverty. It is believed that under this plan Uganda will be transformed into a modern economy where all sectors will actively participate in economic growth.

The PEAP is grouped under five 'pillars': (1) Economic management, (2) Production, competitiveness and incomes (3) Security, conflict-resolution and disaster-management (4) Good governance and (5) Human development. The four core challenges for PEAP implementation are (a) the restoration of security, dealing with the consequences of conflict and improving regional equity (b) restoring sustainable growth in the incomes of the poor (c) human development (d) using public resources transparently and efficiently to eradicate poverty.

With regard to human development, the PEAP document reported that recent years have seen major improvements in the following areas:

i. Education and literacy, through the introduction of Universal Primary Education and functional adult literacy programmes;
ii. HIV/AIDS prevalence rates stagnated between 6% and 7%;
iii. Child nutrition, together with infant and maternal mortality; health reforms and the construction of health centres in rural areas;
v. Improved access to public services through decentralisation;
vi. Infant and Maternal Mortality strategy to address child and maternal health. The key interventions in this strategy are: Improving the quality of health care and the treatment of malaria, sanitation, community mobilisation, and family planning;
vii. Improved access to water supply.

The expansion of production and incomes in rural areas is addressed by a large number of interventions, which are grouped under the **Plan for the Modernisation of Agriculture (PAM)**. This plan focusses on agricultural modernisation and commercialisation by a multi-sectoral approach to addressing the constraints facing agriculture-based livelihoods. In September 2001, the government launched the **Strategic Exports Programme (SEP)** aimed at increasing competitiveness by stimulating value added investments in selected sectors of the economy and removing bottlenecks that hindered the private sector's ability to take advantage of emerging trade opportunities under various initiatives including African Growth and Opportunities Act (AGOA) of USA and Everything But Arms (EBA).

7.1.3. Local Governance Policy and strategy

Decentralisation in Uganda has been implemented for over 12 years now, guided by the Local Government Statute of 1993, the 1995 Constitution and the 1997 Local Government Act. This was based on the conviction that decentralisation comprehensively facilitates the realisation of development and political objectives for Uganda through democratisation, equitable distribution of resources between and within districts and improvements in public sector performance. Democratic participation advocates popular participation, empowerment of local residents and regular local elections. Decentralisation is intended to improve transparency and accountability in local governments and promote good governance and participatory democracy.

The system of local government in Uganda is based on the District as a Unit under which there are lower local governments, the Administrative Unit Councils. Elected Local Government Councils which are accountable to the people are made up of persons directly elected to represent electoral areas, with special seats for persons with disabilities, youth and women councillors. There is a legal requirement that 30% of the Parliament and Local Councils should be comprised of women representatives in addition to provision for representatives of young people and people with disabilities.

The Local Government Council is the highest political authority in its area of jurisdiction. The councils are corporate bodies having both legislative and executive powers. They have powers to make local laws and enforce implementation. On the other hand Administrative Unit Councils serve as political units to advise on planning and implementation of services. They assist in the resolution of disputes, monitor the delivery of services and assist in the maintenance of law, order and security.

There are five tiers of local government in Uganda. Most executive decisions are taken at the Local Council 5 (district LC5) or Local Council 3 (sub-county LC3) level, although the Local Council 1 (village LC1) level has important responsibilities, for instance, in administering the Local Council courts.

Local governments are empowered to make and approve their own budgets and development plans. They raise their own revenue from a range of local taxes and allocate expenditure on decentralised and transferred services. They also recruit and manage personnel and make bylaws. Local governments receive financial support from central government in order to supplement their recurrent and development budgets. In this regard, they receive three types of grants namely, unconditional, conditional and equalisation grants. This financing arrangement is stipulated in the Constitution and the Local Governments Act.

Bilateral and multilateral donors have also continued to support local governments, through the Ministries of Finance, Planning and Economic Development and Local Government, in order to deepen the process of decentralisation and socio-economic transformation. The donors include the World Bank, African Development Bank, European Union, DFID, DANIDA, USAID, Irish Aid and the Dutch Government to mention but a few. Without this support, decentralisation would have taken longer to take root.

Some reported progress in improving service delivery under decentralisation are as follows:

i. Decentralised primary school classroom construction has demonstrated substantially reduced unit costs and faster construction rates than previous centralised programmes.
ii. The economic evaluation of the Local Government Development Programme (LGDP) quotes research by UNCDF, DANIDA and others showing Social Returns on Investment (SRI) for investments by local governments ranging from 12% upwards and which compares well with returns on central government investment.

In the further implementation of decentralisation, the government's objective was to increase local autonomy while strengthening upwards and downwards accountability, so that the autonomy is used to meet the needs of the population. Other issues being addressed are the restructuring of local governments to make them cost effective and efficient, computerisation, establishment of standards for service delivery, improving urban planning capacities, financial management, gender mainstreaming and legal reform. This would include the revision of laws such as the Country and Planning Act (1964), the Public Health Act, the Trading Licensing Act, and the Markets Act which need to be revised to make them consistent with the Constitution and the LG Act (1994). A review is also needed of the legislation which governs poverty reduction activities such as the Local Government Act 1997, LG Financial and Accounting Regulations 1998, the Internal Audit manual, the Town and Country planning Act 1964, the LG Rating Decree 1979, the Trading Licensing Act 1964 and the Markets Act 1942, to bring them in line with the changing environment.

7.1.4. ICTS STATUS, POLICY AND REGULATORY FRAMEWORK

The government of the Republic of Uganda recognised the important role information and ICTs play in national development. To this end, the Uganda ICTs Policy framework was finalised in 2002 and adopted by Cabinet in 2003. Its vision is "a Uganda are national development, especially human development and good governance, are sustainably enhanced, promoted and accelerated by efficient application and use of ICTs including timely access to information".

The main policy objectives were:

— To sensitise and create awareness among the general public and all stakeholders about the role of information and ICTs in Uganda's development process.
— To increase the level of ICTs functional literacy and build human resource capacity.
— To promote and enable the building and establishment of an appropriate infrastructure that supports ICTs development and at the same time meets universal ICTs access goals.
— To promote fair competition and private investment in the ICTs sector with particular emphasis on development and encouragement of local participation including specific incentives for investing in ICTs.
— To identify and establish innovative financing mechanisms that address the specific needs of ICTs development.
— To promote the use of ICTs in the stimulation of production, storage, and dissemination of in-country information and knowledge in both the public and private sector.
— To facilitate the broadest possible access to public domain information, especially development information.
— To promote a conducive environment for media pluralism that will enhance cultural identity and national sovereignty.
— To promote multilingualism and other efforts to provide access to information by the disadvantaged groups and communities.
— To ensure gender mainstreaming in ICTs development.
— To provide for the establishment of an enabling and desirable, legal and regulatory framework that among other things takes into account the convergence of technologies.
— To encourage and support Research and Development in ICTs.
— To accord due regard, recognition and protection of intellectual assets.
— To enhance collaboration and co-ordination in ICTs development at the local, regional and international level.

The ICTs Policy has led to several ICTs initiatives and investments in the country. Each sector, including local governments, is required to develop ICTs implementation strategies in conformity with the National ICTs Policy.

Further, an e-Readiness Assessment Study was conducted in 2003, to pave the way for the promotion of e-government in the country. Currently, the **e-government Strategy Framework** is being finalised in 2005. Its main objectives are:

1. To continuously improve the efficiency of, and access to, government information and services.
2. To use the successful development of the e-government initiative to promote Uganda as an Information Technology centre in Africa.
3. To address privacy and security issues related to e-government implementation.
4. To ensure sufficient revenue streams and funding that enable the development of core e-government competencies.
5. To establish leadership and partnerships that advance e-government services.
6. To develop and maintain a seamless and comprehensive e-government interface.
7. To manage the cost of e-government implementation through effective use of technology.
8. To institutionalise the use of e-government information and services through the adoption of appropriate organisational models.

The Uganda Communications Act, 1997 (Cap 106 Laws of Uganda) established the Uganda Communications Commission (UCC), and the rights and duties of the state, enterprises, institutions, organisations and individuals in the use and management of the means of communication, in the establishment and management of communications networks, in the rendering of communications services as well as the general responsibilities if there is violation of the law. Regulations made so far under the Act include the Communications (Establishment and Management of the Rural Communications Development Fund) Regulations of 2002; and the Uganda Communications (Enforcement Procedures) Regulations of 2004.

Other ICTs related legislations in place include:

1. The Press and Journalist Statute 1995 (Cap 105), The Statute extended Article 29(1) *(Freedom of expression)* of the Constitution to the print media. It also created the Media Council, the National Institute of Journalists of Uganda and a Disciplinary Committee within the Media Council. The Council is responsible for regulating eligibility for media ownership and requires journalists to register with the National Institute of Journalists of Uganda.
2. The Electronic Media Statute, Cap 104, Laws of Uganda provides for the establishment of the Broadcasting Council that licenses radio, television and video rental licences. The purchase, use and sale of television sets is also subject to licensing by the Council.
3. The Access to Information Act, 2004, that makes provision for access by individuals and/or corporations to information of interest relating to a public company.

Proposed legislation due for consideration include:

1. **National Information Technology Authority—Uganda (NITA-U) Bill.** The proposed Act establishes an Authority as a co-ordinating, monitoring and supervisory body to promote National IT development in support of the principles of modernisation within the context of poverty eradication; to provide a national IT-policy framework and technical support for IT related services for government-wide use; and for other matters incidental to these.
2. **The Electronic Transactions Bill, 2003** proposed an Act to provide for the use, security, facilitation and regulation of electronic communications and transactions and to encourage the use of e-government services. It intended to *inter alia* promote e-government and e-commerce in Uganda.
3. **The Electronic Signatures Bill, 2003** proposed an Act to make provision for and to regulate the use of electronic signatures. It attempts to do this through provisions relating to the establishment of the Public Key Infrastructure for authenticity and security of documents.
4. **The Computer Misuse Bill, 2003** proposed an Act to make provision for the safety and security of electronic transactions and information systems; to prevent unlawful access, abuse or misuse

of information systems, including computers, and to make provision for securing the conduct of electronic transactions in a trustworthy electronic environment.

The ICTs needs for Uganda are identified in the National ICTs Policy (2002), and the Uganda e-government Strategy Framework The Uganda e-Readiness Assessment Study revealed the following as the main ICTs needs in the country:

i. Conducting a study at every central and local government office to identify information system needs.
ii. Development of ICTs infrastructure.
iii. Need to reduce connectivity costs and promote universal access.
iv. Equipping every desk with a PC and every government office with email, and office productivity and collaboration software.
v. Setting up a metropolitan network to connect government offices, with gateways to connect to the Internet and the telephone networks. This network should link central and local governments.
vi. Setting up pilot e-government kiosks (starting with existing telecentres) to test the newly developed content and e-delivery mechanisms as well as the economic and technical sustainability of the proposed kiosks.
vii. Setting up the ICTs co-ordinating agency for the government.
viii. Setting up a payment gateway and public key infrastructure to enable online transactions.
ix. Development and standardising ICTs education and training.
x. Setting up an ICTs incubator for encouraging investments in the sector.
xi. General sensitisation on the benefits of ICTs and e-government to public servants, citizens, business, civil society and other groups.
xii. Legal and regulatory framework to promote and safeguard ICTs.
xiii. Promotion of ICTs in schools.
xiv. Development of local content.
xv. Addressing problems of multilingualism.
xvi. Development of a sustainable and affordable alternative power supply to electricity, especially in rural areas to address the limitations of the electricity grid.

xvii. Financing of ICTs development activities.

To address some of the problems mentioned above, the **Uganda Telecommunications Sector Policy** (2005) proposed to undertake the following specific initiatives by 2010:

i. To ensure the ubiquitous presence of telecommunications infrastructure and services that will enable sustainable human development through the ease and affordability of access to relevant, accurate, and timely information (actual content being the responsibility of the various public sectors as well as civil society and private sector initiatives).
ii. To facilitate the delivery of the high level information and service needs to all sectors of society, especially the marginalised sections of society that comprise rural or poor communities, women and people with disabilities, through close integration with the following: IT sector, Broadcasting sector, Media sector, and Postal sector.
iii. To promote the growth of the production and service sectors related to or closely supported by the telecommunications industry in Uganda (research and development, fabrication and manufacturing, training, consultancy, outsourcing services, etc).
iv. To ensure that all aspects of processes and operations in the sector take full account of the following cross-cutting issues: Gender concerns, the physically disadvantaged and sustainable exploitation of the environment.

Although there has not been a comprehensive survey of human resources in ICTs in Uganda, it is fairly obvious that the need for some ICTs skills exceed the current supply. Various levels of skills are required and the existing training institutions are meeting some of the training needs.

There is need to assess the national requirement for ICTs skills, establish how much of this is available, and then determine the best strategy of meeting the appropriate ICTs skills demand. However the ICTs skills that will be needed, and therefore the kind of training that will be required, depend very much on the ICTs policy adopted by Uganda as a nation, and by the Government in particular. For example if government should adopt a policy of information sharing using modern ICTs, Local Area Networks (LAN) and Wide Area Networks (WAN) will be introduced in government Ministries, Departments and Agencies. This would require government employees to acquire a range of ICTs skills that would otherwise not be required.

In order to ensure equitable geographic distribution of telecommunications services in the country, UCC developed and is implementing the **Rural Communications Development Policy**. Having identified the challenges to the achievement of the 1996 Policy targets, the following common challenges and interventions were adopted under Uganda's Rural Communications Development Programme:

1. Awareness and literacy – support a vanguard training institution in each district to create literacy and awareness about the potential of ICTs; support district websites to demonstrate some benefits and use through relevant content;
2. Access – support an internet PoP in each district; set up a national IXP; ensure the provision of a phone in each sub-county (the smallest local administrative unit in Uganda)
3. Affordability – give outright one off grants to small start-ups and partial one off grants to bigger rural operators; permit or require asymmetrical interconnection settlements in favour of rural telecoms operators.

A 1% levy on all telecoms service providers is the main funding driver for the Rural Communications Development Fund. Development partners have also come in to give additional support, including: International Development Research Centre (IDRC) which supported the policy and strategy research (Canadian $200,000); The World Bank which has given a grant of $5 million (under the Energy for Rural Transformation Project) towards actual implementation.

Through subsidies from the Fund to various companies, the following projects have so far been implemented:

(a) 20 internet PoPs were established in various districts.
(b) Establishment of 26 district websites (www.dip.go.ug)
(c) Establishment of 4 Internet cafes.
(d) Establishment of 3 ICTs training centres.
(e) Provision of 66 public payphones.

The following projects are in progress with most of them nearing completion in 2005:

(a) Establishment of 30 district websites.
(b) Provision of Internet cafes in 11 districts.
(c) Establishment of ICTs training centres in 45 districts.
(d) Provision of 200 public access points.

In April 2005, at the Women of Uganda Network (WOUGNET/OWA) consultative meeting in Kampala, participants identified the following issues for Uganda with respect to the WSIS and the National ICTs policy:

i. Financing mechanisms: Rural Communications Development Fund (RCDF), National Budget from the Ministry of Finance & Economic Planning and Development, Development partners, Private sector, Financial institutions.
ii. A centralised ICTs co-ordinating agency should be established to collect funds in one centre. This centre should co-ordinate other matters relating to ICTs.
iii. On the issue of Internet governance, there should be a regulatory framework as cyber crime is becoming a concern in Uganda.
iv. Need for capacity building in both ICTs use and application
v. Need for sharing of experiences: both best practices and failures.
vi. Need to review the ICTs policy with a view to mainstreaming gender within the policy
vii. Need to put emphasis on mainstreaming ICTs in the agricultural sector
viii. Need to mobilise the involvement of communities in ICTs-related activities in their respective areas.

7.1.5. Vision 2035: Towards a Modern Industrialised and Knowledge Based Society

In March 2005, the ICTs/e-government Inter-Agency National Planning Team was established, under the co-ordination of the National Planning Authority. The main goal of this team was to discuss ways and means of ensuring that ICTs/e-government services were undertaken by the Government of Uganda as one of the core priority sub-sector in the execution of the proposed **"National Vision 2035: Towards a Modern Industrialised and Knowledge Based Society"**.

To realise this vision, and consistent with the new policy reforms for the transformation of the Ugandan economy suggested by Hon. Dr. Ezra Suruma, Minister of Finance, Planning and Economic Development, it was necessary to spearhead the process of ensuring that ICTs/e-government Sub-sectors are given due and quick attention under the National Development Planning Framework. As a result the Inter-Agency Team was set up and asked to involve informed members from various sectors (Government, Private, Civil Society and other stakeholders) in discussions in a participatory and transparent manner and to come up with realistic and acceptable National ICTs/e-government frameworks in the perspective of long and medium term Master Plans for implementation.

The Inter-Agency Team is chaired by the National Planning Authority (NPA) that also ensures the monitoring and evaluation of the overall process following the same participatory model. The team held its first two meetings on 24th. March, 2005 and 20th. May, 2005. During these meetings, the main challenges which faced the ICTs/e-government initiative implementation were outlined and discussed. These included:

- Inadequate funding for ICTs/e-government initiatives both in the national Recurrent and Development budgets, as well an inflexible and ineffective budgeting process;
- Inadequate ICTs/e-government basic infrastructure;
- Inadequate awareness of the benefits of ICTs/e-government in national development;
- Lack of co-ordination leading to duplication of efforts;
- Very minimal standardisation of ICTs infrastructure across institutions;
- Lack of integration and harmonisation of ICTs systems, initiatives and activities (leading to wastage of financial, material, human and other resources);
- Limited levels of e-Championship at the highest political and technical levels;
- Widening digital divide between rural and urban communities;

- Lack of enabling legal frameworks (e-transactions, Public Private Partnerships, etc.);
- Lack of a functional and effective Monitoring and Evaluation framework for ICTs/e-government initiatives;
- Limited operationalisation of the National ICTs policy;
- Inadequate practice of the participatory/all-inclusive national planning process;
- Lack of scientific, transparent and universally agreed upon national prioritisation Framework that would facilitate ranking of national development priorities for each planning and development period;
- Inadequate capacity (human, institutional, technological and financial resources).

Within this context, the Inter Agency Team recognised the importance of ICTs in national development, being central to the pursuit of productivity driven growth in all sectors of the economy, hence, having a cross-cutting impact, and stated the need to develop a long-term comprehensive national programme to promote ICTs awareness, confidence and utilisation in public and private sector institutions including those of communities.

The Inter Agency Team had the objective of co-ordinating activities intended to make the National e-government Strategy framework operational. This was prepared under the guidance of the Inter-Ministerial Committee, formed to spearhead the formulation and implementation of the National ICTs Policy 2003. The Committee is co-ordinated by the Uganda National Council of Science and Technology (UNCST) and its secretariat is at the Uganda Communication Commission (UCC). Other initiatives carried out by the Committee include the establishment of the e-government Task Force, under the chair of the Ministry of Works, Housing and Communications (MoWHC).

During the first two meetings of the Inter Agency Team, the need for involvement of all interested stakeholders, and the commitment at the highest political level was underlined. The participation of the Office of the President is a positive contribution to the possibility for increasing the minimal e-Championship of the Presidency so far.

The participants also called for a greater appreciation of ICTs in the country by integrating ICTs in the National Development Planning Framework. It was also resolved that the committee should take advantage of the ongoing national budgeting item in their medium term and annual plans and, on a long term basis, it was recommended that the government should be lobbied to designate a Ministry solely responsible for the ICTs sector regulation and development, in line with the recommendations from regional and international organisations.

In order to implement these decisions, participants called for a national round table meeting involving all stakeholder institutions to harmonise and rationalise ICTs sector development policies, plans and activities. This process would lead to the formulation of Vision 2035 and multi-annual, annual national and sectoral plans of action.

7.2. THE DISTRICTNET PROJECT

7.2.1. Background and Justification

Districts, counties, sub-counties and parishes have been empowered by the Uganda "Local Government Act 1997" to be self-governing. This means that planning and implementing projects, identifying revenue streams and managing revenue and human resources, budgeting and control are now done by local governments and not central government. In the local government structure, the district acts as a focal point to account for resources while lower councils act as centres for implementing district programmes.

The District Local Government (LC V) and the sub-county local governments (LC III) are the most important administrative units in the district local government, as per the Local Government Act 1997. At present there are 56 Districts with over 900 sub-counties in Uganda.

A lot of financial resources (from both donors and the government) are going into financing various projects at local councils level in various districts. The concern in all cases has been that money must be used for the purpose for which it was intended. The overall management of a local council now requires that the council make considerable investment in human resources and infrastructure to manage these increased responsibilities.

To discuss these issues, a Roundtable Workshop with the theme "ICTs for Rural Development" was held in March 2001, in Jinja, with participants from rural and upcountry institutions in the public and private sectors. Four pilot districts of Kayunga, Lira, Mbale and Mbarara were represented, including senior district officials. A number of ICTs projects were proposed and prioritised. One of the six projects selected was the District Administrative Network Programme (DistrictNet) at the district headquarters and lower local government and council level.

A project proposal was then finalised by the districts to support and complement the ongoing process of policy decentralisation and public participation.

The major problems identified during the workshop and which resulted in the DistrictNet project were:

- Lack of a convenient mode of communication between the district and the lower local governments, leading to poor follow-up and co-ordination of activities, which further resulted in delays and inaccuracies;
- Poor delivery of public services due to inefficient record keeping of a variety of paper based data and information, including council minutes and statistical data. This resulted in records being lost and those which were available were in a form that made it difficult to find and share information;
- Financial records were maintained and processed manually, and often not up-to-date and inaccurate leading to a lack of transparency and accountability;
- Public information on government programmes was lacking due to an absence of information in a publicly useable format, resulting in limited transparency and public participation.

To mitigate these problems DistrictNet was designed and implemented, as an attempt to support the overall objective of the decentralisation programme by providing the district and lower councils with tools and infrastructure to handle increased responsibilities and, at the same time, promoting transparency and improving the provision of public information.

DistrictNet is funded by the International Institute for Communication Development (IICD) in collaboration with the Department for International Development (DFID) of the United Kingdom, the Ministry of Local Government and the beneficiary Districts.

The districts manage the project, with the support of the Ministry of Local Government, as pioneers for the benefit of a future possible national approach.

7.2.2. Strategy and Objectives

The project aim was to improve the performance of local governments by establishing functional data/information management and public communication systems for effective and efficient decentralised service delivery.

Based on the analysis of the administrative activities at the district/Sub-County headquarters and the findings on the infrastructure available then, DistrictNet was conceived to improve performance in a number of specific areas:

- To reduce administrative costs by providing a quick and direct means of communication between districts, lower councils and central government.
- To improve the overall efficiency of the district by introducing a common and shareable databank that could be used by all officials (the executive and civil servants) at the district and lower governments level.
- To provide interface/linkages with external parties and sources of information so that information is available to all key stakeholders.
- To train local government staff in basic ICTs skills and on the technical solutions being provided under the project.
- To improve on the accuracy of service delivery data; and
- To enhance transparency and accountability and strengthen the public information function in local governments.

7.2.3. Rationale and Structure

During the first year, the project was planned to be implemented in the four pilot district headquarters and 11 sub-counties. External donor funding was secured to finance the first/pilot year's investments and some of the operational costs. The districts and the Ministry of Local Government (MoLG) also contributed to some of the set up costs in the pilot year.

The four pilot districts were selected so that there would be one from each of the four 'regions' of Uganda. Additionally a 'new district' was required to have the experience of the unique challenges of such districts, hence the choice of Kayunga District. They contain a total of 112 sub-counties, distributed as follows:

- Kayunga District: 09 Sub-counties
- Lira District: 25 Sub-counties
- Mbale District: 31 Sub-counties
- Mbarara District: 47 Sub-counties

During and following the pilot year, it was expected that the benefits of the project would emerge, and useful lessons learned. The project also provided for a seminar to share experience, with other districts, but it was not within the scope of the project to roll out to all districts and sub-counties. However, it was planned that 11 more sub-counties were to be covered during the second year, and a further 21 sub-counties in the third year, in the four pilot districts only.

Moreover, considering that many government programmes and projects were already focussing on building the capacity of local governments to manage their affairs more efficiently and more transparently, the project proposed to set up a Steering Committee to, among other things, liaise with other districts and other Ministries to ensure rollout of the project to the remaining sub-counties and districts. In the pilot phase, the project plan was to:

- Introduce data and voice communication links between districts and lower local governments; and
- Introduce electronic data processing in financial management, data communication, data storage and analysis.

The technical solutions to be adopted involved:

- Installing a Local Area Network (LAN) with a file/email/internet server and at least 10 personal computers (PCs). In addition, installing one PC in each sub-county.
- Installing a data/voice communication link between district headquarters and the pilot sub-counties. The minimum requirement for data is access to an email service. A variety of technologies were proposed to be used, depending on the connectivity infrastructure present. Connectivity solutions included a fixed land line with a modem, mobile phone with data accessories, HF radio with data

accessories, Broadband wireless radio with data and voice channels and VSAT terminals.

- Setting up a computerised data bank, vote books, work plans, financial accounting and report preparation; and
- Starting a training programme for users in basic ICTs skills, and use of computerised applications.

The districts were intended to fund investments and operational costs from their budget after the pilot year, including all sources of revenue for the districts, which include Internal (District) tax collections, budget support from central government and donor funding.

7.2.4. Organisation and Management Arrangements

The Project owners are the District Local Governments of the pilot districts.

The Chairman of Kayunga District Local Council, Eng. Stephen Dagada, had the responsibility of co-ordinating project implementation between districts for the first year, a role that was planned to rotate to other District Chairpersons annually. Actually, given the quality of the leadership of Eng. Dagada, he was reconfirmed as Co-ordinator of the project for the entire period of execution and for its future implementation.

DistrictNet's organisation was innovative within the public sector. In order to be successful, it required sufficient staff time with external support. It was fundamental that District Councils allowed for sufficient staff time. The project was planned to be implemented as a mainstreamed activity within each pilot district, and the District Executive was to oversee its implementation as part of its normal duties. A Project Implementation Team (PIT) of three persons was formed in each district, headed by the Chief Administrative Officer. The implementation team consisted of executives of the district council together with the civil servants of the pilot districts and sub-counties in the pilot districts. The PIT had to spend at least two person-days each per month on project implementation during the first year. A "Technical Manager/User Support Officer" was hired in each district on a fulltime basis in the first year to ensure adequate human resources to start the project. However, the Ministry of Local Government (MoLG) was involved in the implementation of the project as external "Technical

Figure 1. Eng Steven Dagada and Gianluca Misuraca at the Nile River after visiting the Project's site in the Kayunga District.

Advisor", and providing facilitators and materials for awareness seminars and ICTs skills training.

The financial plan has been drawn up showing investments, expenses and revenues over a five-year period. The project started with ICTs installations in a limited number of sub-counties, to be expanded later. Investments were to be made in the four districts' headquarters and 11 sub-counties in the first year, with an additional 11 sub-counties in the second year and completion in the third year. Development of information management and sharing mechanisms was planned to take place in the first year, with more district officers benefitting from the results as the project progressed. The total budget is shown below. It includes both the financial contribution of the donor agency (DFID through IICD) and the Ministry of Local Government and Districts.

DistrictNet's Project – Budget:

Description	Cost (in Uganda Shillings)
Operational Revenue	0
Finance: District Budget	480.123
Ministry of Local Government Contribution	144.863
Finance: Donors	289.000
TOTAL INFLOW	**922.986**
Investments	417.833
Operational Costs	504.006
Interest on Loan	0
TOTAL OUTFLOW	**921.839**
Cash-flow	1.147
Accumulated Cash-flow	5.409

Source: IICD, DistrictNet (Pilot Phase), Finance Account, 2004.

The external funding was originally ensured for eighteen months, but a second refinancing by IICD was decided in 2005.

An important role in the project was played by the Chief Administrative Officer of each of the pilot districts, this functioned as the Technical Project Planning Group.

One of the main challenges arising from this project was how to rollout to other districts and sub-counties. One way to assist the rollout process was to ensure co-ordination of the leading role of the four pilot districts and other relevant stakeholders, including other districts, Governments Ministries and development agencies with similar initiatives. For this purpose the project proposed to establish a **Steering Committee** with the following membership:

- The Four Pilot Districts (Represented by the Chief Administrative Officer);
- Ministry of Local Government;
- Ministry of Finance, Planning and Economic Development;
- Uganda Local Authorities Association ;
- National NGO Forum;
- IICD (with advisory role).

The role of the Steering Committee included:

- Promoting the harmonisation of ICTs solutions, especially software implementation;
- Ensuring harmonisation with existing projects similar to this project;
- Ensuring that the lessons learned in the 4 pilot districts will be shared with other districts.

The Ministry of Local Government functioned as a "secretariat" for the Steering Committee.

7.2.5. Activities and Results

a) Strategic and Technical management support

The implementation of the project followed a detailed project implementation plan, under the wise leadership of the project's co-ordinator, the Ministry of Local Government and IICD.

The first activity was the appointment of a steering committee comprised of the Permanent Secretary of the Ministry of Local Government, a representative of the Permanent Secretary, Ministry of Finance, Planning and Economic Development, Uganda Local Authority Association, Chief Administrative officers and the chairpersons of the pilot districts.

Under the four pilot districts, different officers were appointed to be part of the project technical implementation team (PIT). These included; the District Planner, Information Officer, PIT co-ordinator, Sector Heads of Departments and a representative from the Chief Administrative Officer's office. A district PIT Co-ordinator was appointed. A communication by each district on the composition of the PIT team and its co-ordinator was submitted to the Permanent Secretary, Ministry of Local Government.

In addition to the PIT, dedicated ICTs support officers for each of the pilot districts, instead of one Technical Manager handling all the districts, were recruited by the Ministry of Local Government to ensure full time backup, technical support and guidance to the local governments.

To ensure sustainability and ownership, all the four pilot districts opened up DistrictNet project accounts. Each district made a contribution of 8 million Ugandan shillings for the local project operational costs. The main project account was opened by the Ministry of Local Government to which funds were transferred from the IICD.

b) Sensitisation and awareness creation

DistrictNet Project's awareness was carried out in all the pilot districts and other fora by the technical implementation team i.e. the National Co-ordinator, the Project Technical Manager, ICTs officers and the district project implementation teams.

A one day awareness seminar in each of the four pilots was held. The district officials were sensitised on the importance and uses of ICTs and the benefits of the project in general.

Dissemination of information about the project were also ensured by IICD and specific informative workshops were held at the beginning ("kick-off"), medium term and final stage of the first phase of the project.

To reinforce awareness building, for this and other initiatives, IICD contributed to establishing the I-Network Uganda, the main objective of which is to advocate the use of ICTs for rural development, especially considering that Ugandan poverty largely occurs in rural areas, varying from 60 to 70 percent.

c) Installation of equipment and development of databases

Soon after the "kick-off" of the project, an ICTs infrastructure site survey was carried out in each of the pilot districts by the ICTs officers together with two engineers from One2net (a local company) both at district and sub-county levels. During the survey different solutions for the LAN, internet/email connectivity and telephone intercom were proposed, taking the distance into consideration, an Internet point of presence (POP) and electricity structures among others. A report with the findings (technical specifications) of the required items was produced. This provided a guideline on what hardware and software solutions to acquire.

Based upon the results of the survey, the installation of a Local Area Network (LAN) and a Wide Area Network (WAN) started, including email and internet systems, as well as data and voice communication networks within district headquarters, and between these and the pilot sub-counties and the central government headquarters (Ministry of Local Government).

In some cases, solar panels were installed in those sub-counties which had no power, apart from Lira Local Government whose sub-counties are still faced with insecurity. User acceptance tests were carried out and acceptance certificates issued by the local governments after completion of the works by the contractors who carried out the installations.

Figure 2. A satellite dish for communication, installed in a District in Uganda (photo made available by Arjan De Jager, IICD)

Also database systems were developed and rolled out to the districts to facilitate data collection, entry, analysis and generation of reports for planning and decision making functions. These database systems included:

1. Local Government information communication System (LoGICS)

LoGICS is a database system, designed to help Local Governments (LGs) monitor their own performance. Although the reports LoGICS produces may be useful to Ministries and outsiders (such as donors), the system was primarily designed to benefit local governments by providing them with data for use during planning and other decision making functions.

2. Local Government Financial Information and Analysis System (LoGFIAS)

LoGFIAS is a database system that stores, processes and analyses revenue and expenditure data. This system enables LGs to track their performance with regard to revenue and expenditure processes and projections.

3. Lower Local Government Revenue Master (LLGRM)

LLGRM is a database system designed to assist sub-counties and to collect and analyse data on Graduated Tax (GT) collections. This tool enables management of GT up to the village level, helping to track tax defaulters and duplicate tax tickets among other items.

In order to develop and implement the databases and the relative information gathering process, an Information Flow Analysis within local governments was carried out by the technical team of the Ministry of Local Government, with the backup support of two IICD Consultants. The main objective of carrying out the information flow analysis was to strengthen information dissemination in local governments. The output of the exercise provided an insight in the flow of information from the databases for officers involved in information dissemination at Higher Local Government Level (LC5 and LC4) so that they could strengthen their linkages with the planning Offices at LC5, LC2 (Parish or ward) and LC3 (Division, sub-county or town council)

d) Capacity Building and technical training

An important aspect of the project was that, through DistrictNet, the Ministry of Local Government initiated an extensive training programme for users (district officials) in basic ICTs skills and the use of basic computer applications.

A first "Information and dissemination skills training workshop" was organised with a main objective being to equip key district officials involved in the dissemination of information within and outside the district (i.e. the District Planners, Community Development Officers and Information Officers) with information dissemination skills.

The specific objectives of the training were to:

1. Equip participants on how to use existing database systems e.g. LoGICS to generate and disseminate information about their districts;
2. Equip participants with desktop publishing skills;

3. Equip participants with skills in website updating;
4. Train participants in media and information packaging;
5. Enlighten participants on the different methods of information dissemination e.g. print and electronic media.

At the end of the workshop, participants developed an action plan and a workplan on how they would carry out what had been learned during the workshop, in their respective districts. Some funds were assigned for this particular purpose. Follow up activities by the technical team were carried out to ensure that the expected outputs were attained.

After the first workshop, a training needs assessment was carried out, in all the four pilot districts, which formed the basis for the development of relevant basic computer application training materials. Development of the training materials was carried out under the guidance of a local consultant (International Data Network). As an output of the assessment, training manuals were designed covering four modules including; computer appreciation, Windows operating system, Microsoft Word and Excel, the Internet and email.

Figure 3. A training room equipped in a District in Uganda (photo made available by Arjan De Jager, IICD)

Following this, basic ICTs skills training of the district staff was carried out in the pilot districts, a four day programme per district.

The district headquarter staff was trained first since there were already easily available computers at the district which had been supplied under other existing projects and programmes. Each district had fift of its staff trained. The participants were trained on the four modules for which the manuals were developed.

Also basic ICTs skills training for the pilot sub-county staff was carried out in the Local Governments of Mbale, Mbarara and Kayunga. Due to the insecurity in the Northern region, training of sub-county staff in Lira was not conducted. The sub-county staff were trained at the district premises using the computers procured under the District-Net Project. Three members (Chief, Accountant and Chairperson) per sub-county were invited for the training. The participants were trained on the four modules mentioned above.

At the end of each session, participants evaluated the training. Key responses from the evaluation were: there was a need for more training on the internet/email, training time was too limited, there was the need for customised training packages especially in financial management, database management and statistical analysis among other things.

7.3. CONCLUSIONS

7.3.1. Impact on decentralisation policy

ICTs in local governance in Uganda have been identified as major tools for achieving socio-economic development. In order for government to implement the long term national development programmes, timely and relevant information must be available at all levels of implementation. The National ICTs Policy Framework (2003) was intended to stimulate more participation in the socio-economic-political and other developmental activities, so as to lead to improved standards of living for the majority of Ugandans and enhance sustainable national development.

So far, the four pilot districts where the project was implemented have made savings in administrative expenses thus freeing these funds to be used for other more pressing economic activities geared towards economic development initiatives. This is also due to the fact that, in addition to improvement in the communication channels, users now have easier access to useful information for planning purposes.

In social terms, the communities in the districts covered by the project have been sensitised to the usefulness of utilising ICTs and how these technologies can bolster development. One of the main results is that there is now an increasing demand for accurate and timely information, from technical staff, by the politicians to support their decision making functions.

A project evaluation report was released in January 2005. It was based upon answers to a questionnaire distributed to forty end users of the DistrictNet: 83% were staff and the rest Heads of Departments in the Ministry of Local Government.

50% of the respondents gave a positive feed-back, due to the improvement of their ICTs knowledge; 35% saw an improvement in the flow of information and communication with the Ministry of Local Government, and 15% because of the possibility of having access to a broader information and knowledge-base via the Internet. A total of 38% of respondents said that they had already benefitted from the project: 50% because of the improvement in their work and 50% due to the improvement in using ICTs.

In describing the positive impact of DistrictNet, 53% of the respondents said that the project enabled them to improve ICTs awareness, while 25% claimed to have been empowered to make informed decisions in their departments using their new ICTs skills. In addition, 25% thought they had been motivated by the decreased costs in their work and 20% had seen an improvement in reporting, documentation management and levels of transparency.

Thus, higher levels of ICTs awareness are now helping development and this success has been duly noted: Members of the Parliament have in fact promised to ensure the resources to roll out DistrictNet to the rest of the country.

In fact, the project has now achieved a strong appeal in other districts. Reinforcing ICTs infrastructure and capacities is really viewed as a key component in the development of local governance systems. Once completed, the transformation of a district's administrative structure and general operating systems, the districts are in a position to communicate fully with sub- counties and the central government through increased used of computers for documentation, storage, transfer of information and file sharing.

This allows for a reduction in the costs of communication (e.g. transport and production of documentation) and an increase of public information and service delivery, as well as easier and more accurate data collection through the use of standardised pre-designed forms.

All this will allow the constituents (citizens and private companies) to better interact with the local government, thus enhancing their capacity to produce socio-economic development at the local level.

Figure 4. Department of Education, Kayunga District Council; one of the sites of the DistrictNet Project.

7.3.2. Obstacles and challenges in implementation

Despite the success of the project in its pilot phase and the mentioned interest in replicating similar initiatives in other districts and some sub-countries not covered, it is critical that the pilot project is recognised as a success by completion of the implementation. In fact, some obstacles have been encountered in the implementation of activities, delaying its completion.

One of the main problems is related to the delays in the procurement process (government procurement systems) that resulted also in delays of contractual arrangements and in the supply of equipment by some providers.

This produced a limited impact of the training activities, since in some cases training was not supported by the presence of equipment.

There were also some delays in carrying out scheduled training due to busy schedules in the districts, as well as delays in releasing project co-funding by the districts.

Moreover, the training workshops lasted only two days and this was considered not sufficient for learning the system. A number of staff needed additional training to master the specifics of the packages and programmes. Limited ICTs skills in the pilot districts and sub-counties still remain, and so some of the equipment was underused due to lack of knowledge. Another obstacle came from the inadequate transport facilities for the ICTs support officers to go to the various sub-counties for follow-up and back stopping. This necessitated some full time technical staff being seconded from the Ministry of Local Government to go to the districts for trouble shooting.

Financial resources resulted in not being fully adequate to purchase technical equipment not previously budgeted for i.e. technical support equipment for maintenance purposes, and there were limited options for connectivity solutions especially in sub-counties.

Internet connectivity is still a problem in all the districts, although it has been tested in Kayunga, Lira and Mbale. In the specific case of Lira district, problems of insecurity threatened the effective implementation of activities. In particular, despite the need to link up with the sub-counties, technology compatibility is still not achieved, and as a result the effective connection with sub-counties is not yet a reality.

In all, despite the sub objective being fulfilled, the project (at the time of the mission) was not yet completed. The success of the project is perceived to be measured by Internet connectivity and the sub-countys' ability to communicate with the districts' Chief Administration Officer (CAO).

It was also noted that the sub-county Chiefs were not fully informed of the planned activities and benefits of the project. Some were not aware of the equipment expected on completion of it. Moreover, the PIT did not meet regularly to review the progress of the project, only the technical managers met regularly. This was despite the fact that it was necessary for monitoring and policy advice for the PIT to meet on a quarterly basis, as well as having a more regular external and independent assessment based on clearly identified indicators.

7.3.3. Lessons Learned

The pilot phase of the project, and in particular its assessment and evaluation, outlined a number of recommendations and lessons learned that should enable the completion of the activities still to be fulfilled in a successful manner, and provide elements for further implementation and generalisation, through replicability. These elements apply to this project, but also have a broader relevance.

First of all, despite the very positive approach undertaken since the beginning, with the full involvement of all relevant stakeholders: political and technical staff of local and central governments, what has to be underlined is the need to enhance the role of the National Co-ordinator in the policy implementation and monitoring of the completed and uncompleted activities.

Ownership of the project is important to be claimed at the district level. Therefore a specific process of transfer from the Ministry of Local Government to the districts is required, eventually identifying a Technical Manager employed by the four districts, who will report directly to them.

Specific attention has also to be given to the management of funds, and the tendering process, that should be shifted to the local district boards.

The districts should be in position to supervise the contractors employed to implement the project or install equipment. Central reporting leaves gaps in the response to some of the project objectives. This is also valid for the procurement of equipment. That however should be given to a third party, to ensure impartiality and efficiency. Nevertheless, the Ministry of Local Government should have a role as Technical Supervisor.

Communication between the district staff and the Local Ministry staff should be improved to allow all stakeholders to share in the implementation snags.

At the same time, leaders at the district should be educated about the project before the junior staff, so that they can promote and encourage staff to adopt and use the system. This will in turn increase their appreciation of the programmes.

To avoid problems due to limited technical skills for maintenance, a specific budget line to take care of maintenance should be identified and made available also when there is the need to purchase unplanned for equipment. This should be complemented by the design of a specific maintenance strategy and technical backstopping plan. At the least each district should have a dedicated maintenance officer in order to avoid importing technicians from the central government based in Kampala or using incompetent technicians in the towns.

A policy on information backup should be developed and adopted by the district to safeguard data storage. Staff in the district registry were still reluctant about the new development due to their feelings about the unknown cost of information loss. This should be handed over to a fully fledged information department which is headed by a competent ICTs manager with at least one or two support technicians who have knowledge of data storage and network troubleshooting skills.

With regard to the training of staff, a structured training programme is required, so as to engage in an effective "transfer" of skills from trained to other officials. This could be done through holding some "training of trainers" courses, in addition to the technical training, guaranteeing that enabling staff learn from the job and have a continuous update in new technologies. Eventually, it could also be complemented by having a specific resource person who works for more than one district.

Finally, the assessment and evaluation exercise should be more frequent and be supported by the development of monitoring and evaluation frameworks, both at district level and at the Ministry of Local Government. This will also facilitate building awareness of the importance of the project among community leaders, thus ensuring long-term sustainability of the activities.

7.3.4. The way forward: the future of DistrictNet

By the start of 2005, the project had entered into a mainstreaming phase, and has now acquired private sector partners in addition to local and central government, IICD and DFID.

During the **Final Workshop of the Project, (Ridar Hotel, Seeta, 17th.-18th. May, 2005)**, the activities of the Pilot Phase of the Project, from its inception to its conclusion, and the final report of evaluation were presented, assessed and discussed. The workshop also discussed the main challenges and obstacles encountered and the need for improvements to complete the Pilot Phase (by an extension of the project) as well as to plan the way forward. This was done through presentations and discussion in plenary sessions and workgroups. The workshop was attended by about 30 participants, including the Chairpersons of Kayunga, Lira and Mbale Districts. As a result of the overall implementation of the project, it can be said that today, there is a fast growing realisation in Uganda that e-governance can bring individuals into close contact with decision makers and officials in the government, especially at the local level.

But e-governance can only be implemented effectively if the right human, technological and financial resources are available and the citizens are ICTs literate and sensitised. As a result, the government is currently in the process of acquiring more funding to extend the project to other districts.

This is based on the lesson that is learned by many projects all over the world "think big, start small, scale fast"! The pilot activities are in fact now under analysis in order to be replicated in other projects and implemented in other districts, through a national programme.

However, the growth and significance of the project will depend on the effort by the Ministry of Local Government, working together with other ministries and districts, to integrate all operations and, in particular the database, to avoid duplication.

It is therefore important that the Ministry of Local Government should maintain control on the design and choice of technologies so as to ensure standardisation and interoperability.

It is also pivotal to reinforce the dissemination activities, through advocacy campaigns and specific national and local workshops. In particular, the importance of data collection and information management should be raised, especially at the lower level of government.

Hopefully a result of the process in the action to "scale up" DistrictNet, will be the possibility of creating a "multiplier effect", encouraging local governments (both districts and sub-counties), to invest their own resources in ICTs equipment and training, as well as to develop planning and assessment activities at the lower local level.

To have a greater impact, it is also envisaged that districts and the national government will continue to follow the participatory model that is at the heart of "DistrictNet", and include all stakeholders and beneficiaries when designing the projects.

The current approach of "networking-communities" developed for example in the "I-Network Uganda", as well as the national Inter Agency Team, is promising, but there is still the need to undertake research in appropriate technology that is free or affordable, especially for the marginalised groups like the disabled, the illiterate, and use ICTs for rural transformation. It is also important to research on how ICTs can effectively transform the agricultural sector in Uganda and increase household income. This will involve the implementation of large-scale projects, which call for research in areas such as information system design and management in order to minimise project failures.

There is also the need to undertake research on how ICTs can improve health service delivery especially among the poor in the rural areas. These could be some additional components of a further broader "DistrictNet" Programme in Uganda.

References

Baryamureeba Venansius, State of ICTs and Local Governance, Needs Analysis and Research Priorities in Uganda, Report to the CAFRAD/IDRC LOG-IN Africa Pre-Project Consultative Meeting, Nairobi, 3rd.-5th. September, 2005;

Bitwayiki Constantine, Ministry of Local Government, District Administrative Network Programme, Implementation Report, draft - September 2004;

Dagada, Eng. Stephen, District Net Chairperson – Communications to the Local Government P. Secretary;

De Jager, Arjan, IICD, Programme Manager, Presentations to the "District Net Final Workshop", Seeta, Uganda, 17th.-18th. May 2005;

FIT Uganda Consultants, DistrictNet Uganda: Output to Purpose Review, Draft Report by Robert Kintu & Enoth Mbeine, 4th.October 2004;

FIT Uganda Consultants, DistrictNet Uganda: Project Completion Report, by Robert Kintu & Enoth Mbeine, draft May 2005;

International Institute for Communication and Development (IICD), and the District Local Governments of Kayunga, Lira, Mbale and Mbarara, ICTs Round Table Process, Project Proposal: District Administrative Network Programme, Kampala, 11th. February 2002;

International Institute for Communication and Development (IICD) and United Nations Economic Commission for Africa (UNECA), "i-connect collected: experiences in ICTs for education, livelihoods and governance in six African countries", October 2005;

I-Network Uganda Newsletter, Volume 4, N.1, April 2005;

Laws of the Republic of Uganda. Revised Edition. Vol. I. 2000

Ministry of Finance, Planning, and Economic development, Poverty Eradication Action Plan 2004/05 – 2007/08

Ministry of Local Government, Ministerial Policy Statement for Financial Year 2003/2004. Kampala, June 2003.

Ministry of works, Housing and Communications, National ICTs Policy. Kampala, 2002

Ministry of works, Housing and Communications, National ICTs Policy for Uganda Implementation Framework, Final Draft Report, Feb 2005

National Planning Authority, e-government Strategy Framework for Uganda (Draft). Kampala, August 2005.

National Task Force for the Development of the ICTs Master Plan, Final Report on e-government Strategy and Action Plan.

Uganda Communications Commission, Telecommunications Sector Policy 2005

Uganda, Telecommunication Sector Performance and E-Usage, Draft Final, Research ICTs Africa, April 2005.

Weddi David, "Transforming local government: e-governance in Uganda, in "i-connect collected: experiences in ICTs for education, livelihoods and governance in six African countries", IICD/UNECA, October 2005.

8

CAPE TOWN'S "SMART CITY" STRATEGY IN SOUTH AFRICA

CASE STUDY OVERVIEW

It includes a number of projects and in particular the Ukuntinga Project.

Location: Cape Town, Western Cape, South Africa,

Funding Institution: City of Cape Town and, in some cases Provincial and National Governments

Executing Institution:

City of Cape Town

Project Manager:

Ms. Mymoena Sharif (Manager e-governance, Smart City Project, City of Cape Town

Total Budget: South African Rands (SAR) 355 million (it refers to the Ukuntinga Project).

Project Start Date: 2001

Project End Date: 2005

Administrative Information and Contacts:

City of Cape Town

Cape Town Civic Centre, Cape Town, South Africa

Tel. (021) 400 1111 – Fax (021) 400 1332,

email: mymoena.sharif@capetown.gov.za

Web site: www.capetwon..gov.za

8.1. CONTEXT AND POLICY

8.1.1. South African economic wave and the role of Public Sector and ICTs

While South Africa represents only 3% of the continent's surface area, it accounts for approximately 40% of all industrial output and 25% of gross domestic product (GDP) of all Africa. More than half of the electricity generated in the continent and 45% of mineral production is from South Africa.

The growth of the South African economy has averaged 3.2% a year over the past four years and there are expectations of it improving over the next three years to between 4% and 4.5% due to the sound macroeconomic performance and monetary management and improved competitiveness, among others. The inflation rate has generally declined over the past year and the Consumer Price Index (CPIX) inflation measure was expected to average 4.8% in 2004. The prime overdraft interest rate has declined from 17% at the beginning of 2003 to 13.5% at present, and the Reserve Bank expected to meet in 2005 its inflation target of consumer price inflation between 3% and 6%, after falling to 4.3% for the year 2004. Real income per person over the past decade has increased by 15% and, with an average growth projected at more than 4% a year over the period ahead, real per capita income is expected to rise by at least 30% in the second decade of freedom. Empowerment targets and transformation initiatives in education, employment and procurement are contributing to better racial and gender representation. Corporate restructuring and equity participation schemes have brought changes to the ownership, management and strategic direction of many companies.

However, the income distribution remains highly unequal and the unemployment rate is about 40% of the working population. There are many constraints due to the high rate of HIV/Aids, infrastructure weaknesses, a deficit in industrial and trade policy, technological backlogs, skills shortages and poor flows of Foreign Direct Investments (FDI).

This complex situation must be looked at, also considering that South Africa became a democratic, non-racial state in 1994, after a protracted liberation struggle against the Apartheid regime, which had been characterised by colonialism, racialism and repressive laws.

Following the demise of apartheid and transition to democracy, the new constitution (**The Constitution of the Republic of South Africa 1996, Act 108**) provides for a common South African citizenship, with all citizens having equal access to the rights, privileges and benefits. South Africa is also one of the few countries on the continent with a constitution which entrenches democracy, eliminates all forms of discrimination, promotes and protects human rights but also strives to attain socio-economic rights for all.

The fact that the South African government has placed the need to address poverty and inequality firmly at the centre of its development strategy agenda is reflected in the various development policy documents and strategies that have been developed in the few years that the government has been in power.

The government development strategy was first articulated in 1994 in the original **Reconstruction and Development Programme (RDP)**, 1994-1996, in which the African National Congress (ANC) sought "to mobilize all our people and our country's resources towards the final eradication of apartheid and the building of a democratic, non-racial and non-sexist future". The programme envisaged to attain socio-economic growth and basic needs delivery, while at the same time addressing the legacy of injustice. The RDP put emphasis on "people-centred development", "integrated development" and "sustainable development" that is democratic and participatory.

The RDP proposed several dimensions that should be addressed to achieve socio-economic transformation of the South African society. It further set out various socio-economic commitments and targets for delivery, providing an overarching policy for sustainable development, which sought to transform South African society.

The **White Paper on the Reconstruction and Development Programme**, 1995 refined the 1994 RDP document and identified five goals that needed to be addressed in order to achieve socio-economic transformation of South African society. The fundamental goals of RDP were:

- To create a strong, dynamic and balanced economy in order to eliminate poverty and meet the basic needs of every South African;
- Develop human resource capacity of all South Africans;
- Ensure that no one suffers racial or gender discrimination in hiring, promotion or training situations;
- Develop a prosperous, balanced regional economy in Southern Africa; and
- Democratise the state and society.

The RDP was expected to engineer growth, through increased public expenditures on social service provision. The RDP put emphasis on programmes to meet basic needs and enhance human resource development, placed a major emphasis on social infrastructure and development programmes that address poverty and inequality.

The RDP was also reinforced and supported by a number of implementation strategies, such as the Anti-Poverty Strategy, Integrated Sustainable Rural Development Strategy and Urban Development Strategy. These policy documents formed the core of local economic development (LED) policy.

Thus, during the 1994-1996 period, the RDP was viewed as the cornerstone of government development policy, a yardstick against which the success of the government development policy could be assessed. However, according to many policy analysts, as a development policy document, the RDP had a number of shortcomings. First, it looked more like a "wish list" than a strategy document focusing on opportunities and constraints. Second, it made no attempt to set priorities; or to assign responsibility for the implementation of each programme component. Third, it lacked mechanisms for inter-departmental coordination. Finally, local government, which has been assigned constitutional responsibility for promoting socio-economic development, did not have adequate planning and implementation capacity.

In any case, while the government appeared to have been satisfied with the RDP's broadly humanitarian thrusts, problems began to surface from 1995. The economy, in particular, was not growing at the envisaged rates. The sluggish performance of the economy in turn impacted negatively on the RDP, with achievements falling behind expectations. The welfare orientations of the Programme also came under critical scrutiny as investors and international financial institutions began demanding greater clarity on national economic policy. The release (in 1995) of the White Paper on RDP reflected the beginning of a significant shift towards economic pragmatism, specifically, towards increasingly free-market leanings.

This resulted in the development, in 1996, of the **Growth, Employment and Redistribution (GEAR)** framework. GEAR was introduced as the guiding force for government economic policy. It did not completely depart from earlier government policy but committed government to accelerating aspects of existing policy, albeit with a very significant compromise to the neo-liberal policy. Consequently, some of the policies initiated in the RDP were incorporated in the GEAR which subsequently replaced RDP in 1996.

The goals of the GEAR package of policies were:

- a competitive fast-growing economy which creates sufficient jobs for all work-seekers;
- a redistribution of income and opportunities in favour of the poor;
- a society in which sound health, education and other services are available to all; and
- an environment in which homes are secure and places of work are productive.

GEAR was designed to achieve high rates of economic growth, to expand the private sector, to improve output and employment, achieve fiscal reform and encourage trade and investment. Furthermore, GEAR sought to achieve redistribution and improvement in basic living conditions as a result of generally, revitalised economic performance. GEAR rests on the assumption that the expansion of the private sector would have a substantial impact on the economy, whilst the role of the state would largely be a facilitative one. The evolving thinking was that the re-distributive role of the RDP was to be attained by a more circuitous route.

In order to facilitate economic growth and the expansion of the private sector, the government undertook to reduce state spending and the budget deficit; reduce corporate taxes and relax foreign exchange controls. It further pledged to control inflation; promote privatisation, and encourage wage restraint: all goals which are prescribed as universal panaceas for development by the Bretton Woods institutions such as the World Bank and IMF.

According to GEAR, the results of such a strategy would be an economic growth rate of 6% per year by 2000, which in turn would generate up to 400,000 jobs per year, boost exports by over 8% per year and lead to a drastic improvement in social conditions. It was thus anticipated that in the period from 1996 to 2000, 1.35 million jobs would be created. Critical to the attainment of the goals was a significant increase in private investment and non-gold exports, together with increased state expenditure on social infrastructure.

Unfortunately, according to many analysts, much of the gains expected from the adoption of the measures were not achieved. In spite of the macro-economic changes established, South Africa's economic performance has been generally disappointing. GEAR failed to effectively attain many of its goals.

In spite of the South African government's commitment to development and reconstruction, explicitly stated in the various development policy documents since 1994, and that allowed the reform of development and sectoral policies to overcome the legacy of apartheid and consequently, to put in place the policy, legislative and institutional framework, however, a significant number of the population still is in greater poverty, and an ever-increasing percentage is unable to afford and/ or access basic needs.

In this context, there is a growing and deeper understanding of the importance of the role of public policy in shaping the distribution of income and opportunities through setting developmental objectives. These take into consideration the balance between direct income support, improved public services such as education, health and municipal services and investment in social infrastructure such as housing, water, sanitation, roads and public transport.

The issue of speeding up the pace of investments in communication, transportation, water and energy networks is a priority in the economic development of the country. There is also the need to strengthen the links between further education and training and workplace requirements through upgrading educational institutions and bringing industry and commerce into the governance system, ensuring that funds for skills development are more effectively used.

Some of these priorities are exclusively or mainly the responsibility of government; but, in some areas, and especially when it comes to the use of ICTs for development, it is clear that the public sector seeks to complement and reinforce private sector growth and initiative. In particular, this was required to improve the alignment between public investment for infrastructure and business development opportunities, especially if we consider that in 2004 about 60% of the national expenditure on ICTs (about 8 Million SAR) came from investment by government departments in ICTs solutions and, it was expected to grow in 2005 and in the following years.

In his **State of the Nation Address to the first joint sitting of the third democratic parliament on 21st. May, 2004, the President of the Republic Thabo Mbeki** addressed the urgent need for the public sector to leverage the significant amount of innovation created by private sector organisations in recent years and, in particular, enabling improved service delivery to the citizens.

This ambitious goal of transposing modern corporate practices into government operations is not new to the ears of the citizenry, as Mbeki's illustrious predecessor **Nelson Mandela** held a similar vision for the future of South African government. And although this utopian system is some way from being fully realised, the public sector has in recent years made great strides in building an improved service delivery platform from the legacy - and proprietary system dependant - quagmire of historic inefficiency.

Service delivery is now at the forefront of government agencies' minds. High customer service is no longer a goal but a minimum requirement and ICTs solutions can be deployed to move government from an assisted service to a more "self-service" model while creating a more efficient and less costly operational environment.

The journey towards an e-governance model is therefore a long one, with challenges for both the public sector embarking upon it, and the private sector, which is to provide the underpinnings of this venture. Along with the peculiar historical and infrastructural South African challenges, this process will require all the innovation and co-operation of both public and private ICTs organisations to achieve the desired end goal.

Within this framework, a pivotal role in transforming the public sector with its influence on procurement activities and driving government IT strategies from an holistic overview perspective is played by the State Information Technology Agency (SITA). This is to ensure that all agencies work towards similar goals on platforms that interoperate at an internal communications level.

Although the theory behind this mandate is good, private enterprises have had cause for concern in the past as SITA vacillated between fulfilling this role as facilitator and being at the same time a provider of essential services itself, thus playing on both sides of procuring and delivering ICTs services to the crucial public sector. However not being independent from it, the private enterprises with which it was meant to build mutually beneficial partnerships were put at a disadvantage in the actual delivery of the required services.

Under its new leadership, however, there seems to have been a complete turnaround with the redefinition of the deliverables and the core business of the Agency itself. This allowed the confidence of the private sector to be restored and enabled the Agency to focus on addressing the significant challenges that lie ahead on the public sector's road to transformation. The road that brings improvement of service delivery successfully in the public sector entails fostering meaningful relationships with the private sector to leverage the experience and skills effectively in these organisations for the benefit of the economy and of the citizenry.

8.1.2. Local governance Policy and Strategy: from exclusion to inclusion

Following the end of the apartheid in 1994, South Africa was given a rare and historic opportunity to transform local government to meet the challenges of the twenty-first century.

Apartheid was not the beginning of geographic, institutional and social separation at the local level. Segregation was already a policy by the time apartheid was introduced in 1948. However, the Group Areas Act, the key piece of apartheid legislation, instituted strict residential segregation and compulsory removal of black people to "own group" areas. Through spatial separation, influx control, and a policy of "own management for own areas", apartheid aimed to limit the extent to which affluent white municipalities would bear the financial burden of servicing disadvantaged black areas. The Group Areas Act restricted the permanent presence of Africans in urban areas through the pass system, and reserved a viable municipal revenue base for white areas by separating townships and industrial and commercial development.

Since then, apartheid has left its imprint on South Africa's human settlements and municipal institutions.

Transformation required an understanding of the historical role of local government in creating and perpetuating local separation and inequity and the impact of apartheid on municipal institutions. Equally important is the history of resistance to apartheid at the local level, and struggles against apartheid local government. Various attempts were made under apartheid to introduce "own management" structures for black residents at the local level. This was in part to compensate for restricted rights, and in part to bolster the political and economic privileges of racial exclusion. To some extent these forms of "own local government" acknowledged the permanent presence of black people in urban areas. However, they were designed to reinforce the policies of segregation and economic exclusion. But none had resources to make any real difference to the quality of life of their constituents.

As the 1984 uprising gathered momentum, civic and other community bodies started to organise, calling for social and economic conditions in townships and Bantustans, and protesting systematically against the way human settlements were spatially and economically distorted.

In the late 1980s the apartheid state attempted to prop up collapsing Black Local Authorities and calm political tensions by redirecting funds to disadvantaged areas. A system of ad-hoc intergovernmental grants was developed to channel resources to collapsing townships. Regional Services Councils and Joint Services Boards were established to channel funds to black areas. However, these interventions were "too little too late". By the late 1980s most townships and many homeland rural areas were effectively ungoverned, and it was clear that Black Local Authorities (or any similar structures) would never be viable.

The crisis opened up by the collapse of the apartheid local government system eventually led to the realisation that a new deal was needed. White municipalities, experiencing the financial impact of organised consumers, service and rent boycotts, began to enter into negotiations with township representatives. Initially these fora were little more than crisis management structures. However, these initial talks formed the basis for later local negotiations and the system of the current local government.

Local fora recognised that the legal constraints which separated black residents from the municipal tax base had to be addressed nationally. The popular slogan, "One City, One Tax Base", could only be realised through national legislation. Local fora collectively pushed for the establishment of a national forum, the Local Government Negotiating Forum.

Therefore, the crisis in local government was a major force leading to the national reform process which began in 1990. The Local Government Negotiating Forum framed the Agreement on Finance and Services, writing off arrears to Black Local Authorities. It also negotiated the Local Government Transition Act of 1993, which did not provide a blueprint for a new local government, but only mapped out three phases of transition that has then resulted in a wide diversity of forms of local government.

The Local Government Transition Act effectively "deracialised" the system of local government through the amalgamation of former racially-based structures. However, real transformation was yet to occur. The weaknesses of the Local Government Transition Act, such as its urban bias and the lack of structured support processes to enable municipalities to manage the change process, were reflected in the gap between municipal and rural areas.

While newly elected councils in many areas had made significant progress in addressing backlogs and extending services, they were still facing many constraints. The huge infrastructural disparities and inequalities resulting from apartheid local government remained. The transition process has clearly shown that delivery on new municipal mandates could not be achieved within the existing institutional framework.

So, the new Constitution of the Republic of South Africa (1996) envisaged a complete transformation of the local government system. In terms of the new Constitution, local government is a sphere of government in its own right and no longer a function of national or provincial government. It is a distinct sphere of government, interdependent and interrelated with the national and provincial spheres. Municipalities have the right to govern, on their own initiative, the local government affairs of their community, subject to national and provincial legislation. They are required to give priority to the basic needs of the community, promote the social and economic development of the community, and participate in national and provincial development programmes. Local government has thus been given a distinctive status and role in building democracy and promoting socio-economic development. Its functions are in fact to:

- Provide democratic and accountable government for local communities.
- Ensure the provision of services to communities in a sustainable manner.

- Promote social and economic development.
- Promote a safe and healthy environment.
- Encourage the involvement of communities and community organisations in the matters of local government.

This mandate places local government at the centre of building local environments in which communities can develop and grow. The task is daunting: apartheid has fundamentally damaged the spatial, social and economic environment in which people live, work, raise families, and seek to fulfil their aspirations. Local government can only rise to the challenge of reversing the legacy of the past, and constructing sustainable living environments for the future, if municipalities are financially and institutionally empowered. It was therefore critical to transform and build the capacity of local government.

Local government must also promote the Bill of Rights, which reflects the nation's values about human dignity, equality and freedom, and uphold the principles enshrined in the Constitution.

Within the framework of the Constitution, the vision for local government is that it should be developmental. It should exercise its powers and functions in a way which maximises the social development and economic growth of communities. It should plan and manage development in an integrated and sustainable manner and promote spatial and social integration.

Local government should be responsive and accountable and deliver services which meet community needs in an efficient and equitable manner. It should seek to promote democratic values, both within the community and within its institutions.

But the process was still incomplete: so, in 1997, The Ministry for Provincial Affairs and Constitutional Development embarked on a policy process to give effect to this new vision of local government and which culminated in the "White Paper on Local Government" of 9th. March, 1998.

In the development of this White Paper, every effort was made to ensure that the process had been inclusive, interactive and transparent. A three-phase approach ensured that all stakeholders were included in the consultative process. The first phase of consultations resulted in a discussion document published in April 1997, containing the initial strategic questions to be addressed in the White Paper. The second phase, which consisted of issue-focussed research processes, provincial and local workshops and other consultation mechanisms, resulted in the "Green Paper on Local Government", which was released for public comment in October 1997. The third phase, consisting of Portfolio Committee hearings, a local governance Summit, public submissions and sectoral consultative conferences, resulted in the "White Paper on Local Government", which was approved by Cabinet. Appropriate legislation was then prepared to enact the policy directions contained in the White Paper, establishing the basis for a new developmental local government system, committed to working with citizens, groups and communities to create sustainable human settlements, providing for a decent quality of life and to meet the social, economic and material needs of communities in a holistic way.

The White Paper on Local Government is in a certain way unique, as it does not deal with a sectoral policy, but with an entire sphere of government. It can almost be regarded as a "mini-Constitution" for local government, as it will affect all South Africans. Local government is the sphere of government that interacts closest with communities, is responsible for the services and infrastructure so essential to peoples' wellbeing, and has the task of ensuring the growth and development of communities in a manner that enhances community participation and accountability.

Actually implementing the policies contained in the Paper needs a supreme effort, tremendous resilience and constructive participation of all role players and very specific commitment and effort from national and provincial governments and, not least, from councillors and administrators within local government.

In this context, the implementation of any ICTs for development and e-government strategies are likely to have a strong bias towards cities and provincial towns, where the majority of the population resides. Notwithstanding this bias, President Mbeki noted in his 2004 State of the Nation Address (see above), that "the Departments of Public Service and Administration, Provincial and Local Government, and Communications will work to ensure that modern information and communication technologies (ICTs) are introduced in these development nodes as quickly as possible, to assist in all their developmental and governance efforts." Efforts in this regard have yet to deliver major results and therefore it is crucial to focus on approaches and strategies that address the needs of citizens in local government and, in particular, in urban and rural and remote areas".

8.1.3. The policy framework for ICTs and e-government

The use of ICTs within government, whether this is for the purpose of improving service delivery to citizens or to enhance back-office operations has been significant for at least the last two decades. At the national level, there are currently several large information systems, including the National Population Register, a deed register, the National Transport Information System (NATIS), systems to manage welfare grants, subsidies as well as systems to manage tax collection and liabilities which have been implemented in the last 10-15 years. The responsibility for these systems resides within the appropriate government department that manages the introduction of the systems through budget allocations made to it directly.

Over the last few years, there have been numerous efforts that have been implemented or which are in the process of being implemented by individual government departments. These included the creation of systems that enabled the tax authorities to have a single view of taxpayers, a major upgrade and modernisation of NATIS now known as eNATIS, the introduction of systems to manage better co-operation between the police services, the justice system, correctional services and other government departments, and finally, moves to introduce Smart Cards by the National Department of Home Affairs which was due for roll-out in 2006.

In addition, national government has put in place large 'internally-facing' transversal systems to manage the internal operations of government like payroll, financial management and supply chain management. However, these are mainly applicable to the national and provincial levels of government. Currently there are some 20 primary and countless minor systems in use in the government's transverse systems domain with an annual cost to the state of about SAR1.1 billion.

The existence of primary systems for the payroll function for all employees at national and provincial levels and large parts covered by a common financial management and supply chain management was largely due to the requirement imposed by central co-ordinating departments like the Department of Public Service and

Administration(DPSA) and the National Treasury that these would be the systems that would be used.

Over time, a number of challenges have emerged with the current transversal systems including the fact that they are not able to deal with current realities. On this basis, a process is underway to create an integrated financial management system (IFMS). The move to the new system is likely to take between 5-7 years to implement.

At the municipal level, the picture is less clear. Due to the history and fragmentation and the recent creation of the current 284 municipalities, the deployment of ICTs's varies substantially between these municipalities. In general, it would be the larger urban municipalities, covering large areas which would have the systems in place to manage payments, rates and taxes, registrations, as well as manage their own internal operations. New municipalities and those that exist in marginalised areas are likely to have very few systems in place to assist the municipality. A large scale survey and audit was conducted by a private research agency in 2004 and has been repeated in 2005 (but being done in close association with government). This survey and audit revealed major ICTs deficits in many marginalised local municipalities including the lack of basic ICTs facilities like a stand-alone computer. In addition, many of these local authorities did not see ICTs as crucial when they were facing more basic needs such as housing, water, sanitation, roads, etc.

In 1999-2000, there was an acknowledgement that despite the considerable initiatives in place, there were still many challenges that needed to be addressed if the information systems were to deliver on the development priorities of the new state. These included concerns about inter-operability, duplication of efforts, not achieving economies of scale, and security. In addition, the arrangements were not conducive to the creation of seamless access to government services and these will need to be assessed. For this purpose, the post of a Government Information Technology Officer (GITO) was established in each department, to facilitate the use of ICTs's for meeting the business objectives of government.

In terms of formal legislation, the Department for Public Service and Administration (DPSA) (through the Public Service Act) has the authority to determine policy and strategy on e-government and the use of ICTs within government. This was exercised in a strong way in

2001 when the department released an e-government framework. In the terms of the framework, each government department is required, as part of their strategic planning processes, to develop an information management plan and strategy. In addition, the policy framework suggested the creation of a Gateway portal where all government services could be found in such a way that the services are according to the needs of citizens and not the other way round. Finally, the department issued minimum interoperability standards.

In the implementation of the first phase of the e-government over the last few years, considerable gaps and weaknesses were identified. As a result, a policy review process is underway. Draft policy proposals were developed by the DPSA and presented in July 2005 to the GITO's that identified a number of concerns. As such, it was unclear what policy direction would finally be taken and how this would differ from the previous policy framework. It is important to note that the jurisdiction of the DPSA does not extend to local government and as such the policy proposals do not extend to local government level.

Over the last few years, government has identified a need to harmonise conditions to co-ordinate the three spheres of government as well as public sector agencies and entities. Although the debates have been strongly driven by human resource considerations (i.e. harmonising conditions of service, enabling the easy transfer of staff, etc.), it is likely that governing frameworks on e-government and technology use will also feature in the discussions and policy proposals. Once again, these policy processes are currently underway and it is difficult to tell what the final outcome would be.

To supplement the evolution of the e-government strategy, the Centre on Public Service Innovation (CPSI) produced a research report that dealt specifically with the development of an access framework to support the e-government strategy. The report proposed a multichannel approach including the use of intermediaries. It proposed that local governments should play a greater role in designing an access strategy as they have the best sense of the needs of the community, are responsible for spatial planning, and are a major role in overseeing overall socio-economic development. However, there are major capacity constraints in many local authorities and such an approach would require a minimum 10-year implementation strategy. This model was under discussion within the DPSA and the Governance and Administration cluster at the time of the mission. At the same time, SITA was also studying how to include the local government level in the new "Enterprise Architecture" system which was developing to improve the provision of ICTs services to the overall government and the public sector at large. The debate about the "form" of the state is also discussing the best organisation of the "developmental state", that according to Ms. Geraldine Fraser-Moleketi, Minister for Public Service and Administration, should not be seen as a "centrist state" but, as a "spider web", with many concentric circles. It is the lines that cross the circles and come together in the centre that give strength to the web and hold it all together. ICTs can play a pivotal role in developing and reinforcing the web, thus linking the local to the national level of the governance system.

8.2. BUILDING A KNOWLEDGE SOCIETY IN THE WESTERN CAPE

8.2.1. The Cape Information Technology Initiative (CITI)

The Western Cape Province is a SAR120 billion annual economy that has recognised end embraced the important role ICTs play in poverty reduction and economic growth.

Considering that in the primary and secondary sectors, growth and employment are either stagnant or in decline, not only as a peculiarity of the province, but as a global trend and in light of the "fundamental shift" from an industrialised to a knowledge-led economy, the provincial governments have taken numerous steps to ensure that its 4.5 million people will have the opportunity to embrace the new paradigm.

For this reason, in 1998, the **Cape IT Initiative (CITI)** was launched. CITI is a not-for-profit networking and cluster development organisation that brings together people, ideas and capital to grow the Western Cape ICTs sector. CITI's goal is to promote Cape Town as a global IT hub and gateway into Africa, thus facilitating the creation of jobs and prosperity through IT. CITI identified three main goals to shape the direction of the organisation: 1. enhancing the development and collaboration in the ICTs cluster; 2. promoting the ICTs industry; and 3. making CITI the pre-eminent industry information source. The objectives of CITI are to identify, facilitate and assist entrepreneurial ICTs business in the province through research, networking, collaboration, promotion and marketing activities. These objectives are closely aligned to that of the provincial and local government that also provide funds to CITI and were involved in its creation. But CITI also receives funding from the private sector, thus it cannot merely be considered a Public-Private Partnership. CITI plays a more central role in the context of the government's overall development. CITI's initiatives in fact are built around fostering linkages between firms in the Western Cape through, for example, arranging and facilitating networking events to encourage competition and collaboration, as well as actively bringing together firms, government and education institutions. CITI proved to be indispensable to the development of the ICTs industry in the Western Cape. Since its founding, the number of IT companies in the province have increased from 248 to over 1,200 and which employ about 27,000 people, making it the second largest employer - next to tourism - in the province.

8.2.2. The Cape Online Strategy and the Centre for e-Innovation (Ce-I)

A White Paper published by the Provincial Government of the Western Cape (PGWC) in 2001, titled **"Preparing the Western Cape for the Knowledge Economy of the 21st.Century"** contends that "In the new millennium, economic opportunities will increasingly lie in people and the knowledge they have, rather than in capital or natural resources". In addition to this shift, almost two-thirds of the output of the provincial private sector is threatened by international competition, especially from emerging economies, such as India, China, or the nearby "small" Mauritius. Given that these challenges were embedded in the transition from industrial to knowledge society, the PGWC elaborated a further e-government Strategy, or **"The Cape Online e-government Programme"**. This strategy is based on the assumption that, "to speed the transition to a society based on the availability and leverage of knowledge, it is necessary to change and adjust to the imperatives of the knowledge society". In preparing the programme, however, the already existing initiatives underway were considered, since the IT infrastructure and website had already been developed at national, provincial and local level.

The strategy has therefore been developed through a "discovery" process, during which all available materials and information were sought and analysed, followed by an "exploratory phase. It involved engaging representatives from all key stakeholders to assess the overall current state of activities, and to understand their various perspectives and priorities. The following phase of "decision", involved the identification of key projects and tasks, as well as the initial specification of the resources required for the implementation of the programme.

The vision of the Cape Online Programme is "to develop an innovative environment that facilitates a competitive, knowledge-based economy that promotes economic growth and enhances the quality of life of the people". This is to be realised through "Enabling government to harness the capabilities of the Internet to grow the appropriate use of ICTs, increase internal efficiencies and provide better service to its citizens as a pathway to e-government".

In order to achieve its goal, the Cape Online Programme has been designed around a number of "core" projects that address the internal government structure, and its capacity to deliver the services. Complementary to these, there are some "Online Community Projects", which are intended to have an impact on various communities of interest, involving specific groups of citizens and organisations, other than the Provincial Government. The Programme is completed by some "External Projects", which are non-governmental in nature, and yet have an impact on the online environment for the improvement of business organisations and individuals.

In order to better co-ordinate the Cape Online Programme implementation, the Information Technology (IT) and e-government (KEEG) units of the Provincial Government of the Western Cape joined on 1st. April, 2004 to form the **Centre for e-Innovation (Ce-I)**.

The Centre's purpose is to provide ICTs services to the PGWC, including driving its e-government strategy. The role of the Centre is: 1) to provide and support the basic ICTs infrastructure upon which most of the government's activities depend; 2) To provide and support applications that improve the efficiency of government administration, lower costs and reduce the scope for corruption; 3) To provide and support applications that enable the government to deliver better services; and 4) To build an inclusive Information Society.

The main projects currently under implementation, include the following:

- The **Khanya** Project, a joint venture between the Ce-I and the Western Cape Education Department, uses ICTs to support the educational curriculum throughout the Western Cape by providing content for teachers and learners and supporting e-literacy. Of 432 schools in the province, 276 had been equipped with an ICTs lab by the end of January 2005, many of them in rural areas such as Merweville, Baartmansfontein and Wellington.
- **Schools Administration Management System Project (SAMS)** aims at providing a way for even the most remote and isolated schools to upload administrative information to a central server automatically and fast. This not only cuts the paperwork burden for schools, it also supports better planning and administration. There is also a project underway to make all management information available over the web, so it can be accessed anywhere, anytime by those who need it.
- **Maternity System (CRADLE)**, intends to support the important efforts of the public health system in reducing maternal and infant mortality and improving the health of mothers and babies. To achieve these objectives, health care practitioners and managers need accurate, timely and comprehensive information. CRADLE is one element of the extensive system that Ce-I is building to supply this, collecting data on mothers and babies during pregnancy, labour and delivery and early infancy. The information is used for statistical and research purposes, and it enables officials to track problems and intervene where necessary. It is linked with the Health Information System, which provides consolidated electronic health records for patients across the provincial health system. CRADLE has been piloted in Gugulethu, and will in future be rolled out to all provincial hospitals.
- **Networking Community Health Centres (CHCs)**. Although an important component of the primary health care system the CHCs are often isolated. Because of their important role especially in implementing and monitoring anti-retroviral treatment for people living with HIV/AIDS, the CHCs are now being networked and linked with other health care systems to provide accurate information for health workers . By the end of March 2005, 28 out of 33 CHCs in the Western Cape were networked. In future, the network could enable additional services like improved administration systems and wireless outreach programmes.

- **Social Service Electronic Document Management System (EDMS).** One of the biggest problems in the Department of Social Services & Poverty Alleviation, which administers grants and pensions, is that applications take a long time to process through its old paper-based system – and too many files get lost. The Ce-I is helping the department to convert all its existing records to electronic format, as well as generate all new files electronically. This not only eliminates the problem of lost files, it also offers drastically reduced scope for fraud and corruption. Once the system is well established, the department and the Ce-I will introduce more benefits. Recipients of disability grants and old-age pensions, for example, currently have to travel long distances to government offices to make applications. In future, community workers may be able to travel to people's homes, capture data directly using the EDMS system and wireless technology, and submit applications instantly to the head office for approval.
- **FleetMan**: The provincial government owns a fleet of around 4,000 vehicles including ambulances, fire engines and passenger vehicles. FleetMan is helping fleet managers track and take care of this several hundred million-rand investment. The asset management system, for example, supports automatic logging of vehicle use, enabling departments to be billed promptly and accurately. This improves cash flow and financial accountability, as well as eliminating many disputes. FleetMan is web enabled, so government employees can quickly and easily book pool vehicles or track vehicle movements.
- **e-Fuel**: The fuel management component brings together bank, fuel supply and vehicle tracking systems to ensure that government fuel purchases are tightly controlled. The combination of electronic fuel pumps and vehicle identification means it's no longer possible to fill non-authorised vehicles using a government garage card. The system has all but eliminated fraud, leading to expressions of interest from several other provinces.
- **Cape Gateway**, the Ce-I's most publicly visible project, provides government information to Western Cape citizens via a web portal, a call centre and a walk-in centre in Cape Town's Long Street. Demand for the service has been growing strongly since its official launch in March 2004: by January 2005 the portal was receiving around 50,000 visits, the call centre around 14,000 calls and the

walk-in centre around 500 visitors per month. The most popular queries from members of the public are about social grants and pensions; other popular services include access to the office of consumer protection and information about car vehicle registration procedures – the volume of calls to the traffic department has dropped by 60% since Cape Gateway's launch.

- **Cape Access**: Information has no value if people can't access it; so, to complement Cape Gateway, the Ce-I is also rolling out programmes to provide computer access and skills in rural communities. e-Community Fora have been established in six pilot communities, where ICTs activists are being mobilised around existing physical and ICTs infrastructure. In Oudtshoorn, Struisbaai and Bitterfontein libraries are the focal point; at George and Elim this role is filled by schools in partnership with Khanya, and a multipurpose community centre is being used at Vanrhynsdorp.
- **e-Literacy**: As Cape Gateway staff point out, it's pointless and foolhardy to offer access to ICTs without also offering training so people can use facilities effectively. The Ce-I is developing a series of community training and e-literacy projects, including training modules that will be free for anyone to adapt and use for themselves.

Of course, none of the projects presented would be possible without a robust, well-run and up to date ICTs infrastructure, with its vital hardware and software services linking the information backbone to the officials so that they are able to perform their tasks efficiently. At present, the ICTs infrastructure is dependent on a Wide Area Network (WAN) that provides connectivity to 9,000 workstations in 108 buildings. More than 11,000 officials continually used one or more of the 377 custom developed applications in conjunction with commercial software packages (this is confirmed by the 5,000 Help Desk calls per month and the 120,000 emails per day). To improve its "ICTs backbone", the Ce-I is planning a forward-looking project to ensure that the PGWC has the right infrastructure in place to take advantage of "next generation" technologies. This is the **Project Foundation** initiative that aims at realising an ambitious programme of integration of the current Local Area Networks (LAN) and the WAN, provided by the State IT Agency (SITA), and to prepare to be a "model" for future IT-governance planning.

8.2.3. Strategy Alignment and Holistic Governance in the Western Cape

The Western Cape's Premier's Department has set out a **draft strategy for Holistic Governance**, in which it sets out its intention to realign and reorganise itself to be more relevant, effective and efficient in managing the activities and delivery of a modern government service within a developmental African state. The vision of the Premier, Mr Ebrahim Rasool, is that Holistic governance is about .... "optimising the potential of networked governance and organisation. It is premised on the view that fragmentation is a problem that can be overcome, not a condition to be lived with". The three key aspects of such governance are:

- **Alignment**: planning and operational activities are explicitly based on policy instruments such as the "iKapa Elihlumayo", the provincial strategy.
- **Co-ordination:** in which the different role-players act in concert with each other, and
- **Integration:** in which collaboration and co-operation are built into systems and instruments to effect holistic governance.

In consistency with the Premier's strategy, the Centre for e-Innovation has developed an **"Ignition Strategy"** which lays out in detail the strategic direction for the Centre, taking into particular consideration the alignment with the Provincial Development Strategy, the **iKapa Elihlumayo**, its key priorities, objectives and action plan.

The aim of the Centre is to ensure that its strategy is in line with the Premier's Departmental Strategy by demonstrating good practice and current activity in areas of collaboration, centralised strategy and policy development, with the Provincial government as well as with the City Administration.

In this regard, of particular interest is the collaborative framework agreed upon by the Centre for e-Innovation and the Information Technology and Economic Development and Tourism Directorates of the City of Cape Town. This agreement **"Working Together – Learning Together"**, established in 2004 after discussions and practical collaboration already started in 2002, aims to align the e-government Strategies of the provincial and the municipal government.

Although the two governments have worked together in the past, there was the need to develop and formalise a collaborative partnership in order to ensure that the agreed objectives are met and that the City of Cape Town and the Western Cape are strategically positioned for the future.

The partnership between the two institutions, eventually open to other departments and players, has the objective of establish a mutually beneficial relationship, to realise the following:

- provide strategic direction in terms of e-government initiatives;
- target key customers' needs through programmes and projects;
- access, use and deploy scarce resources;
- share implementation lessons and practices; and
- allow for more focussed and structured interaction with other external and internal stakeholders (including the national government, other local authorities, potential donors, the private sector, other non-governmental and civil society groups).

The partnership document therefore outlines the purpose and principles to be used to guide the collaboration; the specific goals and objectives; and the management framework. It also indicates the collaborative projects already conducted and the planned activities for the future, thus becoming an effective "road-map" for implementation of activities at different level of governance.

Within this framework, the **"Smart City" Strategy of the City of Cape Town**, represents an example not only of successful implementation of an ICTs-driven re-engineering of the City government, but a way to address the twin challenges of poverty alleviation and globalisation of the overall provincial government, by identifying the way that ICTs can enable economic and social development and enhance good governance, in the City and in the Province, but also in consistency with the national and regional objectives.

8.3. THE CAPE TOWN'S SMART CITY STRATEGY

8.3.1. ICTs opportunities and divides in Cape Town

The City of Cape Town is home to 75% of the provincial population and, with its 94 Billion SA Rands annual economy, makes up 80% of the provincial Regional Domestic Product (RDP) with an average growth rate of 3% from 1995 to 2002, the highest in South Africa. Numerous factors have contributed to this, such as the presence of

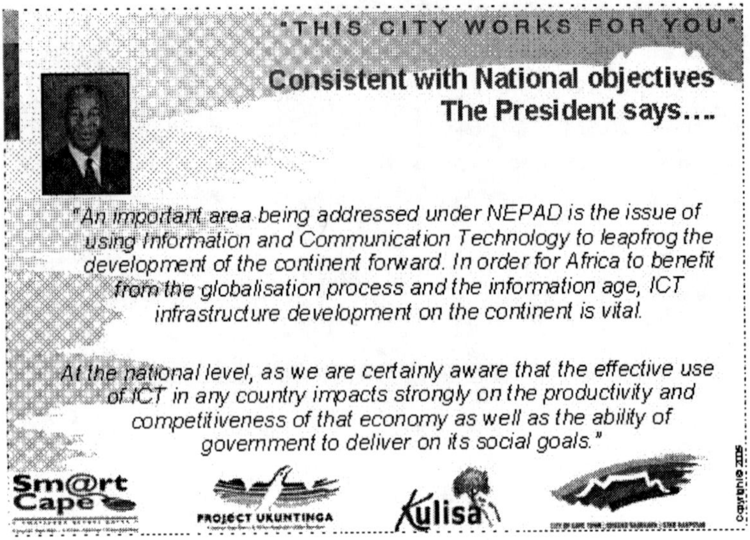

Figure 1 – The Capegateway website reporting the statemement on NEPAD by President Mbeki

the Parliament in the province, a well-developed infrastructure and an expanded skills base relative to other provinces.

Although Cape Town is one of the most productive areas in the country, it recognises that its output per capita is less than one-sixth that of industrialised countries and large sections of the community live in poverty, unemployment and ill health.

The economically active population has grown almost twice as fast as the whole of South Africa (21% versus 11%), however its unemployment rate was at 24% in 2005 which translates into 500,000 people, some 80% of whom are classified as youth.

The City has established that to improve its unemployment rate, it needs an estimated 7% annual Gross Regional Product (GRP) growth.

Thus Cape Town, through its multi-award winning Smart City Strategy, and together with a range of complementary city council strategies, represents the possibility of providing an answer to the challenges of the knowledge-economy and increasing globalisation in South Africa.

Through this strategy, the City administration, since 2002, is focussing on providing ICTs skills enhancement opportunities, access to ICTs and business development opportunities.

At the same time, it developed a policy discussion document on ICTs and Business Development Services and has undertaken a groundbreaking Digital Divide Survey. In fact, recognising that the Digital Divide is having an increasing impact on economic and social development, the City commissioned a survey to determine where its communities, businesses and organisations stood in terms of their access to, and use of, ICTs. Information was collected through 19 community meetings, with 1,852 attendees generating 826 questionnaires resulting in that:

- 67% of respondents had never used a computer;
- 10% or respondents have PC access at home and 11% at work;
- 14% have access to the Internet;
- 44% did not know of an access point to ICTs;
- More people have access to cell phones than to fixed-line phones;
- Majority of low-income residents can't afford to pay for basic services, so ICTs remain out of their reach;
- Most viewed ICTs as critical to the future of their organisations;
- ICTs activities and programmes are mostly unavailable or are perceived to be ineffective in Cape Town's communities.

The study underlined that there is a great enthusiasm for ICTs in general, but a feeling that some communities are being left out of the Information Society. According to McConnell International, South Africa needs to focus on improving its basic infrastructure, human capacity and overall regulatory environment. This is of particular importance in Cape Town where, however, the activities under implementation were going in the direction of filling these gaps.

8.3.2. Vision and Strategic Framework

The vision of the City Council for Cape Town, is "to build a City for all, a City in which no-one is left out". The Smart City vision, is that of "a Smart City populated by informed people connected to the world and each other by the technology of the information age".

The long term objectives set up, are to have:

- A city where 80% residents, businesses and institutions are connected to each other and the world;
- A city in which all residents will have access to digital information and communication and the skills to use it thus bridging the digital divide in the present and future;
- A city where 80% of the population will be able to interact with the city administration through the use of ICTs.

To achieve these ambitious objectives, the City Council developed in 2001/2002 the "Smart City" Strategy that is a strategic framework aimed at positioning Cape Town as a leading city and region in the global knowledge economy. The strategy focusses on transforming the way local government delivers its services. The five pillars of the strategy are the following:

1. **Leadership:** Leadership in technology policy and strategy should be located at the most senior levels in the organisation, both politically and administratively. Other leadership areas are in business, in interaction with citizens, in non-profit organisations and in other collaborative initiatives.
2. **Development Strategy:** ICTs should be used to foster the city's economic and social development, through the growth and retention of the ICTs industry, creation of employment potential through the use of ICTs as a skill, and the use of ICTs for social development.
3. **Policy and regulatory environment:** the entire city's legislation needs to be reviewed and all new legislation passed by the city needs to be designed to ensure digital age appropriateness.
4. **Digital democracy:** the city should make a concerted effort to ensure more equitable access to, and spread the benefits offered by, ICTs to all. For local government, communities and business to take full advantage of the benefits offered by ICTs there is an overall need for infrastructure, skills development, and planning.
5. **Administrative/e-government:** ICTs should be used as strategic tools to transform local government to:

   Create a highly efficient and effective organisation;

   Reduce transaction costs;

   Allow service to citizens anywhere, anytime;

Allow citizens to deal with local government services in an integrated manner, via "one-stop-shops";

Make local government more customer-friendly and citizen-oriented;

Improve decision making by providing easy, timely access to relevant, accurate Council information.

Moreover, it is important to underline that, as already mentioned above, the city works in close partnership with the Provincial Government as well as other stakeholders, to ensure that Cape Town has the best opportunities to use ICTs to support the growth and development of its business, organisations and communities, taking advantage of synergies and common goals.

8.3.3. Activities and Results

Although Smart City has five focus areas, it is important to understand that it is an integrated strategy, aimed at a common end point. In this regard, it was imperative to create a world-class IT organisation that together with other City Services and Directorates, supports the achievements of the overall "Smart City Strategy". For this Strategy, Cape Town is recognised as a leading local government in South Africa, and was awarded the "African ICTs achievers e-government award", in 2002 and 2003.

To this end, the Directorates of ICTs, Social Development and Economic Development and Tourism, started implementing a number of projects, from both "externally" and "internally" focussed perspectives.

The **"externally" focussed projects**, are the following:

- **Smart Cape Access:** This is a pilot project making computers with free Internet access available in six public libraries. The pilot project was a success and it is now being rolled out to all City libraries in a phased two-year programme. Smart Cape computer facilities are provided by the city administration for use by any citizen. Users must be a member of the library and have a valid library card (www.smartcape.org.za). It won the Bill and Melinda Gates Access to Learning Award 2003.

Figure 2 – The logo of the www.smartcape.org.za initiative

- **Library Business Corners:** Based in 33 of the City's public libraries, these corners provide accessible information on starting and running small businesses, as well as resources and access to support services and other national, regional and local small business support networks. An example of which is B.R.A.I.N. the Business Referral and Information Network. It also focusses on youth entrepreneurship awareness.

Figure 3 – Internet users in the public libraries in Cape Town

- **Digital Business Centres:** based in Khayelisha, Guguletu and Langa, each centre includes telephones, faxes, scanners, photocopiers and printers, and will cater for business services such as accounting, legal, tourism, e-business, graphic design and business management.
- **ICTs Sector Support:** In consistency with the overall Provincial strategy, the ICTs sector has been identified as one of the key priority areas which will promote economic growth and job creation. The City of Cape Town thus supports the development of the sector to ensure that it becomes globally competitive, through supporting CITI- Cape IT Initiative.

- **Kulisa Project / Training learnerships in ICTs:** this project offers exciting training opportunities to 130 previously disadvantaged individuals to acquire ICTs skills. It is directed at unemployed matriculants and it is sponsored by ISETT, SETA and other partners, including CS Holdings and the City Administration.

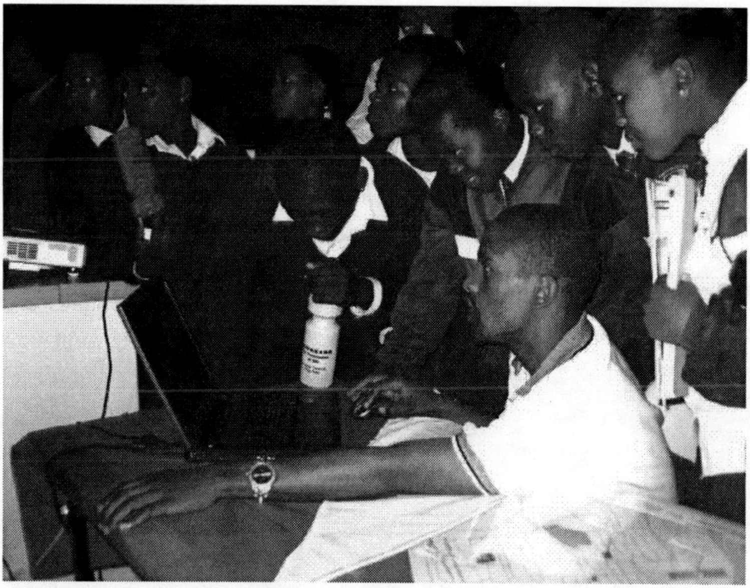

Figure 4 – ICT training learnership session

But the "starting" big effort conducted so far, with the most rewarding results achieved, is in the area of **"internally" focussed projects**. In particular, already in 2001/2002, the City administration started the rationalisation and standardisation of the IT services within the organisation, as well as enabling internal electronic communications (intranet, emails,); developing the City government Web Site and providing training on ICTs, through the **Councillor ICTs support project**, a training activity addressed to councillors, to enable them to effectively utilise the ICTs facilities provided.

In 2001, the implementation of the **Ukuntinga Project – MySAP.com** also started: this is the largest SAP-Enterprise Resource Planning (ERP) implementation and staff training initiative for Local Government in the world, and won the 2004 Computer World

Honours Award as the most significant IT project in a Government and Non-profit making organisation.**8.3.4. The Ukuntinga Project**

The Project Ukuntinga, meaning to soar and rise above in isiXhosa (one of the official language of South Africa), is about the design and implementation of an ERP (Enterprise Resource Planning) System that offers a comprehensive solution for managing financial, revenue, human resources, operations and other services (in practical terms its "back office" systems) on a single integrated IT system.

The city's ERP programme is a key component of the Smart City Strategy as the foundation on which its e-government capabilities will be built.

The reasons why the City of Cape Town implemented this project are the following:

1. **To facilitate the merger of the previous Municipal Local Councils into a unified City of Cape Town.** To do this, it was necessary to implement standardised, integrated financial, human resources, maintenance, revenue, procurement, inventory, assets and customer contact policies and procedures within an integrated system, as well as to consolidate and normalise all data objects on a single data base. However, legacy IT systems differed for each of the previous administrations and did not adequately meet the requirements of the unified city.
2. **To transform Local Government**: By creating an organisation based on standardised and best practice business processes, and replacing back office systems which were deemed to be outdated, functionally inadequate, not integrated and not able to render the level of service the city had committed to offering its citizens and visitors, as well as allocating scarce resources to value adding and service delivery activities.
3. **To unlock Financial Value for the City of Cape Town:** The lack of cost transparency in legacy systems made it difficult to determine where money was spent and what the city was getting in return; by improving and identifying new revenue and income streams, the efficient utilisation of scarce resources could be ensured.

In order to realise these objectives the City of Cape Town elected to implement an ERP system, using the proprietary solution SAP. The current implementation project has focussed on merging the 7 previous Municipal Local Councils and standardising the entire organisation's back office functions and business processes across the various organisational units. In brief, the ERP system implemented has created a platform from which future strategic imperatives are to be realised.

Approximately 300 end-to-end business processes have been designed, documented and implemented through the system. These processes relate to the following functional areas:

- Financial Accounting (Financial statements, treasury and cash forecasting).
- Asset Management (Asset accounting and control).
- Management Accounting (Financial planning, job costing, cost distributions and activity based cost allocations etc.).
- Plant Maintenance (Maintenance Management of infrastructural and moveable assets).
- Materials Management (Inventory management, procurement, accounts payable).
- Real Estate Management (Lease-out of municipal land and property holdings).
- Customer Interaction Centre (Customer account queries, task allocation and monitoring and infrastructure defect reporting).
- Human Resources (Organisational management, recruitment and staff development, training and facility management, personnel cost planning, leave management and payroll).
- Industry Solution for Utilities (Utility consumption, meter reading and management, invoicing and debt management).

Through the implementation of this system the complexity of corporate processes has been reduced. Duplication has been minimised, manual processes have been automated and location and distance are no longer limiting factors as the system does not hinder the location from where a service can be delivered.

This project has enabled the city to facilitate the merger and transformation of the ICTs systems of seven previous autonomous local authorities. More than 113 legacy systems and 70 interfaces were replaced with a single, functionally rich ERP-SAP system to streamline operations, reduce costs and enhance service delivery. This has been

Figure 5 – The SAP Centre at the IT Department of the City Council

achieved by reengineering and standardising more than 300 end-to-end business processes on a single integrated transactional system and by training 6,500 staff members to transact on the new system.

This new IT platform has enabled the city to manage its resources more efficiently and help create a citizen-focussed environment. Access to the city's new system is available from more than 500 sites across the city, where all citizens have access to a consistent level of service.

The city's ERP programme aimed to capitalise on the output of the organisation by optimising the way it deploys its resources, aligning business processes and by exploiting appropriate ICTs. No one component was more important than the other; the success of the programme hinged on how well these three dimensions worked together to achieve the strategic objectives of the administration.

Prior to implementing the ERP's system a study was undertaken to determine if the project would have a positive return on investment (ROI). Senior staff members identified the Value Creation Opportunities (VCOs) they believed the project would create and the benefits this would bring about were then quantified. VCOs were opportunities that the organisation can pursue to deliver value through increased revenues, reduced costs or improving the utilisation of assets.

Opportunities in areas that did not have a direct financial return, such as improving service delivery or advancing social upliftment, were also considered value creation opportunities, but were not used in the cash flow analysis as it was very difficult to quantify these benefits.

In fact, in order to calculate the "pay-back" period, a detailed financial model was developed. This indicated that, by the end of the 2003/04 financial year, the total 3-year long project cost of SAR355 million would have been reduced to 50% of the project costs seeing that benefits with a value of SAR232 million have already been realised, and would continue to produce benefits in the future. The city in fact now generates accounts through the ERP system to a value of nearly half a billion Rands each month. Improved visibility and transparency of information on the new invoice, the possibility for citizens to pay their accounts at any municipal pay point and the implementation of a call centre to address billing queries has enabled the Revenue Directorate to implement income recovery actions. This had improved the ratio between the value of municipal accounts sent out and payments actually received.

In total, after implementation of the ERP system, there is a net return per year of SAR40.6 million; and it will allow a financial break even in 2009. Considering the additional opportunities to create financial value, in addition to the benefits already achieved, in the financial year 2004/05 the project cost had already been fully recovered. In fact, in every part of the organisation there are opportunities to make financial savings and it is every person's responsibility to ensure that they are realised.

The project design phase commenced in March 2002, and the completed project was implemented in two releases. The first release focussed on the expenditure related aspects of the business and was commissioned during December 2002, with the second – income related functionality – being commissioned during September 2003.

Through this ERP programme the city has created a modern transactional and management information system. It will enable it to build a flexible and responsive organisation which will continually improve its efficiency and effectiveness in delivering its programmes and services to the benefit of more than 3,2 million people.

Internally, 6,500 staff members have been trained on how to transact on the new system and its associated business processes. This was after more than 1,650 were directly involved in the various design and implementation stages of the project.

A subset of these staff members was the project implementation team of 120 staff members. They were drawn as volunteers from all levels of the organisation and worked with external resources to design, test and build the new system. Prior to joining the project these people had no SAP knowledge and through a process of knowledge transfer have developed significant new skills which will enable them to form the core of the system support structure.

Six months after the implementation of Release 1 the acceptance level of the new system was tested by performing a user acceptance survey. The overwhelming response indicated that users believed that the organisation is better equipped to address the challenges facing the city as a direct result of implementing the ERP system. Although many of them still lacked confidence in their ability to optimally use the system a level of excitement and pride within the organisation in what it had achieved, was evident.

This business case shows that implementing an ERP programme for the City Administration can provide a positive financial return. In addition to the financial benefits it creates, it enables the organisation to achieve its amalgamation, transformation and service delivery objectives through enforcing a uniform business process.

Implementing the ERP system was a corporate-wide project and, by creating value through the system, demanded the collective efforts of all the stakeholders. The ERP project team supported the organisation in the use of the system and where financial value was realised.

This programme, therefore, did not emphasise the implementation of new technology as its sole objective, but focussed on using ICTs to bring about sustainable transformation in local government with far reaching benefits to the citizens of Cape Town.

8.4. Conclusions

8.4.1. Impact on local governance

The Smart City Strategy, and its ICTs-enabled administrative reorganisation foundation, the Ukuntinga Project, clearly demonstrate the successful use of ICTs as an enabler of transformation, whilst merging seven municipal authorities into a single administration with 28,000 payroll members and serving a population of 3.2 million citizens.

This was not purely about the implementation of an IT system, but about the relationship between the technology, the city's business processes (contained within the system) and how the organisation structures itself around these processes – which the ERP system aims to optimise in support of the strategic objectives of the city. Any change to a single dimension should result in changes to the other two.

The overall impact of the new system has been felt across three areas, namely:

- **Organisational:** the transformation impact of the project has been significant. Prior to embarking on this programme staff operated in their respective functional and regional silos with a great deal of suspicion and guarding of information. During the design phase of the project more than 1,600 employees from diverse backgrounds rallied around to create a common design for the future business processes of the city, thereby laying the foundations of a new organisational culture and service delivery model.
- **Human Resource:** for the city's staff, the introduction of modern technology and integrated systems has improved peoples' pride in their jobs. The integrated nature of the system has provided staff with a greater insight into how processes and tasks relate to each other and the impact their actions have on the outcome. This has enhanced accountability and clearly defined roles, with a greater width of responsibilities that have now being allocated to individuals.
- **Citizens:** for the citizens of Cape Town the distributed nature of the system means that an increased number of municipal services are now available at more convenient locations. No longer will citizens be forced to engage the local authority in the area where they live, but are able to transact at any municipal office within the greater metropolitan area. This is particularly important in a city were a large percentage of citizens do not have access to public or private transport.

This project has provided the City of Cape Town with a single, integrated system. To date the emphasis has been on getting the basic processes right across the organisation, giving the city a robust, stable platform for further developments.

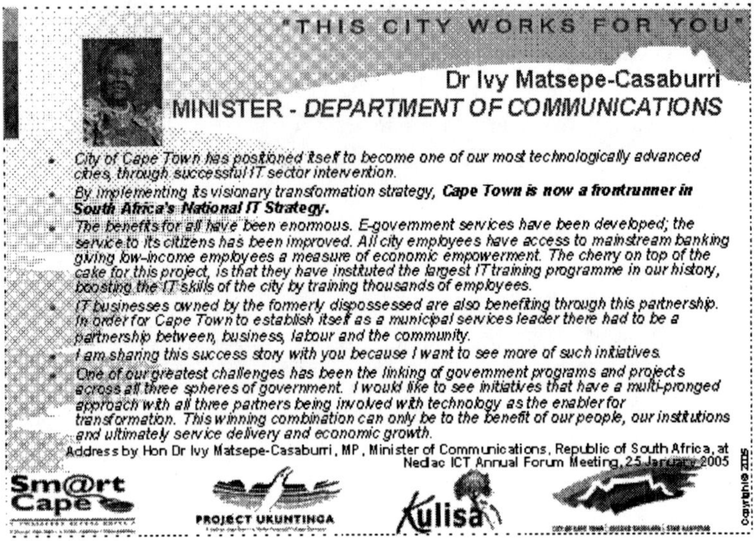

Figure 6 – Recognition of the success of Smart City by the Minister of Communication

Key opportunities identified by the city fall into three broad categories, namely:

- Making local government accessible 24 hours per day, 7 days per week to the citizens, visitors and businesses operating in the city. This includes the ability to query or pay municipal accounts, log electrical faults, apply for a new connection or disconnections for water or electricity, report potholes, or complain about parks, beaches and other recreational facilities across the city;
- The new system also provides a unique opportunity to re-engineer Revenue Services and Customer Care, focussing on tariffs, taxes and grants, arrears incentives and sanctions in a manner that significantly enhances the city's income; and
- The new system also provides an opportunity to holistically address poverty and indigence in the city, given that the system touches nearly every aspect of local government business that has an impact on the lives of poor people, such as the provision of basic services, public housing and municipal infrastructure.

The greater reliance on ICTs-enabled business processes has fundamentally changed how tasks are performed. In the past citizen interactions were characterised by front desk staff only being able to receive requests and then passing them to the back office for action. Significant delays and repeated requests for the same service were necessary as paperwork got lost.

The intention now is to ensure that as many tasks as possible can be concluded at the point of citizen contact and where necessary to escalate the task for action - this gets done via workflow. Queries and requests for information are handled via a centralised call centre and convenient walk in centres will be established across the city. Staff can now be moved from the back office to the front office to improve the level of service – but most importantly tasks will be initiated electronically or concluded where possible at the point of citizen contact.

These changes will unfold over an extended period, but only after structural changes have been made to the city's fixed establishment will their full benefit be realised.

One of the benefits of having so many automated business processes is the improved visibility this gives management. A breakdown in a process or a backlog in a service can now be managed and remedial actions implemented based on objective indicators. The city is now able to monitor its service offerings centrally, but has the freedom to deliver them through devolved structures. Remedial action can be taken proactively, based on objective measures and no longer will the number of people who complain or the length of the queue be the only insight into the demands being placed on a service. A more comprehensive set of performance indicators is to be introduced and the ability to report on these will drive the new performance culture for the city.

8.4.2. Key factors of success and difficulties

The successful implementation of ERP systems in private enterprises is proven world wide. This is however the first time that a full scale ERP system has been implemented in the South African public sector and is considered to be one of the world's largest (if not the largest) SAP installations in local government. Thus its **originality**.

One of the key social objectives of the programme was black economic empowerment and the up-skilling of previously disadvantaged individuals. A progressive implementation contract was prepared.

This sought to provide emerging ICTs vendors, who were previously excluded from projects of this nature, with an opportunity to share in the economic and skills development opportunities. Both financial penalties and rewards associated with meeting empowerment objectives were specified and tracked for the duration of the programme. Through this, the city ensured that its investment in this programme benefited its local ICTs community and that previously marginalised groups were not excluded. The significant risk associated with a project of this scale was lessened by contracting an experienced, international, implementation partner and who were bound contractually to ensure that the city's affirmative programmes were realised.

The **uniqueness** of many aspects of the system can be identified in the support to the city's social and developmental objectives. These include:

- The need to manage property as a primary object for the purposes of billing;
- The raising of property tax and the implementation of progressive utility tariff models which makes provision for the economic realities of citizens and provides for the indigent;
- Creating a financial accounting system which complies with the Generally Accepted Municipal Accounting Principles being introduced in South Africa;
- Providing system generated documentation in all 3 official languages of the Western Cape.

Although the project was implemented in record time it was conceived through a deliberate process spanning many years and with the **involvement of all the key stakeholders**. During 2000 a strategy was developed to enable the city to get off an increasingly dysfunctional platform created by its disparate and non-integrated systems. The implementation of an ERP system to facilitate the merger of the separate local authorities and drive its transformational agenda was envisaged. The need to obtain the buy-in of all stakeholders was identified at an early stage resulting in a detailed and inclusive process being followed to identify system requirements and software / implementation partner selection.

During the implementation phases of the project a multi-tiered governance structure was established to steer the project and keep it on track during the turbulent times associated with a young and unstable organisation.

Of course, as can be expected with a programme of this size and complexity numerous difficulties had to be overcome during the project life cycle.

Challenges both of a functional and technical nature were experienced. These were made even more demanding due to the large number of social objectives, in addition to the business requirements and local government specific legislation with which the programme had to comply.

The technical problems were, however, insignificant in comparison to the organisational challenges which had to be overcome.

- Midway through the implementation phase of the project the political leadership of the city changed - resulting in the restructuring of the executive management level of the organisation. Three different CEO's were employed during this period.
- The city's administration was in a state of flux. The original requirement that a new organisational structure be developed and populated prior to go-live - was not met. The new uniform ERP business processes had to be implemented without being allowed to amend the organisational structures of the previous 7 administrations resulting in new business processes having to be implemented on an old organisational structure.
- So as not to preclude any staff member from future employment opportunities in the city all potential system users had to be trained in terms of the roles they performed in the previous administration. This resulted in a significantly more training effort than originally anticipated.
- The line management structure of the city was ill-defined and no reliance could be placed on it to ensure that instructions would filter down to lower levels of the organisation. To mitigate this risk the ERP programme had to create its own structures with a comprehensive communication and change management plan to ensure that its target audience was kept informed and acted on instructions.

- In many areas of the organisation IT was being introduced for the first time and basic computer literacy, as a pre-requisite to ERP training, had to be provided.

These difficulties were overcome with a high degree of success, but the City of Cape Town still faces a number of challenges in moving forward:

- Ongoing training and education on SAP, teaching staff more advanced SAP functionality that increased the usability of the system and allowed them to make better decisions based on the information available. The set-up of cross directorate user groups would support this process and also ensure ongoing ownership.
- Ongoing focus on breaking down the silo mentality that existed between some directorates and functional areas. Through the ERP implementation, significant progress has been made in this area but will require ongoing focussed attention.
- Deepening senior management understanding of the information that was now available to them and their ability to access and interpret this information. Workshops with the directors had already started. At each of these, the focus was both on broadening understanding of available information, as well as building hands-on capability.
- A SAP Competency Centre staffed by people with a good understanding of the city's processes, transactional systems and future strategies would have to be resourced in order to support the directorates in driving out the benefits of the system as well as supporting them to overcome the challenges in going forward.

The resistance to a project that called for such a large financial commitment (SAR355 million), especially when seen in the City of Cape Town context, was significant. The city faced financial constraints and a large backlog in basic services in previously marginalised communities. Investing so significantly in ICTs systems was questioned from both internal and external sources.

In order to overcome these challenges and obtain the necessary funding the project was positioned within the overarching 'Smart City Strategy'. The importance of getting the back office in order to achieve financial sustainability and the need to create a transactional platform from which other service delivery and developmental objects can be pursued, was debated extensively. The final approval was however only given after a compelling business case had been prepared and it was shown that the project would provide a positive financial return on investment.

Obtaining initial funding was however only the first step. In a programme that spanned three financial years the importance of ongoing stakeholder management can not be over emphasised. Especially in a political environment the need to ensure that this support spans party political boundaries is essential and the creation of a multi-party political steering committee was crucial to the success of the programme.

A further key obstacle to success is that a programme of this nature could be misperceived to be a Finance or IT project (or any other part of the organisation for that matter), whereas in fact it is an organisational transformation project addressing end-to-end business processes. The support and buy-in from all sectors of the enterprise is crucial. This can only be achieved with the full support at an executive management level. For this reason the successful implementation of the ERP project was a key performance area in the performance contracts of each executive management board member.

The external challenges to the project were addressed through debating its merits in the public arena and the implementation of a pro-active communication plan. Prior to any release which could have an impact on external stakeholders, press releases and other channels of communication were used to make the citizens of Cape Town aware of this in a pro-active manner, highlighting potential risks and asking for continued support and so making it possible to mitigate any emotional response if there was a danger of this happening.

8.4.3. Lessons Learned

As in many cases in Africa, the City of Cape Town operates as two distinct societies – one wealthy and developed, and the other poor and underdeveloped. The key challenge faced by the city is the notion of "inclusivity". The poor and disadvantaged must be catered for no less than anybody else. This has generally not been the case. By the same token, the city recognises that an approach that seeks to cater for the special needs of the poor and vulnerable in a manner which impacts unreasonably on the interests of any other segment of the city is also not supported. Therefore, any project, including the ERP system, needed to ensure that it enabled the city to work for all its citizens and effectively address the inequalities of the past.

A serious concern surrounding the introduction of such an ERP system, was that it is a "first world" solution and only benefits the wealthy, developed communities in the city. This can result in exacerbating the "digital divide" across the city, and in the process leave poor communities further behind. As a city, Cape Town needed to ensure that the poorest communities were able to keep pace with the latest technology developments.

Hence, the approach followed has been focussed on solutions that provide equivalent benefits to all communities, addressing the needs of the broader society, rather than focussed on the needs of any specific segment. An example of this was the translation of the municipal accounts from English into isiXhosa (a local national language). The Ukuntinga Project, moreover, has to be considered as part of a holistic strategy that, in addition to reorganising the back office for better service delivery, sought to address the "digital divide" challenge by, for example, providing free access to computers and the Internet to the people of Cape Town at municipal libraries (the city's Smart Cape Access Project), or providing training on ICTs to disadvantaged people (the Kulisa Project). A further example of this challenge was the ability to get small, micro and medium enterprises to embrace ICTs in order for them to more effectively do business with the city (Library Business Corners; and Digital Business Centres).

However, a well-managed and optimal use of the ERP system can enable local authorities to comply with statutary requirements relating to transparent governance, financial, resource and performance management. Through this system the city aimed, first of all, at optimising and enhancing service delivery to the citizens of Cape Town but, at the same time, the system especially proved itself to have been the key enabler of transformation of local government in Cape Town.

The functional objectives of this programme were enabled through technology, but the impact and structure that implementing a technology solution had on the transformation objectives of the city were even more profound.

Moreover, government authorities in South Africa have a reputation for being good in developing strategy, but fail when it comes to implementation. This programme, through the demands associated with a binary system, forced strategic intent to be converted to operational plans and key decisions having to be taken. The project plan spanning 18 months from design concept to implementation demanded that these decisions were taken against an aggressive time line.

Although many people referred to the project as an ERP implementation project, it was in essence a transformation project, driven by the technology implementation. The technology forced the execution and implementation of the new processes and organisational design. It forced the City of Cape Town administrators to make and implement decisions that may have been postpostponed, were it not for the aggressive implementation plan.

It is therefore important to underline the need to have a strong and capable leadership capacity as well as the involvement of the necessary expertise.

Another criticism that could be made of the project is the fact that a proprietary system was chosen instead of open source software. The return on the financial investment seems to show that this was not the main issue and the city decided to use already proven technologies, taking advantage of the professional advice that would come with the technology, instead of embarking on an even more complex operation.

The Project Ukuntinga itself can also be used as a showcase in terms of the development of historically disadvantaged individuals. Through the innovative partnering and deal structure between the City of Cape Town and the international consulting and technological private company contracted, the project gave the opportunity to more than a hundred historically disadvantaged individuals and small and medium sized companies to build ERP and SAP capacity and experience. These individuals gained from the private companies' experience, methodologies and knowledge through working side by side with the consultants for the duration of the project and have now highly marketable skills in the ERP market for future work.

During the transformation from seven previous administrations to one Uni-city, one of the major obstacles was moving away from several disparate systems (113 legacy systems) into a single system that consolidated all information aspects into a single source.

Not only did the conversion from the old legacy systems consolidate the information, but it also presented the City of Cape Town with the opportunity to conduct structured data cleansing, leading to significantly more accurate data representations. The single source of information enables the citizens to conduct their business with the City of Cape Town regardless of their home location. The developed technology enabled the City of Cape Town to provide service delivery anywhere and anytime, at the convenience of their citizens.

Furthermore, through the transformation project, the City of Cape Town, for the first time, deployed a central call centre which can conduct business with citizens who prefer to use the telephone.

For the first time the leadership of the City of Cape Town is able to extract and view information that is based on a single version of the truth, unlocking insights that were not possible while it had all disparate systems. The consolidation of data is much more than the aggregate of the previous administration data, but has enforced the integration between functions, driving a process based view of information. The impact of the unlocking of this potential will have a radical impact on how the City of Cape Town makes decisions in the future.

The ERP system has been deployed to more than six thousand end-users, working in more than 500 locations. The users range from being very sophisticated through to people for whom working with an IT system was a new concept. All of the deployed users ways of communicating and processing of information changed significantly, allowing them to be now part of a process orientated culture, rather than being isolated in a functional and geographical silo.

Implementing an ERP system per se, is not rocket science and has been done many times before. Implementing a wall-to-wall ERP in a local government in a first world / third world country like South Africa and a city like Cape Town provided many unique challenges and opportunities for the innovative use of technology.

The challenge for the City of Cape Town is now to manage the balance between the city's sophisticated, tourist and investor friendly face to the developed world and its accessible and affordable service delivery to its citizens, of whom many come from historically disadvantaged communities with limited access to first world facilities.

References

African National Congress (ANC). 1994. Reconstruction and development programme: A policy framework. Johannesburg: Umanyano Publication.

Brainstorm, Special: Success by design: in search of enduring excellence in Cape ICTs, June 2005;

Bennett Russell, "Greasing the wheels of government", in Web Brainstorm, June 2005;

Bridges.org, "Taking Stock and Looking Ahead: Digital Divide Assessment of the City of Cape Town, 2002"

Centre for e-Innovation, Provincial Government of the Western Cape, "e-Power to the people", 2004;

Centre for e-Innovation, Provincial Government of the Western Cape, "Supporting and aligning the strategy of the Centre for e-Innovation with the strategy of the Department of the Premier", draft, November 2004;

Centre for Public Service Innovation (CPSI) and the LINK Centre, University of the Witwatersrand, "The State of ICTs and Local Governance in South Africa: Needs Analysis and Research Priorities", Report to the CAFRAD/IDRC LOG-IN Africa Pre-Project Workshop, Nairobi, 3-5 September 2005;

Chikulo. Prof. B. C., "Development Policy in South Africa: A Review", DPMN Bullettin, Vol. X, Number 2, April 2003

CITI, Cape Information Technology Initiative, Annual Report, March 2004–February 2005, 2005:

City of Cape Town and Provincial Government of the Western Cape, "Initial research to inform the design and development of e-government services", e-government Services Research Project, (PMO1035) August 2003;

City of Cape Town and Provincial Government of the Western Cape, "Working Together – Learning Together", Collaborative Framework, November 2004;

Department of Welfare. 2000. National report on social development 1995 ? 2000. Pretoria: Government Printer.

Fraser-Moleketi Geraldine, Minister for Public Service and Administration, "A strong centre holds the web together", Comment on "Business Report", Monday 18th July 2005;

Infonomics South Africa, Evaluation of the Sm@rt Cape Access Pilot Project"; January 2003;

Manuel Trevor, Minister of Finance, "National Budget Speech 2005";

Mbeki Thabo, President of the Republic of South Africa, "State of the Nation Speech", 2001;

Mbeki Thabo, President of the Republic of South Africa, "State of the Nation Speech", 2004;

Mbeki, Thabo 1998. The building has began: Government?s report to the nation, ?98. Pretoria: Government Printers.

Munslow, B., and P. Fitzgerald. 1997. Search for a development strategy: The RDP and beyond. In Managing sustainable development in South Africa, edited by P. Fitzerald, A. McLennan, and B. Munslow, eds. Cape Town: Oxford University Press.

Office of the President. 1996a. Growth, employment and redistribution: A macro economic strategy. Pretoria: Office of the President.

Office of the President. 1996b. The rural development strategy: Putting rural people in charge. Pretoria: Office of the President.

Office of the President. 1998. Poverty and inequality in South Africa: Report prepared for the Office of the Executive Deputy President and the Inter-Ministerial Committee for Poverty and Inequality. Durban: Praxis Publishing.

Omer-Cooper, T. D. 2000. South Africa: Recent history. Africa South of the Sahara London: Europa Publications.

Provincial Government of the Western Cape, White Paper on "Preparing the Western Cape for the Knowledge Economy of the 21st Century", 2001;

Provincial Government of the Western Cape, "Cape Online e-government Program", August, 2001;

Provincial Government of the Western Cape, "Ignition Strategy", draft August 2004;

Rasool Ebrahim, Premier of the Western Cape Provincial Government, Speech to the Cabinet Lekgotla on "Holistic Governnance", 3-4 November 2004;

Republic of South Africa, Constitution, 1996;

Sharif Mymoena, City of Cape Town, "Transforming Government with an ICTs enabled strategy: City of Cape Town's Smart City Strategy, Presentation, 2005;

Sm@rt News, Issue 1, December 2003;

Sm@rt News, Issue 2, September 2004;

Sm@rt News, Issue 3, May 2005;

Statistics South Africa (SSA). 1998. Unemployment and employment in South Africa. Pretoria;

Statistics South Africa SSA) 1999. The people of South Africa: Census 1996. Pretoria: Statistics South Africa.

Stelzner Andrè, Foflonker Mehboob, City of Cape Town, "Overview of the City of Cape Town's ERP Programme: Presentation to the Computer World Honours Award", Washington, DC, 2004;

Thornton Kim, "The Western Cape embraces ICTs for economic Development", Provincial Review: Western Cape Economic Development, electronic Government, Volume 1, Issue 5, 2004;

Xundu, X. 2002. Local Government confronts troubling realities. Business Day, Report of 13, November, p. 4.

Wadula Patrick, "The State of the South African Economy"; 2005;

Werksmans Attorney, "Annual Economic Outlook: South Africa", 2005;

Wesso Harold, Naidoo Raven, Neville Mark, "Technology, e-government and economic development: a background paper to inform the strategy of the Centre on e-Innovation", Provincial Government of the Western Cape, July 2004;

http://www.capetown.org.za

http://www.citi.org.za

www.capegateway.gov.za

http://www.smartcape.org.za

PART III

CONCLUSIONS AND WAY FORWARD

9

ICTS FOR LOCAL GOVERNANCE IN AFRICA: SOME PRELIMINARY CONCLUSIONS

The results of this study show that there is a potential for growth by integrating ICTs at the local government level, although building capacity is a key aspect of that potential. It is also the case that there are still several unresolved issues in discussing the role of ICTs for local governance, such as empowerment at the local level; the needs and priorities of citizens; the roles and responsibilities of the different stakeholders for sustainability; and the nature and level of people participation.

The recognition of the potential of ICTs for Local Governance comes from a few successful pilot applications in a number of countries around the world. Attempts are underway to critically evaluate some of these projects so that the real extent of their impact can be understood and the factors inhibiting impact can be identified. But there still isn't a common framework for evaluation which can specifically address the overall objective to create an environment of lessons to be learned from each other and to inform about the factors of success in relation to poverty alleviation and reinforcing democracy using ICTs.

Some of these pilot applications demonstrate the great potential of ICTs to connect communities and provide a two-way communication channel between the communities and government bodies at both local and national levels. Such communication helps governments in improving service delivery through user-centred development and, in particular, ICTs have been, in some cases, a critical tool in ensuring accountability and transparency of government at the local level. In a few cases, ICTs are also powerful tools in connecting communities and local government officials, thereby enabling citizens' full participation in the decision making process, for example allowing the local authorities to formulate development plans with the full participation of the community. Other pilot applications indicate that access to useful information can benefit the poor in improving the quality of their products or services, obtaining a better price and enabling them to market their products/services beyond the confines of their immediate neighbourhood. This is particularly true in the rural communities and marginalised areas, where long distances and difficulties in transportation can be avoided by effectively using ICTs to have and provide timely and reliable information.

The lessons learned from case studies and empirical analysis of specific projects in using ICTs for local governance in Africa, show the following considerations.

First of all, there is no single way of introducing ICTs in government. The process is dynamic and consists of several stages, especially in Africa: raising awareness about the potential of ICTs for community development; encouraging basic use of ICTs; providing specific products and content to meet local demands (e.g., materials in national languages and products tailored to the needs of specific sectors of the population, such as youth, women or disabled people). This is a challenging situation because it involves the need to be able to adjust to the pace of increasing community needs. Political decision makers are affected by these challenges because they must set up legal and regulatory frameworks that create the optimum conditions for equal access and appropriation of ICTs within and by communities.

Participation is a crucial problem in the process of introducing and promoting the use of ICTs for community development. Appropriation mechanisms should have been initiated within the communities, but finding ways to involve large segments of the population still constitutes a real problem, even when people are aware of the potential usefulness of ICTs. In-depth studies must be carried out to understand the decision making mechanisms of the different community actors with regard to ICTs. It is equally important to try to better understand the attitude of communities toward changes, so as to identify the factors that underlie the adoption of ICTs by poor rural communities.

A specific aspect concerns the fact that women barely use ICTs, and when they do they use these tools less than men, even when they are relatively literate. Knowing that women's involvement, despite some resistance and constraints, is a prerequisite for their participation in the Information Economy and steps should be taken to promote some kind of positive discrimination toward women. Projects specifically designed for women seem to offer efficient ways to obtain this involvement. Women's involvement in project management and the promotion of leadership by women are also important conditions for enhancing their participation and appropriation of ICTs. Research should also be conducted to find information media tools and applications adapted to women's conditions, needs, and roles in the community, and to their mode of thinking. This could help minimise the socio-cultural constraints that limit their access to ICTs [1].

Due to installation costs and the recurrent expenses involved in the use of ICTs, alternative technologies (e.g., satellites, wireless and mobile technology, multimedia tools, etc.) should be considered in the introduction of ICTs, in order to better adapt to the limited infrastructure available, to improve community access. The number of community access points could also be increased to combine the more familiar traditional technologies with the new ICTs. Adaptable and affordable alternative technologies are needed to ensure universal access to ICTs and they can actually contribute to improving the living conditions of the population. It is necessary to assess the amount of real change and to identify and evaluate the effects that the use of ICTs has on income levels (both for individuals and the community).

Finally, due to country specificity and the importance of the institutional context to ICTs project implementation, national approaches should be encouraged to study the use of ICTs for development purposes. A national institutional environment seems to be a relevant framework for conducting studies on ICTs and development.

Taking all this into account, it seems evident that the challenge remains as to how the use of ICTs in local government can be beneficial to all the stakeholders. What have to be taken into consideration are the very real factors such as the digital divide (both international and domestic) and the prohibitive cost of traditional technology. These remain a challenge to full citizens' participation which is necessary for the creation of an "e-inclusive" society. What is difficult is not introducing technologies, but how people can best use the technologies!

The other main challenge ICTs pose is how to balance control and freedom. New "networked" technologies (of measurement, identity, location and efficiency) may enable a transformation of the economic system faced by the poor. But the same ICTs may also enable ubiquitous control and give or enhance the power of few people. Instead of reinforcing participation and democracy, ICTs could reduce them. ICTs can produce unexpected effects![2]

In this connection, political will, community leadership and ownership are key enabling factors, and accurate strategic planning, effective monitoring and critical evaluation are indispensable to identify factors inhibiting impact and to ensure sustainability.

When we talk about local governance, especially in Africa, it is pivotal to consider the development of local content. Provision of ICTs infrastructure and services is mutually reinforcing when ICTs applications are accompanied by local content development.

A first aspect to consider, concerns the fact that having many local languages and widespread illiteracy constitute a barrier to access of information. In this respect, it is rightly believed that, unless ICTs are made available in local languages, the ongoing ICTs revolution will remain incomplete and its benefits are likely to reach only a small section of society who have access to the main languages and, in particular, the "linguafranca" of Internet, the English language. The scenario is, however, undergoing rapid change. For instance, efforts are continuing in India, some with remarkable success, in making ICTs available in local languages, often called regional languages, thus taking the benefits of ICTs to the ordinary people. In Africa this is an even more complicated issue, considering the number of local languages and dialects which exist and the high rate of illiteracy. Moreover, the gap between connectivity and technology capacity on the one hand, and content on the other, keeps growing ever larger. More so, in African countries, where the mastery of technology seems to be an end in itself, almost wholly divorced from the need to solve the many problems of deprived millions.

ICTs have enabled various items of information or content to be placed on the internet in order to share it all over the world, thus opening the doors for content globalisation. Today, huge amounts of information are available over the internet in text or document form like market prices, poverty alleviation government schemes, hospitals, weather, educational institutes' directories, telephone directories and much more. While urban net-citizens increasingly upload the content available to them due to greater awareness on the part of urban centric organisations, what is still ignored or not available is local content available to and for rural communities.

Local content is invariably available in the form of indigenous knowledge that has been inherited by the community over centuries. One important aspect of this indigenous knowledge is the content about the various products that the rural communities produce. These products are part of the "global village economy" and include various types of work and an important element of these is the work of the rural artisans, their creative space and the economics associated with them.

It is therefore important that Africa consciously and successfully develops and exchanges local content. To achieve this, the use of local languages, the exchange of local cultures and the development of local programmes have to be aggressively pursued and supported by governments, businesses and civil society. Africa has a rich legacy of cultural products that could be developed and packaged for new media dissemination both on the continent itself and in the wider world. Furthermore, ICTs should be used extensively to increase general and digital literacy and expertise, especially among the youth and children, while using them, at the same time, to enhance the development of local content. When ordinary people can relate to ICTs in their own languages and when these reflect and are reflective of their cultures and traditions, ICTs are more likely to be embraced and become an integral part of their lives, thus enabling them to benefit more fully from ICTs applications[3].

However before content development can be made viable, Africa must take a serious approach to developing business models for transforming content to viable e-business/e-commerce solutions, especially in rural areas. Incubating and stimulating content industry spin-offs should be promoted and training programmes developed to improve the entrepreneurial skills of local content developers.

The availability of the appropriate skills base is an important determinant of the growth of ICTs supply activities, and these contribute to the more general human resource development. At the same time, the skills base must be understood as an important risk factor in appraising communications network infrastructure expansion and ICTs applications projects. Without available skills to operate and maintain the physical infrastructure, as well as develop and maintain software, users or potential users will naturally be unable to take advantage of the infrastructure, which itself will therefore not be used to its full potential. Another potential risk factor related to building the capacities of the human resources is the "brain-drain" risk, especially when training is not related to the real context. In this case, high-expectations can produce frustration as well as difficulties for trained people, especially if young people are placed at a high hierarchical level. In this regard, it is crucial that capacity building will not only focus on the training of individuals, but on reinforcing the capacity of an organisation (private and public) and especially the institutions at the local government level.

Currently, in Africa, the availability of specialists in ICTs and even training institutions in this area is extremely limited. It is therefore necessary that the sector reforms address this issue of basic training and developmental training so as to ensure the existence of sustainable, quality facilities, accessible to all in the sector, to ensure continued and improved availability of the requisite professional and operational human resources. Forging alliances between private and public sector, including international and multilateral organisations is pivotal. Africa should learn from the Indian experience, where rather than trying to legislate against staff poaching and brain drain, instead introduced policies and incentives for over-training, re-training, re-allocation and motivation schemes. In this way India not only reduced the impact of a brain drain, but changed it to "brain-export". Africa could do the same, and even develop research and manufacturing industries in ICTs, taking advantage of the many assets in the continent that give Africa an advantage over the more expensive economies and congested environments of Northern and Eastern countries. An additional approach to capacity building and institutional development in this area is through the frequent exchange of information, experiences and lessons learned between African policy makers and regulators, including the cross-border use of local experts and professionals[4].

In this connection, an important aspect to take into consideration is the need to overcome the resistance of decision makers as a key factor in the effective involvement of all stakeholders. This can be done only through the promotion of general ICTs diffusion and creating awareness and appreciation as well as e-literacy among populations, especially children and young people, which is also likely to improve the level of basic literacy in Africa, giving it the required pool of people to develop higher skills to use ICTs efficiently and productively.

In conclusion, some questions still remain open, such as: What kind of actions should governments take in order to develop local e-governance systems that produce real public value (e.g. respond to the needs and priorities of citizens)? Which are the processes and competences associated with ICTs that should be developed/enhanced in the local government/public service in order to have a positive impact on "customer satisfaction" (internal customer=civil servant, external customer=citizen)? How to protect, nurture and develop people-participation and information-exchange (two of the basic assets of the knowledge-society)?

Notes

1. Molo Thioune Ramata, (Edited by) Information and Communication Technologies for Development in Africa: Opportunities and Challenges for Community Development, CODESRIA/IDRC, 2003.
2. On this see also John Gage, *Information Technology and Economic Development, in Economic Development,* 1999, Oxford University Press, and other articles and publications.
3. On this see also, Sy, J. Habib, "Critical and Prospective Views on ICTs and Governance in Africa", in "Africa Networking: Development Information ICTs and Governance, United Nations Economic Commission for Africa, UNECA, Addis Ababa, 2004
4. On this see also, Olekambainei Emmanuel and Sintim-Misa Mavis Ampah, "Info-communication for Development in Africa", UN ICT Task Force Series 2, ICTs for African Development, UN, NY 2003.

10

ONE WAY FORWARD: *LOG-IN AFRICA*

One of the way to respond to the above mentioned questions is by the development and conduct of pieces of research to analyse the impact of ICTs on local governance, through evaluating projects and initiatives and applying the results of research to concrete cases, eventually developing pilot projects to be further replicated broadly.

This should also involve the definition of a monitoring and evaluation system and the identification of guidelines (Road Map) for implementation of ICTs Projects at local government level. In addition to evaluating the social impact of incorporating and using ICTs for both management purposes in local governments and communicating with citizens, as well as conforming citizen networks that attempt to become valid representatives of these governments, there is the need to develop a consolidated system of indicators, relevant to the African context, which will be updated on a frequent basis and serve as a reliable and current data source for stakeholders at local, regional, national and global levels.

In this regard, the preliminary findings of this research together with further discussions on the issue of ICTs and local governance in Africa, were presented to the **"International Workshop on Innovative Applications of ICTs for Local Governance in Africa"** jointly convened in June 2004, in Addis Ababa, by the United Nations Economic Commission for Africa (UNECA), the International Development Research Centre (IDRC), also in collaboration with the United Nations Capital Development Fund (UNCDF). The main output of this workshop, attended by some 60 participants from Africa and elsewhere, was a proposal to establish a regional research network to design and undertake applied research on the impact of ICTs on local governance in Africa.

In response to a proposal I presented to the Workshop, I was requested to further elaborate on the research network, proposing that this would eventually be coordinated through the African Training and Research Centre in Administration for Development (CAFRAD).

I therefore conducted further research in this area on behalf of the IDRC. This, combined with other discussions about the development of the research network, provided impetus to the development of the **"Project Idea" for the establishment of a "Local Governance and ICTs Research Network for Africa (LOG-IN Africa)"** that I prepared and submitted on behalf of CAFRAD to IDRC on 4th.August 2004.

The LOG-IN Africa "Project Idea" was subsequently presented for discussion at the 2004 PICTA meeting in Mauritius, the African Development Forum 2004, and the African preparatory meetings for WSIS-II, which all endorsed the idea. Ultimately during an Acacia team meeting in Dakar in 2005, the proposed network was officially included in the IDRC pipeline for support. Subsequent to the team meeting, funding was made available by the IDRC to support pre-project activity and to enable the collaborative development of a proposal including the identification of appropriate institutions and researchers.

I was therefore asked to lead the Pre-Project activities and coordinated, in collaboration with the IDRC Offices in Dakar and Nairobi, the selection of the research institutions. This was done on a competitive basis resulting in the identification of nine research institutions from nine African countries including from almost all of Africa's major sub-regions[1].

This resulted in the **"LOG-IN Africa Pre-Project Consultative Workshop", held in Nairobi, 3rd. – 5th. September 2005**, attended by the identified researchers and institutions. Each selected institution prepared a preliminary analysis of "The Current State of ICTs and Local Governance" in their respective countries in order to identify knowledge and information gaps and research priorities for discussion during the Workshop. In the course of this meeting, researchers agreed on common research issues and methodological approaches, and prepared draft documents upon which the "LOG-IN Africa Project Proposal" was based.

I was then requested to act as Project Leader/Research Network Co-ordinator for the establishment of the LOG-IN Africa Research Network.

Following the Nairobi workshop, I further elaborated the LOG-IN Africa Project proposal, with the support of Dr Michael Gurstein, as a Research Adviser, and in consultation with IDRC, and submitted for official approval on behalf of CAFRAD to IDRC on 11th. November 2005.

The Project Proposal was further discussed during the WSIS-II in Tunis, in November 2005, and finally approved by IDRC in January 2006. A Memorandum of Grant Conditions (MGCs) between IDRC and CAFRAD was finalized on February 2006, and LOG-IN Africa started in March 2006 (www.loginafrica.net).

LOG-IN Africa has the general objective of informing, supporting and orienting African countries and other stakeholders in their policies and practices concerning the application of ICTs to local governance.

The research projects intends to assess the current state and outcomes of e-local governance initiatives in Africa, and in particular how ICTs are being used to realise good local governance at four levels:

a) the internal organizational processes of local governments;
b) the provision of information and service delivery;
c) the promotion of the principles of good governance; and
d) public participation and consultation.

LOG-IN Africa is currently an emergent pan-African network of researchers and research institutions from nine African countries. The Network research partners is drawn from the following institutions:

1. Al Akhawayn University, Morocco (http://www.aui.ma)
2. Cairo University, Egypt (http://www.cu.edu.eg/default.asp);
3. LINK-Centre/Witswatersrand University and the Centre for Public Service Innovation (CPSI), South Africa (http://link.wits.ac.za and www.cpsi.co.za);
4. Makerere University, Uganda (http://www.cit.ac.ug);
5. Societé Africaine d'Education et de Formation pour le Développement / African Society of Education and Training for Development (SAFEFOD), Senegal (www.safefod.org);
6. University of Addis Ababa, Ethiopia (http://www.aau.edu.et);
7. Universidade Eduardo Mondlane, Mozambique (http://dmi.uem.mz);

8. University of Nairobi, Kenya (http://www.uon.ac.ke);
9. University of Technology of Mauritius, Mauritius (http://ncb.intnet.mu/utm).

As a network of research peers, it is coordinated through the African Training and Research Centre in Administration for Development (CAFRAD), ensuring effective implementation; a pan-African outlook; and high-level policy dissemination of research results.

The **"First LOG-IN Africa Kick-Off and Methodology Workshop"** was held in **Tangier, 8th–10th June 2006**, and gathered together a total of 30 participants, from 9 African countries, and representatives of CAFRAD, IDRC, UNDP and UNECA, as observers.

An intention of the first LOG-IN Africa Workshop was to facilitate the creation of a "research network" with considerable degrees of mutual support, research synergies and ultimately collaborative research activities and research outcomes. The Network as currently established, consists of a range of researchers, each with their own professional background, training and experience, working in a variety of locally specific institutional and national contexts. However, through the Workshop, the beginnings of a common baseline was established and directions set for a variety of common data elements (outcome indicators) to be collected.

While respecting the individuality of the respective researchers/research teams the intention of the project has been to create a common overall e-local governance framework within which each of the individual research activities could be "nested" and through which the individual projects could be linked to the variety of other on-going projects. In this way they would be constituted so as to provide a broader basis for moving towards an empirically grounded e-local governance "Roadmap" of value both nationally and on a Pan-African basis.

As a research network its objective is to provide a broad framework within which individual research may be coordinated and integrated in support of knowledge creation and knowledge integration. As a network of researchers its objective is to support the activities of the individual researchers as they undertake their individual research activities.

The broad intention with the creation of LOG-IN Africa, in fact, is to overcome the isolation of individual researchers in the area of ICTs as applied to local governance in Africa. More importantly, it aims to strengthen the quality and significance of applied e-governance research in Africa so as to support the on-going development of e-local governance in the region. The Network begins with a broad understanding that research has a necessary role in social and economic development both as a means to inform policy concerning the outcomes of practical developments and interventions and as a means to inform practice concerning the effectiveness and efficiency of practical interventions and developments.

Through collaboration among the networked research partners, a modular "outcome assessment framework", with specific indicators linked to a conceptual framing of the characteristics of good governance, will be developed. This will be adapted to local contexts in conjunction with training of local researchers. Specific data collection and analysis will be conducted at the local level in large part based on locally determined research priorities, strategies and methods broadly coordinated within the LOG-IN Africa research framework and research objectives.

An integrative process will allow for comparative cross-national and regional assessment of the outcomes of current e-local governance activities.

The Network will generate research findings contributing to more effective policy making and implementation in e-local governance in Africa. National and regional guidelines and an implementation "Roadmap" for how to proceed in this area is also to be developed.

During the two-year of its implementation (March 2006-March 2008), the Research Network is intended to contribute to improved project management and evaluation capabilities of the participating institutions.

The direct outputs of the research project, the outcome assessment framework and the Road Map for e-local governance, will shape the landscape in the theory and practice of ICTs for local governance. The establishment of the Network will also facilitate the gaining of support for e-local governance from the international community as for example, through the framework of the WSIS and the recently inaugurated Digital Solidarity Fund (DSF). The Network, in fact, was also intended to serve as a possible channel for resources from the North to the South, in this area as well as supporting South-South partnerships, and decentralized cooperation. A particular emphasis will be put on the leveraging role of ICTs in supporting local economic development through e-local governance activities as for example, promoted by the African Diaspora and through local-to-local connections (e. g. cooperation among Regions and Cities).

In the longer term, in addition to reinforcing the research capacities of partner institutions in the area of ICTs and local governance and facilitating the sharing of knowledge and experience, the Research Network will reinforce the capacities of local governance institutions and grass-roots communities. In this way the project will potentially have an additional impact through building the skills of young leaders and ICTs professionals, thus supporting the development of human resource capacity at the local level for the implementation of ICTs projects and in turn creating job opportunities and stimulating economic growth in Africa.

Notes

1. Cf. for example GARNET http://info.lut.ac.uk/departments/cv/wedc/garnet/publnew5.html or SARRNET http://www.iita.org/sarrnet/sarrnet/asanet.htm as models of previously IDRC funded research networks and also see the Community Informatics Research Network as a network of independent researchers in a parallel area of applied ICTs http://www.ciresearch.net. More information about LOG-IN Africa area available on request to CAFRAD or IDRC, or at www.loginafrica.net.

ANNEXE

REVIEW OF THE KEY EXPERIENCES OF ICTs IMPACTING ON GOVERNANCE IN AFRICA

INTRODUCTION

This review of key experiences of ICTs having an impact on governance in Africa, is the result of my ongoing effort to analyse the e-Initiatives impacting on the region. A preliminary analysis titled "Overview of e-governance in Africa" was made within the framework of the activities of the "e-Africa Initiative for good governance; building e-governance capacity in Africa" in 2003, I have drafted on behalf of CAFRAD where I was seconded in the period 2002-2004 as Associate Expert for UNDESA/DPADM, within the framework of UNPAN. It is available on www.unpan.org/africa.asp .The analysis takes advantage of the main pieces of research and working papers in the area, and in particular the Background Paper on ICTs for development in Africa, prepared for the Third Meeting of the UN ICTs Task Force (September 30th., October 1st., 2002) by Joseph O. Okpaku Sr. Phd. The present analysis also takes advantage of the UN ICTs Task Force Publication on "ICTs for African Development", Edited by Joseph O. Okpaku Sr. Phd, UN N.Y., 2003 and some analysis and researches available on the web.

In this context, the review of key experiences is a compilation analysis which takes into consideration initiatives at different levels (sub-regional, regional, sectoral, national, and global specifically on e-government) that have a potential impact on local governance in Africa.

GLOBAL INITIATIVES

Digital Opportunity Task Force (DOT Force), and the G8 Africa Plan of Action: established at the G8 Summit in Okinawa (July 2000), represents a new model of international co-operation. Following the G8 Summit in Genoa (June 2001), the DOT Force has been endorsed to implement the *"Genoa Plan of Action"*, to broaden the understanding that ICTs are an effective instrument to reduce poverty and for spurring sustainable development. In this context, the *"G8 Africa Action Plan"*, adopted in the G8 Summit of Kananaskis, Canada, 21st.-22nd. June, 2002, welcoming the *"Declaration on Democracy, Political, Economic and Corporate Governance and the African Peer-Review Mechanism"*, statement of the New Partnership for Africa's Development - NEPAD Heads of State and Government Implementation Committee (11th. June, 2002), underlines the importance of this innovative method of partnership, recognised as crucial for the strengthening of governance and capacity building.

Global Development Gateway (GDG) and InfoDev: this project, executed by the World Bank, within the framework of the UN ICTs Task Force, provides a Global Database Gateway and a window for ICTs projects to respond to the needs of the UN ICTs Task Force. In addition, it is providing support through its Network of Country Gateways. African countries are beginning to take advantage of this opportunity.

Global Development Learning Network (GDLN): this project of the World Bank, has the objective of providing decision makers across the developing world with affordable and regular access to a global network of peers, experts and practitioners to share ideas and experiences to fight poverty.

Global Development Network (GDN): aims at providing policy researchers in developing countries with access to financial support and data resources and helping to strengthen collaboration with their counterparts throughout the world.

Global Digital Divide Initiative (GDI): this initiative of the World Economic Forum intends to build a partnership between the public and private sectors to bridge the digital divide and to make effective use of ICTs to improve lives.

Global Digital Opportunity Initiative (GDOI): started as a joint venture between the Markle Foundation and the United Nations

Development Programme (UNDP), which also has a support mechanism under the International Partners Group, led by the Government of Italy and co-ordinated by the United Nations Department of Economic and Social Affairs (UNDESA). It provides developing countries with expertise and resources to develop national e-strategies.

Global Knowledge Partnership (GKP): is a "network of networks" with a diverse membership base comprising public, private and not for profit organisations from both developed and developing countries. It was born as a result of the preparatory process of the 1997 Global Knowledge Conference in Canada, organised by the World Bank and the Government of Canada. The Secretariat is hosted by the Government of Malaysia and represented by the National Information Technology Council (NITC). The GKP aims at promoting broad access to, and effective use of, knowledge and information as tools of equitable sustainable development.

International e-Development Resource Network (IeDR): this initiative aims at facilitating the supply of regulatory, policy and strategy expertise from both North and South, with the support of national governments, the private sector and international organisations.

Internet Corporation for Assigned Names and Numbers - ICANN: is a technical co-ordination body for the Internet that is specifically co-ordinating Internet domain names, IP address numbers, Protocol parameters and port numbers. In addition, ICANN co-ordinates the stable operation of the Internet's root server system. Africa's participation in the ICANN activities is still limited despite the efforts of international partners to support participation of African countries. In 2002, a stakeholders meeting of ICANN was held in Accra, Ghana, and following the meeting UNECA and ICANN have been discussing the creation of an African outreach programme as part of the African Stakeholders Network.

United Nations ICTs Task Force and the African Stakeholders Network - ASN: the UN ICTs Task Force, whose achievement of a meeting of independent experts from industry, academia, civil society and government, convened by the United Nations in April 2000, and then institutionalised by the UN Economic and Social Council (ECOSOC) in July 2000, found further support in the UN Millennium Summit in September 2000. Set up to support the development of regional ICTs networks by empowering developing nations to establish their own national e-strategies, improving the existing national capacities and exploring new development areas, it has been working to establish and provide a global forum for integrating ICTs into developing programmes. Its focus is on: strategy, infrastructure, enterprise, human capacity, content, application, partnerships and policy and governance related to the digital revolution at the regional and international levels, facilitating the effective participation of all. To co-ordinate the international community initiatives to turn Africa into an information based economy, following the decision of the first working meeting of the UN ICTs Task Force (November 2001), to form Regional Networks to optimise global development of ICTs strategies, the "African Stakeholders Network" (ASN) was set up in a meeting in Addis Ababa (21st.-22nd. January, 2002). The aim of the ASN, organised by the United Nations Economic Commission for Africa (UNECA), is to provide help, through collaborative partnership, in designing a platform for issues on ICTs for development, and sharing experiences by regional and international institutions, in respect of the Common Position for Africa's Digital Inclusion, adopted during Africa's contribution to the G8 DOT Force and the UN ECOSOC panel on the digital divide, (10th.-12th. May, 2001, Addis Ababa).

REGIONAL INITIATIVES

African Development Forum-ADF: since its creation, the ADF has registered significant impact and rapidly gained recognition as an effective forum for informed dialogue and consensus building on urgent development issues of relevance to Africa, and for agreeing on implementation priorities and strategies at sub-regional, regional and national levels. While ADF 1999 focussed on ways to accelerate the information revolution in Africa, and is still used as a reference for African countries and experts doing studies on Africa's ICTs, the ADF III, held in March 2002, on Regional Integration, created an ICTs Focus Group to explore the role of ICTs in regional integration, and a portal was also launched.

African Information Society Initiative (AISI): aims at supporting and accelerating socio-economic development across Africa. It focusses on priority strategies, programmes and projects which can assist in the sustainable build-up of an information society in African countries. A wide range of bilateral and multilateral partners is supporting the implementation of activities within the framework of AISI.

African Technical Advisory Committee (ATAC): is a regional advisory committee composed of African experts representing different areas of activities, including the Diaspora. It was established by a mandate from the UNECA Conference of Ministers Resolution 812 (XXXI), to support the African Information Society Initiative (AISI), and was formally launched during the first meeting in October 1997.

Building Digital Opportunities: this is an joint initiative of the British Ministry of Co-operation and Development and the Dutch Ministry of Foreign Affairs. It is focussed on four main activities: strategies and regulations of the Commonwealth Telecommunication Organisation; support to national strategies by the International Institute of Communication and Development (IICD); the development of radio broadcasting systems by the AMARC International group; and the exploitation of information through the implementation of the "OneWorldOnline" portal. In particular, through the activities undertaken in the context of this initiative, the IICD is co-operating with some local partners in six African countries, to support their efforts in integrating ICTs in the governance process. Moreover, IICD has a particular activity on Thematic Networks, where the focus is on knowledge sharing with local and international communities, empowering local organisations in using ICTs and helping national institutions to become providers of local information and advisory services.

Communities and Information Society in Africa (ACACIA) and Connectivity Africa: these projects are implemented by the International Development Research Centre (IDRC), in partnership with the United Nations Economic Commission for Africa, within the framework of the Canadian contribution to the AISI initiative. Launched in 1997 with the objective of supporting Sub-Saharan communities to integrate ICTs in their development strategies, and helping them to meet their own social and economic development, through research and policy focus, Acacia has invested more than $40 million in research, demonstration and evaluation projects on key ICTs issues. These include how ICTs can be used to reduce poverty, policies to bridge the digital divide and the development of local content and knowledge. At the G8 Summit in Kananaskis (2002), Prime Minister Chrétien announced a $500 million aid package - the Canada Fund for Africa - to support the G8 Africa Action Plan and the New Partnership for Africa's Development (NEPAD). The Canada Fund for Africa is providing $12 million for the implementation of Connectivity Africa to provide Canadian expertise in applying ICTs to education, health and community development. Connectivity Africa has four components: innovation in the use of ICTs; African regional ICTs futures; research and development in African ICTs; and partnership and convergence.

Digital Diaspora Network for Africa (DDN-A), Afrishare and the Africa Social Venture Fund: DDD-A is an initiative designed to tap the value of Diaspora communities in service to Africa. It is a collaborative effort between the UN ICTs Task Force, UNIFEM, UNFIP, Digital Partners and Gruppo CERFE. It aims at promoting development in Africa by mobilising the technological, entrepreneurial and professional expertise and resources of the African diaspora. Among the activities of the DDN-A: 1) AfriShare is an innovative initiative committed to unleashing the enormous potential of ICTs to build a bridge to carry the resources and knowledge of the African diaspora, back to Africa. The objective is to mobilise and organise a cluster of stakeholders with a direct interest in Africa's sustainable development - African and US business leaders, government and intergovernmental agencies, foundations, NGOs and academics - into a "brains trust" that will help identify innovative projects on the ground in Africa and pinpoint ways that ICTs can be used to trigger market-based solutions to the region's poverty; 2) The DDN-Africa Social Venture Fund is designed to provide financial support for entrepreneurial activities using ICTs. The fund is being launched with modest initial aims, but is designed to grow into a collaborative effort supported by individuals, foundations, development agencies and corporations.

European Commission projects and activities: to address the impact of the Information Society on citizenship, education, culture, business and much more, relevant European Commission programmes and initiatives have been established. Among these are: the Europe Action Plan; the Internet Action Plan; ISTweb; e-Content; e-Safety; e-TEN;

IDA (Interchange of Data between Administrations). Moreover, in December 2001, the European Commission, invited by the Council of the European Union, the European Parliament and the ACP-EU Assembly, adopted the Communication "ICTs and Development: the role of ICTs in the development policy of the European Union". The communication has the objective of exploring the practical mechanism of integration of ICTs in the development and co-operation programmes of the European Union. In fact, the EU intends to play a more proactive role in the support and exploitation of the opportunities related to the ICTs for development in Africa.

NEPAD ICTs Projects, the e-Africa Commission of NEPAD: the NEPAD's contribution on ICTs consists of thirteen major projects, as outlined in the Conference on financing NEPAD, held in Dakar, Senegal, 15th.-17th. April, 2002. The projects are the following. 1) Infrastructure Project: aimed at installing 32 optical fibre inter-state links in west Africa; 2) Telecommunications Law and Regulation Harmonisation: aimed at creating a unified and open economic zone through the integration of property, infrastructure and financial services markets; 3) Telecommunications device manufacturing plant: aimed at developing activities around ICTs-related industries, creating ICTs private industries, promoting industrial sub-contracting activities, improving ICTs equipment availability and producing ICTs equipment more adapted to the African needs and environment, in West Africa; 4) Support for ICTs-related facilities: is a transcontinental project to provide support to maintain and upgrade existing ICTs-related educational or industrial centres in Lome, Togo, Dakar in Senegal and Harare in Zimbabwe; 5) PAG-NET, PanAfrican Governmental Network: aimed at establishing a transcontinental secure IP/Ipsec network designed exclusively for African government communications (data and voice transmission); 6) DATAFRICA: aimed at the creation of an electronic database to store various statistics in the field of economics, trading, geography, environment, agriculture, health, population, ICTs and infrastructure; 7) e-Justice Africa: aimed at developing a system to manage justice information in Africa, allowing the exchange of data between criminal justice agencies, courts, law enforcement and prosecutors; 8) e-Customer Africa-ACEN: is intended to be a public-private communications and data transmission system designed to track customs transactions between African countries; 9) ACT-NET or ACTIS: this is intended to be a PanAfrican co-operation tool to prevent and fight terrorism, collecting, analysing and tracking information about terrorists, suspected individuals and their activities; 10) Telemedicine-AHTIS: this is a continental project intended to be a way of building high-quality, interoperable systems for health education, prophylaxis, epidemiological analysis, telemedicine operations, medical care and prevention; 11) e-History Africa: is a programme aimed at supporting and encouraging the production and diffusion of African history on worldwide networks and media; 12) Africashop: is intended to create an electronic online store that aims to be a window on African art and culture, offering crafts, clothing, local food and jewellery; 13) Africa Cybermarket: is planned to be a commodity market that will allow the electronic exchange of agricultural and sea products between African producers and buyers. These ambitious projects and the overall plan of the ICTs of NEPAD has to be managed under the supervision of the e-Africa Commission, established in 2002 within the NEPAD Structure in order to be the NEPAD, de facto, ICTs organ for masterminding its ICTs priorities and programmes.

Partnership for ICTs in Africa (PICTA): is an informal group of donors and executing agencies committed to improving information exchange and collaboration around ICTs activities in Africa. It was formed by the representatives of 17 UN and other development agencies involved in ICTs development in Africa, who attended the donor and executing agency meeting on ICTs for development in Africa, held in Rabat, Morocco, in April 1997. They agreed to make PICTA a forum for donors and executing agencies collaborating within the framework of AISI, setting up common information resources on the Internet for ICTs related activities in Africa. The major current joint programmes of PICTA members include the SCAN-ICTs Project, development and implementation of national strategies (NICIs), the publication of a quarterly bulletin, "iConnect Africa", and a monthly "PICTA Bulletin". Furthermore, PICTA members jointly organise a number of conferences and meetings related to the promotion of ICTs for African development.

Sustainable Development Networking Programme (SDNP): as the countries of Africa seek to develop national and local capacity and effective policies, UNPD promotes the building of partnership networks, such as the SDNP, that focusses on the integration of ICTs in the decision making process and on the promotion of the Internet.

Tokyo International Conference on African Development (TICAD): is an initiative of the Japanese government in partnership with UNDP Africa focussed on the theme of poverty reduction through accelerated economic growth and sustainable development and the effective integration of African economies into the global economy. Recognising the contributory effect of ICTs in bringing emerging economies to the global market, TICAD aims to build on the success of the Internet Initiative for Africa (IIA) (see below) to raise awareness and contribute intellectually to policy and institution building through South-South co-operation with particular emphasis on Asia-Africa co-operation.

UNDP, Internet Initiative for Africa (IIA): UNDP is working in close partnership with key public and private sector players to craft comprehensive regional and country strategies and implementation plans to help transform the digital divide into a digital opportunity. In particular, the IIA launched in 1996, with the objective of improving local ICTs infrastructures and promote national and regional telecommunication networks in the fifteen African countries where it was feasible. Through a cost-sharing partnership with the governments of these countries, this programme established the first national Internet gateway, national backbone infrastructure, increased national bandwidths and established Internet points of presence. It also served to provide an array of policy and technical advisory services and training to national experts to manage and administer the infrastructure and foster sustainability and growth.

UNDP and Microsoft Technology Partnership to Combat Poverty in Developing Nations: UNDP and Microsoft agreed to work together to build capacity in developing countries around the world, by providing technology-enabled training for young people and adults in community education centres. By providing skills training, content, curricula and other new resources, this partnership is intended to help expand UNDP's ongoing development efforts and encourage the exploration of creative, technology-based solutions to the world's most pressing development challenges. The alliance draws on the resources of Microsoft Unlimited Potential, the company's global effort to deliver computer literacy and job skills training to underserved communities.

SUB-REGIONAL INITIATIVES

ICTDAR Programme for Arab States: this sub-regional UNDP ICTs for Development programme is covering 20 countries in the Arab Region, including North African countries. It has the objective of assisting Arab States in harnessing ICTs to reduce poverty and improve both public administration performance and private sector hold and expansion. The main ICTDAR priorities include awareness raising, promotion and stakeholders campaigns, capacity development and strategy implementation, pro-poor growth and employment generation.

Innovation in Public Administration in the Euro-Mediterranean Region (Innov Med): the objective of this project is to contribute, through the exchange of innovative ideas and experiences in public administration, to the improvement of governance systems in the countries of the Euro-Mediterranean area with a view to enhancing prosperity, peace and stability in the region. The project is also intended to promote the progressive harmonisation of public administration systems in the Mediterranean area in line with the Barcelona process established in 1995 as a means through which the European Union supports Mediterranean partners in their political, economic and social reforms. The project is being executed by UNDESA and Formez -Training and Study Centre, an Italian semi-private institution based in Naples (Italy). The project, being implemented from January 2003 to April 2005 and planned in six phases, aimed at improving the governance systems of the countries of the Mediterranean region by assisting governments in assessing their public administration needs in order to undertake appropriate reforms in public administration; by creating synergies among existing programmes for the promotion of exchanges of experience in public administration innovation; by strengthening the capacity of governments and regional institutions to exchange information, knowledge and best practices in public administration innovation; by enhancing the capacity of governments to assess validity and transferability and implement best practices and innovative experiences in public administration; by assisting selected governments of the region to implement best practices and innovative experiences; and enabling governments of the region to acquire knowledge and information on the usefulness of the project.

ICTs for Regional Integration in the Economic Community for Central States (CEMAC): further to the workshop on ICTs for regional integration, organised in Yaounde, in September 2002, the Yaounde Declaration was adopted by CEMAC Heads of State in December 2002. It focussed on harmonisation of the ICTs sector in the sub-region, sharing resources and creating the Central African countries Association of Regulators (ARAC).

Regional ICTs Development in Southern African Development Community (SADC): in addition to being the first sub-region to establish an association of regulators, the Telecommunications Regulators Association of Southern Africa (TRASA), several studies on ICTs have been undertaken and meetings and workshops on ICTs and regulations organised in the SADC sub-region. A Protocol on Transport, Communications and Meteorology and a Declaration on ICTs were adopted by SADC, which also has a Southern Africa Transport and Communication Commission.

Regulatory Harmonisation in the Economic Community for Western Africa States (ECOWAS): in order to facilitate the harmonisation of national sectoral policies in the sub-region, the ECOWAS Council of Ministers established a Consultative Regulatory Committee for Telecommunications to ensure the consistent and co-ordinated regulation of telecommunications within the community. A West African Telecommunications Regulators Association (WATRA) was officially created in June 2002. The first activity was to undertake a study on the harmonisation of West African telecommunications regulations.

UEMOA Declaration on ICTs: in 2001, the Council of Ministers of the UEMOA adopted a recommendation on a programme of action for improving ICTs infrastructure and services in the region. It aimed at harmonising the regulatory frameworks, creating a committee of regulators, and a forum of operators and service providers, promoting ICTs and liberalising the national telecoms markets.

World Economic Forum: initiative on e-Readiness in the Southern African Region: a key partner to the UN ICTs Task Force, is itself vigorously engaged in promoting ICTs development in Africa in a variety of areas. In co-operation with the Southern Africa Development Community (SADC), government institutions and the African individual and institutional private sector, WEF conducted a comprehensive initiative on e-readiness in the Southern African Region.

Southern Africa Capacity Initiative (SACI): this UNDP initiative, now re-invigorated by the alliance with Microsoft, is intended to explore innovative opportunities to use technology to build capacity, facilitate e-government initiatives and improve basic services delivery in countries most adversely affected by the HIV/AIDS pandemic.

SECTORAL INITIATIVES

Access/Skills

Community Access Centres Network (ADEN): is a project funded by the French Government to create a network of Internet community access points for French-speaking countries in Africa. It focusses on the training and capacity building of managers and practitioners, the sharing of North-South and South-South experience and the development of services responding to local community needs

CAR Project: is a project to implement Edu-Telecentres in Malawi, Kenya, Uganda and Zambia. Along with programmes on HIV/AIDS, it provides programmes to address women's empowerment, teacher training, distance learning and skills development.

Catalysing Access to ICTs in Africa (CATIA): is a project to increase affordable access to ICTs across the continent (both Internet and radio), increase Africa's influence in International decision making, and promote the exchange of local African content.

iLearn Project: is a project of Thintana communications, to equip schools with computer networks (computer lab with internet access) and to facilitate an educator development programme to support teaching and learning through ICTs.

ITU, Training on Internet Programme: is an initiative run by the International Telecommunication Union (ITU) to focus on the establishment of training centres on the Internet, to allow citizens and entrepreneurs to develop competence in the use of ICTs

Project for Information Access and Connectivity (PIAC): a project of the Ford Foundation in collaboration with the Rockefeller Foundation aims at promoting ICTs as a cross-cutting theme for programming in South Africa.

Telecentre Infomediary/Help Desk: is a project run by "digital pioneers" in Africa and developing countries in other regions, to provide practical help and advice to technology professionals and managers of community based telecommunications facilities.

UNDP/CISCO Networking Academies: is a strategic partnership to establish facilities in Least Developed Countries, to provide network technology skills and training facilities to prepare students for the 21st. century workplace. CISCO Networking academies have been established in more than twenty African countries.

USAID-Leland Initiative: is a five year project funded by the U.S.A. to ensure access to the Internet in twenty African countries and to create an enabling policy environment and a sustainable supply of Internet services.

Business and Trade

Global Business Dialogue on e-Commerce – GBDe: established in 1999, represents a major step forward in the development of a comprehensive approach to electronic commerce issues, both by delivering a wealth of information through its website and database and by connecting and co-ordinating major stakeholders in the field. It is divided into three regional hubs (Americas, Asia/Oceania, Europe/Africa) and focusses on eight key areas: consumer confidence, cyber security, convergence, digital bridges, e-government, intellectual property rights, trade and taxation.

CEO-Charter for Development Programme: an initiative of the Global Digital Divide Task Force of the World Economic Forum, in partnership with the UN ICTs Task Force. The CEO Charter is based on the pledge of companies which sign up to commit a minimum of 20 per cent of their annual corporate citizenship and philanthropic budgets to support ICTs Development in the developing world with a view to eliminating poverty. This programme holds immense potential for driving ICTs development support in Africa in a consistent and coherent way, especially the support of the indigenous African private sector, the ultimate repository and arbiter of long-term durable industrial and competitive capacity-building and knowledge acquisition in Africa.

Panafrican Initiative on e-Commerce: as a result of the ADF '99, IDRC and UNECA established this initiative with the aim of developing policy and strategy advice for African government. A Ministerial Conference (Libreville, Gabon, November 2000) and some sub-regional level workshops have been conducted on the use of ICTs to enhance the competitiveness of SMEs in Africa.

Digital Factory: is an initiative to create capacity in Africa for the development of software and applications at a global standard to support the global ICTs industry and market, as well as to meet indigenous continental demand. A private-sector initiative between Sun Microsystems, The Telecom Africa Corporation, Epi-Use *plc* and the State of California Technology, Trade and Commerce Agency, the Digital Factory hopes to replicate the software development miracle in India, most notably in Bangalore.

World Economic Forum - Business Endorsement of the NEPAD initiative: the World Economic Forum devoted its 2004 African Economic Summit, expanded from its predecessor the Southern African Economic Summit, and entitled, "NEPAD at Work: Business Engages the New Partnership for Africa's Development", to promoting support for NEPAD by the global private sector. One of the outcomes of the Summit was the "Business Endorsement of the New Partnership for Africa's Development" initiative, a programme by which companies doing business in Africa commit themselves to support NEPAD's objectives by undertaking to observe a set of standard corporate citizenship criteria, such as transparency and proper accounting principles. Although a large number (over 250) companies have signed up for this programme, its value is difficult to assess as signing up does not involve any quantifiable commitment of resources (material or in kind) to Africa or the NEPAD process.

Other indigenous African Initiatives of the SMEs Industry, the Informal Sector and the Civil Society: there are many other indigenous initiatives aimed at building industrial as well as research and development capacity in Africa, mobilising Africa's expert capacity spread around the world. Of great importance in the ongoing drive for ICTs Development in Africa is the active role of Africans and African institutions, both public and private sector, in undertaking often quite bold and innovative initiatives. The potential impact of such efforts is itself greatly enhanced by the close level of collaboration between both sectors, government and private, and between Africans on the continent and in the diaspora. These initiatives range across a broad spectrum of areas, from policy and regulation, to industrialisation, infrastucture, software, content, development communications and capacity-building.

Culture

African Culture Conservation Fund (ACCF): provides support to African communities who wish to implement cultural initiatives. Programmes include the "Banking on Culture" and the "Ghanaian Weavers".

World Project: is a World Bank's Project to help new generations learn about world cultures, encouraging school-to-school project collaboration to, and serving as an information channel for, teachers around the world.

Education and Capacity Building

African Learning Networks: supporting the establishment of school networks, (e.g. SchoolNet), University Networks (e.g. VarsityNet), Networks for marginalised people (e.g. OosyNet), and networks of research institutes (e.g. African Knowledge Network Forum-AKNF).

African Virtual University (AVU): is an innovative educational organisation established to serve the countries of Africa. The objective of the AVU is to build capacity and support economic development by leveraging the power of modern telecommunications technology to provide world-class quality education and training programmes to students and professionals in Africa. After a successful pilot phase, AVU has been transformed from being a project of the World Bank into an independent, reputable, inter-governmental organisation based in Nairobi, Kenya with over 34 Learning Centres in 19 African countries.

IMFUNDO Project: is a partnership between DFID, Cisco Systems, Marconi and Virgin, which aimed at bridging the growing digital divide in African countries. The pilot project has the objective of exploring how ICTs can improve education, through better teacher training, raising skills levels and sharing knowledge.

Information Technology Centre for Africa (ITCA): ITCA, in co-operation with USAID/Leland Initiative, developed a training manual and delivered training courses for policymakers, and, in co-operation with the World Bank's InfoDev Programme and /CISCO Systems, ITCA launched a training course on Internet Networking Technology for African women. Similar activities are now being undertaken in partnership with UNIFEM.

UNESCO Projects: UNESCO developed several projects for promoting the contribution of ICTs to the development of education, science and culture and the construction of a knowledge society. In 2002/03, in addition to other ICTs activities carried out by the different sectors of the Organisation, 13 projects were being implemented with a specific focus on ICTs. Among these were: Open Learning Communities for Gender Equity with the Support of ICTs; ICTs-Based Training in Basic Education for Social Development; Electronic Theses and Dissertations (ETDs); Higher Education; Open and Distance Learning Knowledge Base for Decision makers; and Building Digital Libraries in Africa.

Health

Health InterNetwork: is a project to strengthen public health services by providing public health workers, researchers and policy makers with access to high quality, relevant and timely information, through an Internet Portal.

Twinning Promotion and Facilitation Through ICTs: is a project that uses ICTs to improve the communication of best practices with respect to AIDS programming and to facilitate partnership between AIDS service organisations in Africa.

ADF Portal on health resources and health statistics in Africa: a portal on health resources and health statistics was launched by ADF 2000 after ADF '99 recognised ICTs as an important part of the World Health Organisation strategy "Health for all strategy for the 21st. Century".

Pilot Telemedicine Projects and e-Strategies for Health Sector: some Pilot Telemedicine Projects are being implemented in countries such as Mali and Ethiopia, while Tunisia adopted Telemedicine Plans, and more recently, Mozambique and Senegal are embarking on developing e-strategies for the health sector.

Mapping Malaria Risk in Africa (MARA): intends to promote a Geographic Information System-based Network to monitor the risk of malaria in Africa.

Infrastructure

African Connection and Ministerial Oversight Committee: was created by the African Ministers of Communications during the ITU African Regional Conference, which took place in Johannesburg in 1998, to serve as an institutional framework for the co-ordination of telecommunications development ideas and capacity-building, especially those with regional scope. The African Connection is supervised by the Ministerial Oversight Committee of African Ministers of Communications.

African Telecommunications Union (ATU): is a reconstitution of the Pan-African Telecommunications Union (PATU) by the African Ministers of Communications, and is the de facto African regional telecommunications counterpart of the ITU. ATU, which also reports to the Ministerial Oversight Committee, serves as the organ for the systematic pursuit of telecommunications development in Africa.

African Advisory Group on ICTs (AAG-ICTs): is a group of 12 eminent African ICTs experts from around the world who meet behind closed doors an average of twice a year to provide confidential high-level advice to African Ministers of Information and Communications on strategic, policy and regulatory issues, with no holds barred. It usually meets one day ahead of the meeting of the Ministerial Oversight Committee, whose subsequent meeting its members also sit in on. The AAG also works in close liaison with the African Connection and the African Telecommunications Union, the heads of which two institutions also sit on the AAG. The Advisory Group expects to support the strategic aspects of the activities of NEPAD through intellectual support for the e-Africa Commission.

Sat-3/WASC/SAFE Undersea Optical Fibre Cable Network: shortly after the independence of South Africa, in a dramatic exhibition of continental solidarity, co-operation and strategic common purpose, several African countries, in the euphoria of having achieved the most singular strategic objective of the OAU, undertook to join forces to build a major undersea optical fibre cable to directly link many African countries, and link them to Europe and Asia. Led by Telkom S.A., the 36 participants built the Sat-3/WASC/SAFE cable network. The 28,000 km cable, which cost $650 million US, was launched in Dakar on May 27th., 2002.

RASCOM Satellite Project: the Regional African Satellite Communications Organisation to which most African governments belong, is undertaking to build the RASCOM Satellite, in collaboration with Alcatel. Designed to have a footprint that will cover the entire continent, it is intended to support affordable access to ICTs resources for Africans anywhere on the continent, especially among rural populations.

Comtel Project: is a regional project, undertaken by the member states of COMESA, to build an optical fibre grid to interlink their national networks.

SatCom Project: was instituted by the telecommunications and satellite industry in Africa, as a partnership between indigenous and international players. At the SatCom Africa 2002 Conference held in Midrand, South Africa, in February 2002, the industry embraced the suggestion of PanAmSat that it commits bandwidth, equipment, expertise and other resources to support significant satellite-based projects. Created primarily by Terrapinn Ltd., RASCOM, the Telecom Africa Corporation, Hughes Network Systems, WorldSpace, Sentech, UNISA, the Global VSAT Forum and Mike Jensen Consulting amongst others.

Global Information Infrastructure Commission: is a non-governmental initiative that, with the support of leaders from developed and developing countries, is aimed at fostering private sector leadership and enhanced private-public sector co-operation in the creation of an improved ICTs infrastructure worldwide.

e-GOVERNANCE INITIATIVES

e-Africa Initiative for good governance: building e-governance capacity in African countries: in view of the overall commitment of the NEPAD Heads of State to stimulate the use of ICTs as a driving force to foster social and economic development of the continent, the African Training and Research Centre in Administration for Development (CAFRAD) launched, in 2002, the "e-Africa initiative for good governance: building e-governance capacity in Africa".

The "kick-off" of the e-Africa initiative was the "e-Africa 2002: First Regional Workshop on building e-governance capacity in Africa" (Johannesburg, 28th.-31st. October, 2002). This was organised by CAFRAD in partnership with the United Nations Department of Economic and Social Affairs (UNDESA) and hosted by the Department of Public Service and Administration of South Africa (DPSA), under the banner of NEPAD. The e-Africa initiative focussed on drawing on the strengths in both good governance and ICTs and wished to provide an important contribution to the implementation of the NEPAD Macroplan, for the success of NEPAD's overall vision on Africa's development. It addressed these issues at the level of policy and decision makers, stressing the significant development role and cross-cutting impact that ICTs can have on all aspects of society. To this end, the promoters of the e-Africa conference (CAFRAD, UNDESA and NEPAD), in consultation with other participants and partners, have recognised the need to mobilise the African and global public administration and ICTs communities for e-governance in Africa and have agreed on an overall "Framework for Action on e-governance for Africa". The framework identifies the vision for e-government, the mission that needs to be engaged in by partners, the strategic goals, the impacts expected, a set of strategic intervention areas and examples of outcomes expected. The Framework for Action was further presented to the "4th. Global Forum on Re-inventing Government: Citizens, Businesses and Government: Dialogue and Partnerships for the Promotion of Democracy and Development" (Marrakech, 10th.-14th. December, 2002). In 2003, CAFRAD, UNDESA, and NEPAD, developed a High-Level Strategy and draft Plan of Action. The draft Plan of Action was discussed during the "e-Africa 2003: Expert Consultative Meeting on e-governance" (Tangier, Morocco, 20th.-22nd. October, 2003), organised with the financial support of the Italian Government. The draft e-Africa Plan of Action was then presented for adoption to African Ministers in charge of Public Service during the Meeting of the Pan African Committee of Ministers held in Kampala, Uganda, 27th.-30th. January, 2004, alongside the CAFRAD, NEPAD, UNDESA Workshop on Public Sector Leadership Capacity Development in Africa, again organised with the financial support of the Italian Government.

e-government for Development Initiative: under the banner of the G8, the Government of Italy was assigned the leadership on e-government activities and, with the support of the United Nations Department of Economic and Social Affairs (UNDESA) launched the e-government for development initiative. The initiative was presented during the International Conference on e-government for Development, (Palermo, Italy, 10th.-11th. April, 2002), organised to raise the awareness of the opportunities offered by e-government in the process of economic and social development, and exploring the use of ICTS to foster democracy, efficiency and transparency. For this purpose, an "Open Plan of Action on e-government for development" was prepared. It provided guidelines on the development and implementation of e-government strategies at the national level and captured best practices and lessons learned from experiences. Projects then began in a selected number of African countries.

e-governance Capacity-Building for African Municipalities Project: is a UNESCO cross-cutting project aimed at promoting the use of ICTs tools in municipalities to enhance good governance. Training modules for local decision makers are being developed and implemented according to a prior assessment of needs and opportunities in the two participating regions: Africa and Latin America. The project in Africa is being implemented in collaboration with the African Training and Research Centre in Administration for Development - CAFRAD.

Electronic Distance Training on Sustainability in African Local Governments (EDITOSIA): was a thematic network of 10 African and European partners exploring the potential of Electronic Distance Training on Sustainability in African Local Governments. It aimed at formulating recommendations for policy makers at all levels of government, for donor agencies, training institutes, municipal associations and others concerning the promotion of adequate training methods for building the capacity of African local governments to deal with the challenges of local sustainability. The project was funded by the European Commission, DG Research, and co-ordinated by the International Training Centre (ITC) of ICLEI - Local Governments for Sustainability. The project started at the end of 2001 and was concluded in April 2004 with a symposium organised in Windhoek, Namibia, in which the results of the EDITOSIA project were presented and discussed with a wider audience. Partners in the project were: the Africa Secretariat of ICLEI, the African Training and Research Centre in Administration for Development (CAFRAD), the Polytechnic of Namibia (PON), the Southern African Non-Governmental Organisation Network (SANGONeT), the Zimbabwe Open University (ZOU), the European Distance and E-Learning Network (EDEN), the International Institute for Communication and Development (IICD), the Open University (UK), and the University of Wales, Swansea, Centre for Development Studies.

Regional ICTs Network for Africa (RINAF): established since 1992 by UNESCO, is a "space of co-operation" in the framework of the Intergovernmental Programme on Information technology (PII) with the aim of strengthening the capacities of local administration and civil society to exploit the use of ICTs in Africa.

United Nations Online Network in Public Administration and Finance (UNPAN): The UNPAN Programme was launched in 2000, by the Division for Public Administration and Development Management of the United Nations Department of Economic and Social Affairs (DPADM/UNDESA), which is charged with the overall co-ordination of a group of international regional and sub-regional institutions devoted to public administration and finance in the context of social and economic development and titled UNPAN Online Regional Centres (ORCs), and UNPAN International Centres (OICs). UNPAN's mission is to promote the sharing of knowledge, experiences and best practices throughout the world in sound public policies, effective public administration systems and efficient civil services, through capacity building and co-operation among Member States, to bridge the digital divide, with the emphasis on South-South co-operation and commitment to integrity and excellence. UNPAN's immediate beneficiaries are Public Administration-related regional and national institutions. Its ultimate clients are the citizens of the world, government entities, the private sector, NGOs and academic institutions. The immediate objective of UNPAN was therefore to establish an electronic platform using the online linking of a number of institutions for information exchange, experience sharing and on-the-job training in the area of public sector policy and management. Its long-term aim is to build the capacity of these regional and international institutions to access, process, and disseminate relevant information via up-to-date (ICTs) for the promotion of better public administration. To ensure this, UNPAN was designed to primarily reinforce the required capacity of the regional and international centres partner of the UNPAN Network. The UNPAN Online Centres selected for their prominence as public sector policy and management institutions, are responsible for information and knowledge management within their own geographic areas. In Africa, the UNPAN Network includes three institutions at Regional level: CAFRAD – African Training and Research Centre in Administration for Development; IDEP – African Institute for Economic Development and Planning; and OFPA – African Civil Services Observatory. The Centre for Public Service Innovation CPSI, based in South Africa, was selected as Sub-regional Centre of UNPAN for Southern Africa. At present, UNPAN serves as a portal for public administration and finance and is the only example of such a network in the world today. Since it was launched online in March 2001, (www.unpan.org) UNPAN has been accessed by thousands of interested users from all walks of life around the world, providing ongoing access to the most innovative research, training practices, methodologies and technical assistance. Through their multiple roles as electronic research centre, think-tank, consulting firm and library, the capacity of the regional and international centres will be continuously strengthened. This shall enable them to function effectively as dynamic sources of information and knowledge and to address existing and emerging issues in public sector policy and management. The second phase of UNPAN faces the challenges related to effective information and knowledge management, enhancing governance capacity in African countries. Expansion of the UNPAN Network to sub-regional and national levels in Africa, involving governments and other African ORCs and sub-regional institutions, within the framework of the NEPAD Plan of Action and consistent with the activities of NEPAD and the "World Summit on the Information Society", will play a pivotal role in enhancing governance capacity in African countries.

OTHER INITIATIVES AND SOME PROJECTS AT NATIONAL LEVEL

Many other initiatives and projects are undertaken by **other UN and executing agencies** in their specific fields of expertise, with the general objectives of promoting awareness raising and conducting capacity building activities to assist African countries, which are at different levels of participation in the construction of the global Information Society. Other initiatives are undertaken by the **Informal Sector and the Civil Society** playing a significant role in advancing efforts at building ICTs development in Africa, especially with a view to the use of ICTs applications for dealing with the scope of issues which have become traditionally associated with NGO efforts, These include the eradication of poverty; the social, educational and political empowerment of the disadvantaged or erstwhile deprived, especially women, children; rural and handicapped persons; education; preventative healthcare and the management of illness, especially HIV/AIDS and other communicable diseases; and universal access to basic information and telecommunications services through innovative and affordable technologies or modifications of existing ones. Other important "pushers" of innovation are the **Small and Medium size Enterprises. (SMEs)**. Given the size of the informal component of the African economic landscape, especially as over 70% of the population lives in small and rural communities, and the unique adaptability of ICTs applications to small and micro enterprises, taking advantage especially of the online facilities of the Internet, as well as the development of telecentres, individuals and small groups of African entrepreneurs are setting up a range of businesses, from online marketing of farm products, arts, crafts and clothing, to Internet cafes and telecentres, street corner and marketplace pay-as-you-go phone services, etc.

Here below are reported some examples of innovative projects ICT-related in Africa:

3D technology and Multipurpose Community Telecentres (MTCs) in Uganda: is a UNESCO Project aimed at creating 3D and multimedia programmes to help educate Ugandans about healthy water.

Afrique Initiative, Saint Louis, Senegal: is a project that attempts to combine social purpose and sustainable business by supporting the development of a non-profit organisation focussed on preventative health care, and a for-profit business that intended to offer a range of ICTs-based services to the community, by sharing an Intranet site and related ICTs infrastructure provided by Afrique Initiatives (Belgium). Both have a social purpose, but have evolved different operating models, one to provide preventative healthcare to low-income children in the target age group, reaching the greatest number possible during the critical period of childhood development, the second to try to develop a self-sustainable business.

AfriShare project to Deploy SchoolWeb to Ghanaian Secondary Schools: this project targets computer education for 250,000 Ghanaian young people at the secondary school level in two years. Partners include HP, InfoSAT, Worldspace and Advanced Interactive.

e-Academia, Tanzania: this project, being supported by DDD-A, aims at addressing the high cost and inadequate quality of education in Tanzania via the creation of an online e-learning initiative that will make teaching materials, developed by the "best brains" in the country, available in the local Kiswahili language. It also aims to take advantage of the proliferation of cyber cafes throughout Tanzania to provide

Internet connectivity to subscribers of e-Academy, while CD-Rom-based education will be available to reach those without an Internet connection.

e-government system for the city of Fez, Morocco: this project, executed by the University Al Akhawayn of Ifrane, Morocco, and funded by IDRC, aims at developing a pilot e-government system for the city of Fez, one of the largest cities in Morocco (about 1 million population), to allow citizens to request and receive government services in an easy and efficient way. In parallel, the project also intends to raise a series of research questions concerning the social impact and political implications, as well as the technical feasibility, of e-government projects at local level.

Gauteng Online:, South Africa: this project aims at providing every learner and educator in all public schools with Internet access, e-mail and electronic curriculum delivery, as well as developing a model for large scale implementation of ICTs in school.

Geographic Information System in Mozambique, and Info Techno Industry Knowledge for Development in South Africa: two projects executed by the Canadian International Development Agency (CIDA).

Go with the global flow, Senegal: through this IDRC Acacia project, ENDA Tiers Monde, a nongovernmental organisation in Senegal worked with Acacia in developing a series of "community resource sites" and providing training and Internet access to those living in the most difficult neighbourhoods in and around Dakar. The project has helped transform a grassroots economy to make the social and technological innovations of local groups more visible.

Information to get a fair market price, Senegal: through this IDRC Acacia project, local food producers can use their knowledge of world market prices to more than double the price they receive from intermediaries for their grapefruit. With their cell phone, they check the market prices for produce twice a week. Using wireless technology, they dial into a database of current prices compiled by Manobi, a mobile and Internet services operator. This knowledge enables them to get the market price for their goods without fear that the buyer will go elsewhere and leave them stocked with their produce. Research shows that food producers using this service have seen their incomes increase by an average of 15%.

LoveLife, South Africa: this project intends promoting the use of ICTs for sexual health/HIV-AIDS education through the establishment of Call and Youth Centres and Virtual Studios.

Mandatory ICTs Exposure, Cape Verde: is a project of the World Bank, in collaboration with the Ministry of Education, Science, Youth and Sports, and the Portuguese Development Foundation (PROMEF), to evaluate and analyse ways in which ICTs can be used to improve the education and training systems in Cape Verde.

One-stop business shop, Uganda: through this IDRC Acacia project, women make up more than 45% of small-scale entrepreneurs. They are using the Women's Information Resource and Electronic Service (WIRES) as a "one-stop-shop" to find information on markets, prices, good agricultural practices, and support and advisory services. Based in Kampala and linked to two rural telecentres, WIRES provides information that has been gathered from electronic and print sources and then repackaged in easy-to-use databases in local languages. With this information, women in Uganda are able to hone their entrepreneurial skills, expand their enterprises, and boost their family's incomes.

SATELLIFE and HealthNet Uganda: the PDAs and Better Health in Uganda Project focusses on an area where access to information is scarce and potentially lifesaving resource. It aims at improving the decision making capacity of health professionals by arming them with PDAs that provide them with access to the information they need to make timely diagnoses and provide appropriate treatments. Building on its experience implementing a PDA project in Uganda and Kenya, HealthNet Uganda is poised to introduce this technology on a wider scale in African countries with the support of international partner organisations.

Student ICTs business, Inhambane, Mozambique: through this IDRC Acacia project, a student has set up a community ICTs access centre within his school. Centre use is free for students while walk-in users from the community pay for services. The students and teachers have started small projects such as designing Web sites and recycling and repairing computers. In addition to developing ICTs skills, these projects bring revenue to the centre. As a result, the centre is well on its way to sustainability.

Uganda Connect: an ITU Project which aims at giving students and teachers Internet access and connecting rural communities through High-Frequency radios.

UNESCO assessment and ICTs outlook in selected African municipalities (Zanzibar, Lusaka, and Maputo): The municipalities of Zanzibar, Lusaka and Maputo are being assisted in developing the use of e-governance by UNESCO, as part of its ongoing efforts to support the use of ICTs in the public sector. The initial phase of the project was supported by DANIDA (Danish Co-operation) to provide some basic ICTs infrastructure for the municipalities aimed at assisting in the process of developing an e-governance capacity and providing shared access to ICTs for both local government staff and the public. Some PCs, a LAN, Internet access, a Website and training were provided under the project. Building on these initial activities, a second project is being developed to conduct training in e-governance for the municipalities.

UNESCO Pilot Project on Village e-governance in Tanzania: this project was undertaken by UNESCO in co-operation with the Commonwealth Network of Information Technology for Development Foundation (COMNET-ICTs) They were contracted to commission two computer installations in two Tanzanian villages for the purposes of enhancing local governance and, indirectly, catalysing community development. The project was executed in partnership with the Tanzania Commission for Science and Technology (COSTECH) as implementing partners.

Wind-up radios in Mozambique: is a project which aimed at utilising wind-up, environmentally friendly radios in order to help relay to remote villages the information that could aid their safety and security.

Youth for Technology Foundation, Nigeria: the YTF's TechPreneurship Programme for Rural Women is being supported by the DDN-A at Owerri Digital Village in Nigeria. It attempts to equip women, who run small businesses, with the technology training they need to run small businesses, with the technology training they need to run their businesses more efficiently while promoting coexistence within religious heterogeneous communities. Participants in the Programme learn to use YTF's business management software and database application which was locally developed by YTF's programme members. The application allows women entrepreneurs to track their inventory, revenue and expenses for their small and medium businesses. Workshops are also offered on writing successful business plans, microcredit facilities and credit programmes.

REFERENCES

Bertucci Guido, "Opening Remarks to the UN Ad Hoc Expert Group Meeting on Knowledge Systems for Development", UN New York, 4th.-5th. September, 2003.

CAFRAD, e-Africa 2002: Building e-governance capacity in African countries, 2002, Project Proposal, edited with technical assistance of Mr Gianluca Misuraca.

CAFRAD, "e-Africa: Elements and Principles for a Strategic Plan of Action" - Draft Working Paper, not published, edited with the technical assistance of Gianluca Misuraca.

CAFRAD, NEPAD, UNDESA, e-Africa Framework for Action, Johannesburg, October 2002.

CAFRAD, NEPAD, UNDESA, e-Africa draft Plan of Action, Tangier, October 2003.

Cheema Shabbir and Maguire Linda, "Democracy, Governance and Development: A Conceptual Framework"; Background Paper of the 4th. Global Forum on Re-inventing Government, Marrakech, Morocco, 10th.-13th. December, 2002, UN, New York 2002.

Ciborra Prof. Claudio, U., "Unveiling e-Government and Development: Governing at a distance in the new war", Inaugural lecture at LSE on 24 October 2002

e-Government Policy Network of the Privy Council Office (PCO) ."Transforming Government and Governance for the 21st. Century", 2003

European Union Commission, Communication from the Commission to the Council, the European Parliament, the Economic and Social Committee and the Committee of the Regions – The Role of eGovernment for Europe's Future, 26th. September, 2003

Falk Richard, "On Human Governance", University Park, The Pennsylvania State University, 1995.

Finger Matthias, Misuraca Gianluca, Rossel Pierre, "Governance with and of ICTs: the need for new institutional designs in a changing world", egov Magazine, Volume II – Issue 5th., May 2006.

Finger Matthias, Pecoud Gaëlle, "From e-government to e-governance? Towards a model of e-Governance", 3rd European Conference on e-government, Trinity College Dublin, Ireland, 3rd.-4th. July, 2003

Fukuda-Parr Sakiko and Ponzio Richard, "Governance: Past Present and Future"; Background Paper of the 4th. Global Forum on Re-inventing Government, Marrakech, Morocco, 10th.-13th. December, 2002, UN, New York 2002.

Gilbert Riley Cathia, "The Changing Role of Citizen in the e-Governance & e-Democracy Equation", CceG, 2003.

Gordon T.F., eGovernance and its value for Public Administration", White paper, e-Government Competence Centre, Fraunhofer Institute for Open Communications Systems (FOCUS), Berlin, Germany, May 2006

Gurstein Michael, "From e-Government to e-Governance: an approach from effective use", Canadian Civil Society and the WSIS Conference on Paving the Road to Tunis, May 2005

Gyan-Baffour, George, "Decentralisation as a means to improve governance and poverty reduction: Experience from Ghana", 2003.

Institute on Governance, Ottawa, Canada, "ICTs and Governance: Linkages and Challenges", October 1996.

ITU-International Telecommunications Union, "e-Strategies, Empowering Development", 2006

Heeks Richard, "Most eGovernment-for-Development Projects Fail: How Can Risks be Reduced?", in iGovernment Working Paper Series, No 14.

Kauzya John-Mary, "Local Governance Capacity Building for Full Range Participation: Concepts, Frameworks, and Experiences in African Countries"; Background Paper of the 4th. Global Forum on Re-inventing Government, Marrakech, Morocco, 10th.-13th. December, 2002, UN, New York 2002.

Kauzya John-Mary, "Local Governance, Health and nutrition for all: problem magnitude and challenges with examples from Uganda and Rwanda", Paper presentation to the Global Forum on Local Governance and Social Services for All, Stockholm, Sweden, 2nd.-5th. May, 2000.

Katsiaouni, Presentation to the workshop on Poverty Alleviation and Decentralization for ten West African countries, organised jointly by UNDESA and the Government of Senegal, Dakar, July, 2003.

Khan and Katsiaouni, Presentation to the workshop on Poverty Alleviation and Decentralisation for ten West African countries, organised jointly by UNDESA and the Government of Senegal, Dakar, July, 2003.

Khan Sarbuland, "ICTs as an instrument to Leverage the Millennium Development Goals", in ICTs for African Development, Edited by Okpaku Joseph Sr, PhD, UN ICT Task Force, New York, 2003.

Kemo Conteh and Sheikh E.T Lewis, "Decentralisation and Civil Society approaches as means of improving governance and poverty reduction: The Gambia Experience"; and Sao-Kpato Max-Kyne and Abu Brima "Sierra Leone's experience with deentralisation as a means to improve governance and combat poverty", 2003.

Lenihan Donald, "Realigning Governance: from e-Government to e-Democracy", Crossing Boundaries Paper, Changing Government, Volume 6, Centre for Collaborative Government, Canada.

Mani, Presentation to the workshop on Poverty Alleviation and Decentralisation for ten West African countries, organised jointly by UNDESA and the Government of Senegal, Dakar, July, 2003.

Misuraca Gianluca, Overview of e-Governance in Africa, draft working paper, Tangier, January 2003.

Misuraca Gianluca, "From e-Government to e-Governance: the e-Africa initiative", Paper presented to the International Conference on e-Government, SITEXPO, Casablanca, Morocco, 18-21 February 2004.

Misuraca Gianluca, "e-Africa initiative for good governance: building e-governance capacity in Africa", Encyclopedia of Developing Regional Communities with Information and Communication Technology, IDEA Publishing, May 2005.

Misuraca Gianluca LOG-IN Africa Project Proposal, on behalf of CAFRAD for IDRC, November 2005.

Misuraca Gianluca, Rossel Pierre, "Triggering the governance perspective of e-Government projects: beyond mere digitisation of administration services; or the Change I to Change II shift issue", Lausanne, CDM-EPFL Working Paper, 2006 (forthcoming);

Molo Thioune Ramata, (Edited by) Information and Communication Technologies for Development in Africa: Opportunities and Challenges for Community Development, CODESRIA/IDRC, 2003.

OECD e-book: Citizens as Partners - Information, Consultation and Public Participation in Policy-Making, 2001

OECD, e-Government Studies, "The e-Government Imperative", 2003.

OECD, Development Centre, Working Paper No. 236, "Decentralisation and Poverty in Developing Countries, Exploring the Impact", by, Johannes Jütting, Céline Kauffmann, Ida Mc Donnell, Holger Osterrieder, Nicolas Pinaud and Lucia Wegner, Research programme on Social Institutions and Dialogue, August 2004, DEV/DOC(2004)05

Olekambainei Emmanuel and Sintim-Misa Mavis Ampah, "Info-communication for Development in Africa", UN ICT Task Force Series 2, ICTs for African Development, UN, NY 2003.

Okot-Uma Rogers W'O., "Electronic Governance: Re-inventing Good Governance", Commonwealth Secretariat, London, 2000.

Okpaku Joseph O. Sr., "The Role of ICTs in the African Development Agenda", keynote address to the CAFRAD, UNDESA, NEPAD e-Africa 2002: Regional Workshop on Building e-governance capacity in Africa, Johannesburg, South Africa, 28th.-31st. October 2002.

Okpaku Joseph, Ownership of Problems, Intellectual Property and the Digital Divide: The Enabling Challenge of Solutions - An address to the WIPO Second International Conference on Electronic Commerce and Intellectual Property, Geneva, September, 2001.

Okpaku Joseph, "e-Culture, Human Culture and In-Between: Meeting the Challenges of the 21st. Century Digital World", Address to the ITU Conference on "Creating New Leaders for e-Culture", Coventry, UK, August, 2001

Okpaku Joseph, "Background Paper on ICT-for-development in Africa" Prepared for the United Nations ICT Task Force Third Meeting (September 30th., October 1st. 2002).

Osorio C., "Public Ends by Digital Means: Some Thoughts for Creating Public Value", National Science Foundation, Digital Government Workshop, White Paper 2002.

Rossel Pierre, Glassey Olivier, "La fracture digitale dans les pays du sud et les pistes possibles de sa remediation" (Bridging digital divide in developing countries : possible solutions), EPFL, Cahiers de la Cooperation, n.1 December 2004.

Rossel Pierre, Finger Matthias, Misuraca, Gianluca "Assessing and steering mobile e-Government options: findings and indication proposals", ECEG, 2006.

Rossel Pierre, Finger Matthias, From e-government to e-governance: implications for technology management, 2005

Sheridan, W., and Riley, T.B., "Comparing e-Government vs e-Governance", www.rileyis.com 2006

Stevenson, 1997, in Computing Dictionary.

Sy, J. Habib, "Critical and Prospective Views on ICTs and Governance in Africa", in "Africa Networking: Development Information ICTs and Governance, United Nations Economic Commission for Africa, UNECA, Addis Ababa, 2004

UNCDF, Le pouvoir des pauvres: la gouvernance locale pour la réduction de la pauvreté, N.Y. 2003

UNCRD, Regional Development Dialogue, Vol. 23, N° 2, Nagoya, Japan, 2002.

UNDESA, Economic Governance: Guidelines for Effective Financial Management, New York, 2000.

UNDESA, Report of the workshop on Poverty Alleviation and Decentralisation for ten West African countries, organised jointly by UNDESA and the Government of Senegal, Dakar, July, 2003.

UNDESA, Report of the Capacity Development Workshop on "Decentralised Governance and Poverty Reduction", organised by UNDP, during the 4th. Global Forum on Re-inventing Government - Citizens, Businesses and Governments: Dialogue and partnerships for Development and Democracy, Marrakech, Morocco, 10th.-13th. December, 2002, UN, New York 2002.

UNDESA, "World Public Sector Report 2003: e-Government at the Crossroads", New York, 2003.

UNDESA, "UN Global Survey on e-Government", New York, 2003.

UNDESA, Global e-Government Readiness Report 2005, From e-Government to e-Inclusion, 2006.

UNDESA, Government of Italy, Ministry for Innovation and Technologies, Plan of Action – e-Government for Development, 2002.

UNDESA, Background Papers of the 4th. Global Forum on Re-inventing Government - Citizens, Businesses and Governments: Dialogue and partnerships for Development and Democracy, Marrakech, Morocco, 10th.-13th. December, 2002, UN, New York 2002.

UNDP, Fifth African Governance Forum (AGFV), "Local Governance for Poverty Reduction in Africa", Maputo, Mozambique, 23-25 May 2002.

UNDP, Human Development Report 2001 "Making New Technologies Work for Human Development", UN, NY, 2001.

UNDP, Human Development Report 2002, "Deepening democracy in a fragmented world", UN, NY, 2002.

UNDP, Human Development Report, 2003, "Millennium Development Goals: A compact among nations to end human poverty", UN, NY, 2003.

UNECA, Africa Networking: Development Information ICTs and Governance, Addis Ababa, 2004.

UNECA, Striving for Good Governance in Africa, Addis Ababa, 2004.

UNESCO's medium term strategy 2002-2007, 31 C/4: Chapter on "The contribution of ICT to the development of education, science and culture and the construction of a knowledge society".

United Nations Millennium Declaration, A/RES/55/2, 18th. September, 2000.

United Nations, Road map to good governance and democracy, 2001

United Nations, ICT-Task Force, "The Role of Information and Communication Technologies in Global Development; Analyses and policy Recommendations", Edited with introduction by Abdul Basit Haqqani, UN-ICT-Task Force Series, n. 3, 2003

United Nations, ICT-Task Force, "The World Summit on the Information Society: Moving from the Past into the Future", with Opening Statement by Kofi Annan and Preface by Yoshio Utsumi, Edited by Daniel Stauffacher and Wolfgang Kleinwachter, UN-ICT-Task Force Series, 8, 2005

Weiss Thomas, "Governance, Good Governance and Global Governance: Conceptual and Actual Challenges", Third World Quarterly, Vol. 21, n.5, 2000

Work Robertson, "The Role of Participation and Partnership in Decentralised Governance: Lessons from Nine Local Case Studies on Service Delivery to the Poor"; Background Paper of the 4th. Global Forum on Re-inventing Government - Citizens, Businesses and Governments: Dialogue and partnerships for Development and Democracy, Marrakech, Morocco, 10th.-13th. December 2002, UN, New York 2002.

World Bank Group, Information and Communication Technologies: A World Bank Group Strategy, 2002

WSIS, Declaration of the World Summit of Cities and Local Authorities on the Information Society (Lyon, 5th. December 2003).

Relevant websites

www.accenture.com
www.adele.fr
www.andhrapradesh.com
www.ba.gov.br
www.bridges.org
www.comune.bologna.it
www.developmentgateway.org
www.egov.epfl.ch
www.e-devexchange.org
www.digitalgovernance.org
www.electronicgov.net
www.etampere.fi/infocity
www.europa.eu.int

www.firstgov.gov
www.gartner.group.com
www.gc.ca
www.globalforum.ma
www.governo.it
www.gov.my/MyGov
www.hyperdictionary.com
www.iadb.org/ict4dev/governance.htm
www.iicd.org
www.idrc.org
www.info4local.gov.uk
www.issy.com
www.italia.gov.it
www.kantei.go.jp
www.idea.int
www.localegov.gov.uk
www.loginafrica.net
www.man.ac.uk/idpm
www.nepad.org
www.nua.com/surveys/how_many_online/index.html
www.oecd.org
www.open.metro.seoul.kr
www.ourbrisbane.com
www.palermoconference2002.org
www.pimanagement.org
www.portal-unesco.org
www.presidencia.gob.mx
www.publicus.net/e-government/
www.publiservice.pco-bcp.ga/egov-cybergouv
www.stlouis.missouri.org
tom.riik.ee
www.rileyis.com
www.takingitglobal.org
www.unicttaskforce.org
www.un.org/millennium
www.undp.org
www.unpan.org